Writing from the Margins

WRITING
FROM THE MARGINS

*Power and Pedagogy for
Teachers of Composition*

Carolyn Ericksen Hill

New York   Oxford
OXFORD UNIVERSITY PRESS
1990

Oxford University Press

Oxford   New York   Toronto
Delhi   Bombay   Calcutta   Madras   Karachi
Petaling Jaya   Singapore   Hong Kong   Tokyo
Nairobi   Dar es Salaam   Cape Town
Melbourne   Auckland

and associated companies in
Berlin   Ibadan

Copyright © 1990 by Oxford University Press, Inc.

Published by Oxford University Press, Inc.,
200 Madison Avenue, New York, New York 10016

Oxford is a registered trademark of Oxford University Press

Library of Congress Cataloging-in-Publication Data
Hill, Carolyn Ericksen.
Writing from the margins: power and pedagogy for teachers
of composition/Carolyn Ericksen Hill.
p. cm.   Includes bibliographical references.
ISBN 0-19-506185-3
ISBN 0-19-506637-5 (pbk)
1. English language—Rhetoric—Study and teaching.   I. Title.
PE1404.H54   1990
808'.042'07—dc20   89-36615   CIP

1 2 3 4 5 6 7 8 9

Printed in the United States of America
on acid-free paper

To Larry and our family
for the life stories
we all create together

Preface

For years I thought mourning doves were morning doves, and when I learned their song was supposed to be about endings rather than beginnings, it seemed haunting in a new way. I've kept the "morning" in my mind though, too, and I listen now with a different sort of alertness, letting my mind range over the old and new ways I've heard the story, imagining new stories that might emerge from both.

This book is about a similar kind of attention in the teaching of writing, about our being able as teachers to move through the profession with a sure sense of what its life is about, but also being able to let old understandings double over new ones, the doubling giving us a richer sense of how things can begin and end, whether in the stories we tell about our professional and departmental lives, or our classroom lives, or even our personal ones. They do all become so much a part of each other.

But there is also talk in these pages about the problems of opening old readings to new, about the mental and emotional turbulence that often comes when one meets foreign-feeling others, when some other person, idea, or culture bumps into one's own habits of understanding a life world. Central belief systems—more tenacious than beliefs about doves—can get shaken, moats get built around them, and a dead space so easily set in place.

Writing of most consequence, I claim, starts with a decision to bring one's mind out of that dead space, to the margin between self and other, old ideas and new. There one can read things better, see how lines get drawn, tell new stories, create different kinds of spaces, live at the risky critical edges between one's own values and those of others, have a say perhaps in generating changes in people's minds.

Such a job. But such an exciting idea of writing to give our students.

Others have given it to me, often by challenging what I thought I knew as this book came into being.

Just when I would think I knew what I needed to give to students, for instance, they would turn my head in new directions, giving me texts that demanded new ways of reading and giving me, in turn, readings of things I'd said that would send me back to my computer, revising and revising those oral texts I'd given them. Who has given what to whom? They, most assuredly, have given me an abundance of ideas about writing.

George Dillon showed me ways to read and write I had never thought of. He read draft after draft of early chapters, only once finally losing patience and asking me, "What *are* you trying to say, anyway?" When I decided what it was I wanted to say, my ideas felt like his as much as mine; he had been so willing to talk and listen for so long.

Gene Hammond read too, and gave me some of his good sense of detail about sentence structure, words, and logic. He has given me insights, friendship, and an example to follow always of what good teaching and a humane professional life should be.

Susan Handelman and Marion Trousdale were early readers who provided support and suggestions. The five members of my teaching group and their students were the lifeblood of early chapters: those five cared about teaching with an intensity that kept them arguing with each other long enough for me to record important parts of what they said.

David Bleich read a more recent draft through ears sensitized to voice, and he knew I had given mine away to all the experts I used to support it. What a grand lesson I learned from him, one I now give students in every writing class. My reading of his lesson is that there comes a time when a writer has to look fearlessly into the face of the others who are her sources and her expected readers, and then gather her materials into her own vision. The voice heard in her writing gives evidence of the way she senses herself orchestrating all those whose presence can be felt in her text. Writers who are not deadened to themselves or to others as alive, responsive beings give palpable evidence of who they are in the words they write;

when that evidence grows murky, writing is dehumanized for both writers and readers.

Martha Ramsey at Oxford University Press was a wise and insightful reader. I would like the ability to make marginal comments as graciously and helpfully as she.

Finally, my friends and colleagues at Towson State University have created a stimulating place in which to work and learn and think about issues involved in teaching writing: We talk, we plan, we argue, we challenge each other every day of our lives together. Departmental support, feminist support, and a real commitment there to innovative programs keep our theories and practices from slipping apart, and our Monday mornings moving right along.

Towson, Md.   C.E.H.
May 1989

Contents

Writing from the Margins

1

Introduction

Writers need to seek life at the borders

"You decide; you're the teacher."

From a desk tightly placed against the side wall, a voice was challenging Catherine Wood's directive. She was a new teacher, he one of twenty students in her freshman composition class. She had asked them to choose between working on an assignment in pairs or in one large group; Jimmy wanted her to decide. Nevertheless, pairs were beginning to form on their own, and he moved along with them. During the ten-minute work period, his eyes and his feet seemed restless. Once or twice he got up to ask Catherine a question.

The semester had barely begun, but Catherine was already feeling drawn to Jimmy's warm and volatile personality as well as challenged by it. She was one of five new teachers I was working with; my job as their supervising teacher was to help them cope during their first year in the classroom. Today, visiting her class for the first time, I began to join her interest in thinking about Jimmy—his appeal, his writing problems, the apprehensive look in his eyes.

His writing style and his habits of mind gradually began to make some sense, along with his needs in the classroom. The only son of a Greek immigrant, Jimmy wrote proudly about his father's teen-aged involvement in underground activities against the Nazis. Tortured by the Gestapo, surviving imprisonment and finally the war, the father in his son's eyes "ha[d] lived a very hard life and done it well."

Jimmy was drawn to the authority he sensed in his father; in fact, he seemed to have trouble during the semester *not* writing about him and talking about him with Catherine. He would tell stories, for instance, about how his father guided the direction of topics for his papers. Or, in one of those papers, Jimmy interrupted his description of a supermarket's gourmet deli to tell the reader that his father was the manager of this "Rolls Royce of Giant Supermarkets," and that its thirty-three employees and its visitors from overseas show "how important my father's job is."

When Jimmy needed to write about a topic other than his father, he would often wander down side paths, tell side stories (as in the paper about the supermarket's deli), and forget his point or his purpose. As Catherine remarked on one paper, he would "lose [his] way." He seemed as unable to focus his attention on his writing as on his classwork. Sentence logic, for instance, was often garbled: "Living on campus offers several advantages which makes putting up with occasional interruptions." It was as if he had no ability to follow an independent line of thought when his mind moved away from its source of power, whether the power was Catherine in the classroom or his father at home. It was a mind accustomed to walking in someone else's footsteps, seeking always the comfort of staying safely within that other's conceptual borders.

Living a pale reflection of someone else's life or value system leaves one with few resources for alert and sustained probing of one's environment, no motivation to reach out for answers when the most important question is whether or not one's support system is operative. Writers require confidence that they have the right and the ability to read their own experience in the same way they read anything on a printed page: noticing the details and the patterns that connect those details to each other and to a larger picture. And although drawing inferences is certainly at the heart of this task, so is being aware of the social and cultural context out of which and for which those inferences are drawn—the relationships between reader, writer, and subject that are different from those of others and that give fire to a writer's mind. Besides confidence, then, writers also require an agility in moving between viewpoints—a sense of muscular and mental readiness to move both into their reader's mind and into the midst of their subject area without losing their own voice or purpose in writing. To achieve this rhetorical stance they need the kind of attention that can live on both sides of the border between themselves and others. They must write from a strongly grounded position and then read from outside that position, never fearing to leave the safety net of old, habitual places that feel magnetic to them. New magnets are needed every time they write anew, so that they can question what they have just written from one vantage point and answer from another.

Such agile movements and encounters of the writing mind bring it into the realm of learning, itself a change of mind created when old knowledge meets new. Composition teachers have thought a lot in recent years about writing as learning and have often valued this kind of writing over the "dummy" runs that simply feed back to teachers what is already known or what involves little personal input. Yet teachers who think of writing as involving the kind of movement just described will not make so strong a dichotomy; rather they will see a continuum between dummy writing and writing to learn. All writing changes the quality of the writer's knowledge and understanding in some way (some more, of course, some less) because it takes on a life of its own that forces the writer to respond *as she writes*. Even the most mechanical or uninvolved writing is the voice of someone—or often many "ones" within a single mind (as Mikhail Bakhtin has argued [34–39]). To sharpen their awareness of and control over their writing, students need to notice whose voice or voices they hear; they do this by changing points of view from reader to writer, slowing down, speeding up, zooming in and backing off. Content cannot be separated from the way it is perceived and the way it moves between minds (and "parts" of minds); knowledge is never any more given than it is made, over and over, across mental borders. We would simply hope to encourage more borders, more encounters, more complexity, and therefore more learning.

Jimmy's mind was used to being stuck in one place, one vantage point, in a world that felt ready-made, given, and factual. Other eighteen-year-olds may turn away from parental power to other social spheres (to contemporary role models, for instance), but their habit of dependence is simply less visible than Jimmy's: rather than reaching for freedom to question social or cultural givens, they ordinarily just trade one given for another, so strong are the habits of mind that need rings of protection from conceptual dissonances.

Crossing borders of schemata creates anxiety

Young people cling to those habits with good reason. According to some psychologists, one of the most uncomfortable scenarios in anyone's life is having to move through everyday events without a firm emotional and conceptual grip on what those events mean. "When individuals are uncertain about the symbolic meaning of events, as well as what to do about them," claim psychologists Garber, Miller, and Abramson, "they become anxious" (161). They associate this anxiety with a feeling of helplessness, impotence, and lack of control, all clustering around a person's discovery that "his or her system of interpretive schemata is not adequate for the situation" (161). Depression, with its attendant low energy level, is not an uncommon adjunct to this syndrome, they believe. One need not rely so strongly as do Garber, Miller, and Abramson on cognitive explanations to agree with them that people cluster their experiences into systems of belief, that these systems are structures of viewpoints that create expectations—"schemata" or plans—for future experience, and that the plans may go astray and experience prove less controllable than some people can tolerate with ease. Anxiety and depression result. If losing the support of familiar frameworks of interpretation can have such debilitating effects on *any* of us, we can be sure our freshmen would be looking for even more stable belief systems than most; they have so recently left the cultural scenes of their homes (with all its complexities) for the yet more complex ones of college dormitories and classrooms. If Garber and her colleagues are right that even the ability to give one's attention to the details of a situation depends on a sense of familiarity with what it might mean in a coherent system, does it not seem sensible to encourage rather than discourage students' efforts to keep their minds focused on familiar events and meanings? Might we not simply assume that Jimmy's hold on his parental culture must surely have been loosening, that his volatility might have signaled a desperate holding on to old ways, and that Catherine's job was to support more writing about—and therefore more control over—the old ways? Even though we might object that our job as writing teachers is decidedly not to protect our students from situations that are hard for them to read, many of us want to support them if they are drawn toward writing about their own cultural roots, or for that matter, about any other culture with which they are feeling identified.

Writers should not be protected from anxiety-provoking encounters

I would agree that students' writing should follow the magnets of their minds (at least in classes that encourage free choice of subject matter). But I would not want that writing to exist in a classroom vacuum, immune from all the values and contradictions that can arise when each person is encouraged to follow her own magnet and then jump with it into the ongoing classroom conversation. The very grappling with and untangling of the lines of force after such encounters brighten a writer's mind, drawing it toward the boundary between itself and other minds that are different, facing it with real or seeming inconsistencies which it can learn to set up as problems to be solved.

The trouble with otherwise valuable studies of psychological schemata is that too often they do not model the effects of psychological conflict or social encounter on the way people construct meaning in their lives. To be sure, rich and diverse models of mind proliferate in the field of psychology itself: Charles Hampden-Turner, for instance, charts sixty paradigms of mind, gleaned from a wide range of psychologists and philosophers (*Maps of the Mind*). Many of these models, and even the "schemata" and "frames" shared across disciplinary boundaries in linguistics and the social sciences (Tannen 137–139), have supported work in the area of interpersonal and intrapersonal dynamics and conflicts. But talk of mental designing and schematizing in the field of composition has been dominated by psychology's cognitive process models, devoid of or only loosely linked to such dynamics. (Strongly valued among us, for instance, have been the cognitive planning, translating, and reviewing model of Flower and Hayes [365–387], and the individualistic schemata of Bereiter and Scardamalia [1–64]). Such paradigms for writers seem to produce self-enclosed mental prisons with impermeable boundaries, giving us three-dimensional, single minds processing information inside the containers of heads, rather than interactional events moving in an arena between people.

When a writer's mental processes are not considered *necessarily* connected to those of others, not necessarily containing seeds of conflict, dilemmas, and arguments, those processes lack the interactional dimension that keeps writing and thinking alive and exciting, even though risky. If Jimmy were to think differently from his father, grapple with the questions and contradictions probably already present (though hidden) in his schematized belief systems, he would undoubtedly lose a certain sense of safety. But he might also learn better how to define, compare and contrast, argue, and tell new stories from the margins between himself and his father.

The writing process is rhetorical even more than it is cognitive, alive with both dissonances and resonances between people and their schemata, between their own assumptions about life and those of others. I have watched the eyes of young writers who seem to be shutting down their own mental boundaries, and I am reminded always of cognitive paradigms that cannot address the problem of deadened eyes nor the fear of opening to another's point of view. At such times I also think of the caged panther in Rilke's poem "The Panther," whose sight grows blunt because it is contained behind bars, and whose "mighty will stands stupefied" because what seems to be outside his cage is "nothing merely."

The idea of schemata is a helpful one in that we need to know that writers read everything through already-in-place clusters of beliefs and hang onto those clusters as to lifelines. But such lifelines are surely less than stable, and as the relationship between writer, reader, and subject matter (rhetorical context) changes from one piece of writing to another, those interpretive clusters need to adapt to it. Writers' minds, in other words, need to operate as open systems of meaning capable of learning about relational context as well as simply subject matter. Boxlike models resemble closed systems, numbing and belying our everyday experience of having to cope cognitively, emotionally, socially, and politically with people whose own background knowledge and mental habits differ from ours. These models do not help writing teachers who are faced with students like Jimmy, unable to find seeds of opposition in their own assumptions.

Since writing for readers (all writing, that is, even a diary to oneself) grows directly out of meetings between clusters of different viewpoints (even "within" oneself), we need a way to deal directly with those differences in our teaching. Only then are we able to help writers feel more confident when they dare to confront belief systems different from their own. Anxiety is an inevitable concomitant of the border-crossing that gives life to writing. It is such an odd mixture of both fear and excitement that to avoid it is not only to avoid fear but to avoid a sense of excitement too. Anxiety needs to be welcomed into the classroom as incipient change of mind. Ways to deal with it will be discussed in later chapters. Its avoidance should not be part of our agenda.

Cultural habits permeate schemata

Clusters of viewpoints—"schemata"—take on a more social and usefully interactive tone if they are referred to sociolinguistic, rhetorical, or anthropological traditions rather than the psychological ones in which the schemata appear conflict-free. Once we turn our minds to what happens between people rather than within single heads, we find talk not only of schemata, but of scenes (Fillmore 124), interactional frames (Tannen 142), ideological dilemmas (Billig et al. 31), and even stories. Instead of individual minds, the settings studied are those of social relations, and the cultures that act as clusters of beliefs, values, and attitudes structuring those social relations. As the "minds" of social groups, cultures permeate individual minds so thoroughly, say such anthropologists as Clifford Geertz (55–61), that they pattern the way people perceive the world as well as how they behave in it, the meanings people read or take in as well as the meanings they communicate to others. Cultures are sign systems, habits of reading the world indeed, but ones that cannot easily shut themselves off from change because cultures overlap so much with each other. They spread across minds and groups of minds, joining social with individual knowledge and with desires and commitments and interests. Multiple cultures crisscross through everyone's life, informal ones as well as formal, and according to Edward Hall, it is the often unconscious informal cultural patterns, such as those of men that differ from those of women, that subliminally guide the way people experience their lives (176–181). The many subcultures and informal cultures we live in, then, often create conflicting voices or subterranean beliefs, and the need arises to suppress dissonant ones in order to move through life with a semblance of order.

Writing is a necessarily social and political act

Since our most demanding job is to help our students clear a path for themselves through and with those clamoring voices and view-points they meet, we might consider how their learning for that task differs from that in some of their other classes. Some educators have thought of writing as a skill or set of skills that students learn in order to be able to act appropriately—in this case, to write. These people claim that after all, writing is more an ability to act—like driving, swimming, typing, for instance—than a process of acquiring facts to be memorized, fed back to a teacher as correct answers. Writing, they claim, is an action that demands a much different mindset from the one students so often use in "content-oriented" classes: Those content-oriented students are apt to memorize what a teacher expects and learn only that much, so that they can feed back enough to be right but not enough to cause them to risk self-exposure. Thinking of writing as a skill puts it in a different, less passive mindset, aimed more toward control over actions.

Other teachers, though certainly not wanting students to have "memorizing" mindset, condemn a skills approach to writing because they believe it too context-free and too mindless a concept, one that emphasizes a kind of muscular flexing of mind in little subskills unaffected by content. These teachers believe that writing asks for a far more complex, committed, and functional response to living situations, ones that demand a writer's imaginative and active engagement with subject matter.

A good deal of cultural and intellectual baggage comes along with the arguments on both sides of this (admittedly simplified) issue, the one side often linked to empirical traditions in education or psychology, the other to Kantian and Romantic concepts in a philosophical and literary lineage (e.g., that of Ann Berthoff [*Making* 26–29]). But what both sides have in common is an often unexamined historical link to nineteenth-century visions of what individual minds can do cognitively or imaginatively. Issues between them are often framed in terms of how single minds manage to give form to content, and although interactions are often thought important to learning, they are rarely cited as necessarily connected to what is taught or learned.

What is missing in the skills tradition as well as the Romantic one is a necessary and balance-destroying connection between one mind and another, an acknowledgement that the context of writing is inescapably interactional and finally power-structured or political, with writers feeling tugs on their minds from many sides, many people, many ingrained habits of cultural thinking that tend to govern and socialize that thinking. Moreover, because cultures are not isolated from each other, writers can avoid intercultural influence only by looking away, closing down interactional systems, killing them a little. Living, open systems—biological ones, psychological, social, cultural—cannot otherwise escape influence from others who touch their borders; as a human activity in a world of open systems, writing is an answer to another voice, another place, another time. It can never be, for instance, *only* expository, or *only* expressive, with no political, strategic, or argumentative undercurrents. It exists in a web of interactions that exert influence or force on each other.

Thinking reflects a writer's sense of social context

In order to address problems that result from living and writing being such magnetic fields, writers need to learn not simply skills that help them to act appropriately (the "rules" of "good" writing), but how writers can come together with foreign-feeling readers and data to create a result of that meeting. What happens, for instance, when real writers meet those rules about writing that others have made? What happens when old habits meet obstacles to their functioning? What happens when one culture (teachers for instance) meets another (students for instance) or even one theory in the classroom (nineteenth-century Kantian, let us say) an other (perhaps social and Freirean)? The cultural habits through which people read meaning into their experience can change at the point of contact with others, if questions or controversies about the interaction are allowed to arise there. (If feet are shuffling or heads nodding while someone is reading a paper aloud, for instance, it is not inappropriate to ask "What's going on here?" and pursue historical connections on both speaking and listening sides.) The boundaries between people's usual reading of themselves and of some other person or group will then sometimes shift, so that the interaction or the relation is read in a new way.

But this kind of change is not likely to happen unless students hit an impasse that raises questions along the way in their thinking, writing, or interactions with readers or listeners. And impasses are just the sort of thing they try to avoid, smoothing over or ignoring differences between their own belief systems or cultural habits and those implicit or explicit in the material they are dealing with and the projected readers of their writing.

One of the major reasons writers have so much trouble working smoothly between details and thesis, or drawing inferences from facts, is not their inability to reason effectively or think like an expert, but their difficulty in raising questions and controversies at points of impasse between themselves and their readers and subject matter, questions that they would then expect to be able to research and answer. This rhetorical context, the moving and alive connection between reader, writer and material, needs to wrap itself up into a ball of vision, a desire to answer and solve, a purpose to fuel a writer's attention and thinking. The meaning of any piece of writing reflects or doubles the way a writer conceives of this situation (a situation David Wright of the Health and Human Sciences Department in Washington calls, in his government writing courses, PAWS: purpose, audience, writer, subject). The meaning is not in the subject matter, not in the reader, not in the writer himself, but in the answering of questions about the relationship between all three parts of this triangle. If there is to be a felt purpose, it will be embedded in the desire to address dissonance in life situations: controversies, problems, senses of disjunction between people. All of these motivate writers to think "critically," if they trust themselves to be active agents able to argue, negotiate meaning with others, and figure things out. Critical thinking depends on a certain level of interactive energy, a tension that commands attention. It cannot flourish in environments where cultural dissonance is denied or ignored: not in families, schools, or nations. (Useful discussions about human and affective contexts for critical thinking can be found in Myers [40–53] and Brookfield [5–34, 211–227].)

When writers are not willing or able to open their own minds (sometimes painfully) to the difference *and* the similarities between themselves and those others, they will usually try to kill the differences off in order to fit the others into their own systems of beliefs or try to see those differences as so oppositional that there are no similarities. In effect, they are reproducing selfsame selves, doubles of the systems of thinking they had before any rhetorical encounters, rather than reproducing selves with boundaries changed from a negotiation with someone and something other than themselves.

Two kinds of learning are important for writing

Learning about anything within the confines of one's old system of beliefs is called by Chris Argyris and Donald Schön "single-loop learning"; learning that changes the boundaries of one's old system of beliefs they label "double-loop learning" (85–101). It takes place when old beliefs and values that interfere with a learning task are opened to new possibilities. Let us say, for instance, that a writer's claim about Muslims being a violent people is challenged by an Iranian classmate. If the writer listens to his classmate's argument and questions him further with a desire to learn more and then possibly change his stance, he is using double-loop learning, since, according to Argyris and Schön, "a person engages in double-loop learning when he learns to be concerned with the surfacing and resolution of conflict rather than with its suppression" (19).

On the other hand, if instead of listening to that "other" the writer finds a way to dismiss his argument as prejudiced or ignorant, he is engaged in single-loop learning, which involves learning "new techniques for suppressing conflict" (19). Single-loop learning deals only with challenges that can be handled within existing systems of belief (challenges that usually stay close to a comfort zone: for writers, for instance, "arguing" a case without considering opposing points of view, or even learning about clarity and coherence of documents but not investigating their rhetorical context).

Single-loop learning, claim Argyris and Schön, allows people to function fairly efficiently when they stay within the confines of their habitual patterns of experience, but not when they are faced with dilemmas that challenge the systems of beliefs in which they oper-ate. Single-loop learning will of course always be a necessary part of what we as teachers of composition deal with, but since writers are faced with challenges to their habitual mindsets whenever they contextualize their writing, they need to become practiced in dou-ble-loop learning as well. It asks writers to step into a system of values that contains both their own and those of an other who feels foreign to them or is impinging on their territory for whatever reason, and from there to question their relationship to that other. Instead of staying centered within the margins of their own loops of values, they contextualize those loops by moving their minds into a second loop around the first, a bigger picture that contains both their own and that other's belief system. Response groups, for instance, can simply be asked to raise questions where they seem appropriate: does a writer share any common purposes with a disliked co-worker, say, one the student "cannot" work with to solve a problem at hand? Double-loop learning is social learning because it asks questions to be raised at boundaries between people and their beliefs. Once a second loop is entered and the habit of questioning takes over, third and fourth loops are often engaged.

Double-loop learning is embedded in questions of perspective

Argyris and Schön's ideas about learning can be related to Gregory Bateson's theories of Learning I, II, and III, each level changing the boundary between text and context of what was learned at the preceding level (*Steps* 279–308). Bateson argues that communica-tion always carries information about the relationship that contex-tualizes it, and that habits of thinking change when learners allow themselves to look at those relationships from ever more inclusive contexts, describing the preceding learned "text" from a new "you-plus-me" perspective ("Difference" 4).

A writing teacher who values double-loop learning will be pre-pared to reach into the questions arising everywhere that borders seem to meet and to try to humanize those questions, so that they can be seen as problems of context and relationship, not yet well-defined enough to be inscribed into a text formally (see Carter on problems, 551–565), but indispensible if the more formal problems are to be articulated. At this contextual site, cultural differences should be expected and even looked for: why does this feel foreign? Who is behind this seemingly nonhuman opposition? When did this opposition arise? How? As open systems, cultures have histories and create complex and subtle contexts for every thought we ever think. The more we question our own and our students' assumptions about other ways of thinking, the more sophisticated and revelatory will be our own and our students' writing.

The discomfort caused by the questioning can be at least partly minimized if closure is trusted to follow the opening, if answers are believed implicit in the questions. These openings and closings can be pointed out to students as embedded in the beginning, middle, and end of a composition, and even of parts of a composition, its sentences, for instance. Ron Scollon uses the word "ensemble" to describe the rhythms and tempos of face-to-face interaction; drawing on the work of Bateson, he claims that these rhythms create the bond between people that lets them attend to each other's discourse and its context (342–345). Surely the large and small rhythms of a piece of writing create the same kind of bond between reader and writer. Talk about cultural rhythms and tempos (ones Edward Hall insists characterize every cultural group, formal or informal) can encourage students to think of everything about the way they interact with others as style born of "ensemble": cultures have it and people do, and it can be changed when ways of interacting change (Bateson "Difference" 3–6; *Steps* 128–132).

Not all models of culture encourage questioning and change

E. D. Hirsch's controversial book *Cultural Literacy* has become a rallying point for people in the humanities, both for those who wish to oppose it to their own views about literacy and for those who agree with much of it. Hirsch's works nearly always lend themselves to such clarifications (their messages tend to be clear-cut). My own agenda is to oppose this book's message not because it supports people's learning more about mainstream culture (I support that too), not because it claims learning takes place through clusters of values (I believe that also), or even because Hirsch believes reading is a social and socializing process (I do not question that it is). Rather I oppose his deceptive claim that he is giving the nation a way to read and write better—become more literate—through social and cultural means, when what he seems to me to be doing is giving the nation a way to numb potentially active minds by making sure they stay in little boxes of nouns devoid of verbs and mutual encounters.

Let me explain. First, Hirsch *seems* to stretch models of individual minds into the wider social realm when he urges—as a solution to weak reading and writing skills—that schools inculcate common cultural schemata in order that students can know and "predict the typical attitudes of other Americans" (24), even though this may not mean "forcing them to accept [national] values uncritically" (24). Taking the notion of schemata from psychologists and reading theorists, Hirsch defines them as "somewhat abstract mental entities" by which readers cluster and structure their background knowledge needed for any reading task (51). Hirsch's point is that these habitual mindsets, known variously as "frames, theories, concepts, models, and scripts" (51) are clusters of associations shared by any community of people who need to communicate with each other, and that effective readers and writers will share "the other person's unspoken systems of association" (68), in this case, the schemata of the national community rather than "a local culture" (69). In a sixty-three-page list of nouns and noun phrases ranging from "Constitution" to "the crown of thorns" (with a few adjectives and a handful of sentences here and there), Hirsch gives his readers cues for some mental entities that might start them or others down the road toward literacy in the "mainstream culture." How the list is to be taught is not entirely clear, but Hirsch says the schemata are "facts" and "information" as well as "clusters of associations" that can be taught through dictionary-like explanations.

But however firmly we might be convinced that every student does indeed gain writing power as she learns the conceptual currency of her wider culture, a moment's thinking might also tell us that learning definitions of this list of nouns will tell students nothing about how the nouns are part of social currents, patterned movements with each other rather than self-enclosed entities. There is no consideration of the emotion- and value-laden activities that real people use to shape their experience (which may include reference to the list's words) in real interactions with others, whether or not those interactions are oral or written. Here again is the container model of mind, assumed able neutrally to absorb lists of words and their definitions, giving us what Henry Giroux has called, in a different context, a "warehouse" tradition:

> This [cultural warehouse] tradition mirrors Education Secretary William J. Bennett's view that the purpose of liberal arts is to initiate students into a unitary Western cultural tradition. In this view, excellence is about acquiring an already established tradition, not about struggling to create new forms of civic practice and participation. Culture is viewed as an artifact to be taken out of the historical warehouse of dominant tradition and uncritically transmitted to students. Within this perspective, there is little, if any, understanding of culture as a set of activities lived and developed within asymmetrical relations of power, as competing forms of knowledge and practices that speak to a variety of voices and traditions; moreover, this view of liberal arts is often translated into a defense of high status knowledge and professionalism that maintain an ominous silence, an ideological amnesia of sorts, regarding the traditions and experiences of women, blacks and other groups excluded from the narrative of mainstream dominant culture. ("Liberal Arts" 23)

Rather than introducing students to the complexities, conflicts, and irregular rhythms of life in a democratic society, Hirsch gives us a simple, reductive solution to the undeniable problems our students have with writing and reading. Giving us two terms from which to choose, "formal skills" and "substantive schemata," and announcing that the former has ruled the latter for too long in educational circles, he claims that the skills will follow "once the relevant knowledge has been acquired" (61). This either/or thinking based on a ruling concept may satisfy our need for closure, but it will not give us or our students a way to deal with the inevitable clashes of cultures all around us, in and out of the classroom, and in and out of all our writing.

I believe there is a connection between the kind of thinking that

gives us the noun-like, settled down, and unified schemata of cognitivists, and the kind that gives us such choices as those between
national culture *or* local culture, or between skills *or* schemata. It is
the kind of thinking about entities that associates itself with most
cognitive research, itself concerned with what might go on in individual minds (or in computers) more than between people. No
matter how "process-oriented" cognitive psychology claims to be, it
is as a discipline riddled with a static kind of structuralist thinking
that gives us those schemata and rules and three-dimensional boxes
that are of little help to composition teachers interested in how
minds might learn through multiple contexts, that is, learn to
change each other. Although cognitivists' flow charts may show us
successive stages of a process, the boxed "stages" cannot mingle
with each other on the printed page, and are not apt to move across
each other's borders in a reader's mind either.

This failure to attend to marginal activities connects thinking in
terms of entities and thinking in terms of either/or choices. Both
kinds are modeled on timeless space, and the very language that
grounds our teaching reflects the fact that such a model cannot
even accord with the movements of our own tongues. Noun-entities
cannot separate themselves from verb-actions and still make sense.
Twentieth-century physics reflects this inseparability of space and
time; Newtonian physics did not, and we would do well to reflect on
the political and linguistic assumptions of a model that fails to enter
twentieth-century complexities, fails to consider the *encounters* of a
person or a group's history, the ways one moves with, toward, or
against an other, answering that other and being answerable for
one's own actions. Space is, as Roger Poole points out, ethical, full
of the meanings brought to it by people (5), and I would add that it
is the times and histories and pacings of those people that help it
become so, create that ethical flavor in any space when people bring
to it the interactional rhythms of their meetings, conflicts, unions.

In an age that tends to live in a Newtonian sea of charged but
seemingly autonomous images—"Irangate," "gipper," "new dimension of comfort," "commitment to excellence," "America's favorite"—our students are not used to noticing that noun-like images
threaten to swallow their experience. No list of cultural concepts
can possibly sink into a nation's young heads and make them
"literate" until they, and especially we, begin to notice what those

concepts are *doing* in all our lives with each other and with us.
Nouns without verbs have no way of transferring syntactic power
from a subject through a verb to an object, through a completed
movement of an idea that will pick up steam again in the *next*
sentence. Language in use is nothing if not open, a structured
system with gaps in the structure. I want my students to appreciate
how language tends to reflect the states of their minds and cultures,
how easy it is to let nouns swallow verbs in nominalizations, so like
one mind, one culture, one nation trying to swallow the threats
impinging on its borders and causing it to kill itself a little, wound
the system rather than face the anxiety and the excitement of
looking those threats in the face, those Muslims, for instance, that
just may be no more violent, no less "right" about world affairs than
we. Personal energy and shared social power are born between us
when we refuse even to imagine culture as a collection of concept-
things to be "learned."

Systems of mutual fear can be changed

My commitment to the notion that such energy and power need to
be linked experientially for a writer has admittedly grown out of my
own political life over the years. I have been interested all my adult
life—since the 1950s—in what people try to do to others in order to
govern them in some way, and in how the "governed" react,
whether parents with children, husbands with wives, teachers with
students, or presidents and the nations entrusted to their care. But
how each side supports the role of the other escaped me until very
recently.

   Let me begin with the governed. In the early 1970s Kate Millett's
Sexual Politics discussed how the idea of politics is a way to talk
about the relative status between people in *all* relationships, not just
the very large-scale ones. "The essence of politics is power," Millett
said (25), power being an ability to make things happen, decide
policy, and set rules, and I knew that I had always felt more
governed than governing. Millett's focus, of course, was men and
women: men had power; women did not. I felt indignant then for all
the times I had routinely felt speechless in front of my father or my
husband, and even for the times I had let my sons chuckle at me

condescendingly when I did not understand some football play. Still, even then it seemed to me the picture was complicated, since none of these men or boys in my life had actually prevented me from making more decisive return moves in our interactions. It was *my* mind, heart, and tongue, after all, that could not decide whether to move into action against those I felt dominating me, pull away from them, or approach them with an open trust of some sort, this with an assumption that a change in my attitude might work miracles in the attitudes all around me.

I did know that power was something I had often sensed as coming toward me rather than from me, tugging me toward the people—often indeed men—in whom the power seemed incarnated or toward the places and events around them. But it tugged in a way that split my mind in two and seemed to put me into a state with nothing to say, or sometimes something false to say, though I had only a fuzzy idea of what would have been true to say. Sometimes the power had seemed embedded in my father, sometimes a boyfriend, a minister or teacher, or later even my husband. Usually my saying nothing, or my false saying, seemed simply a slight misrepresentation of my thoughts, an expedience that made me the suppliant, asking the other for knowledge I probably already had. But that other would feel better, feel appeased somehow, thinking he was giving me the knowledge, I thought. I barely realized then that my habit of catechistic talk was giving me a governed self, inseparable from its language.

Or perhaps I would shut down other kinds of language, some nonverbal, in the presence of a power needing to be appeased, and my habit of attributing that power to someone other than me was so ingrained that the governing ones could certainly be women or children as well as men. There were so many ways I wanted to connect with others, so many languages I felt close to using well if "given" the chance: piano playing, painting, conversing in the sciences, mothering. But in high school when I wanted to play the piano like a friend (male) who did it so well, my own hands would forget where to move on the keyboard when he was around. In college my mind gave up learning biology and chemistry after I watched others (male and female) mastering it so quickly and so well. I switched from the sciences to art only to notice how beautifully my roommate (female) painted. I soon began, of course, to grow nostalgic for the sciences, to slip away from striving for artistic competence to contemplating (from a comfortable distance) my previous life in the labs, a life that seemed freer to me now that I did not need to incarnate those who governed the space and movements of life in those labs. As a young wife in the late 1950s I longed to go back to the schools I had left, though it seemed easier to long to do so than to imagine ways in which I might actually do it. Then as a mother of two daughters and two sons over the next two decades, I walked not very confidently through their youths, wondering at how little control I had over their fates on their bicycles or their behavior in school. My reaction was often either to go limp with resignation or to protest loudly but ineffectually.

One night I dreamed that as I was standing in the midst of friends at a party, I screamed "Won't anybody listen to what I have to say?" Nobody did.

I was not without either rationalizations or remedies for being attracted to giving up control and being mentally debilitated by it. I read childrearing books and fit myself semi-comfortably into their recommended laissez-faire stance. I "did" therapy, finished school, taught art and music—all in Puerto Rico where most of us from the States felt ourselves at the edges of and between two cultures, neither outside the one nor inside the other.

But those green and sunny edges did something other than decenter those of us who lived in Puerto Rico during the 1960s and early 1970s. Living on the margins between Spanish and American worlds forced us to deal in our daily lives with both at once, and to feel on the one hand a helplessness when we could not join in linguistically mixed conversations, but on the other hand, an invigorating sense of rhythmic competence when we could, when we began to find our Spanish tongues. Gradually being able to speak and think and move through daily life from two places at once was, I was finding, somehow training in me not only a listening ear but an answering voice, one that was no longer only asking, and one that began to count in some everyday situations. I who cared not a whit for my lost vote in national elections (we displaced continentals were denied that vote by our residence there) began caring a great deal for the more immediate kind of "votes" in smaller circles: at bicultural parties, for instance, where I might have a say in the direction of a conversation, or in what we should all do next, or in who does what, simply because I was starting to glide fairly smoothly *between* cultures, between Spanish and English, or even between the merengue and the waltz, capable, then, of sensing body and mind together negotiating moves. I felt somehow less governed, more governing, and therefore, more politically able, and the ability was one I cannot imagine separating into cognitive, affective, physical, and social components. They all came together for me in an attitude, a stance, a gesture toward people in my life.

It may seem unusual to juxtapose such power as the vote in a democratic society with the activities at a social gathering. Yet one point of this book is that such analogies can help us all better understand the workings of power, particularly when one speaks in experiential terms: People need to know what power feels like in a given situation, feel its energy with an embodied sense of engaged awareness, ready to move and speak, and ready to stand and listen. They need to experience viscerally this sense of both active and passive timing in order to imagine translating it to other places in their lives.

It was in those days, pulling together all those instructive experiences—the feminist perceptions and perspectives, the confronting of the passive world I had experienced, the language learning, that I realized I had not simply been a passive recipient of an imposed political status, but that I had chosen it, too—subliminally perhaps, unconsciously perhaps, but chosen it nonetheless. I saw other people who seemed able, after all, to act and to decide policy, however small the group within which they acted. Many had fewer resources than I and certainly more forces pinning them down: a friend with no art training at all, for instance, who became a fine painter and still managed to be a competent and affectionate wife and mother, or immigrants with no money and no knowledge of the language who moved right into their new lives and learned not only the language but a profession, finding then places for themselves in their new communities; even figures in island politics who had risen from hard beginnings in the barrios. I knew too that a vast world of people from time immemorial had learned more than one language and gained thereby at least a little more status, and that there were many *kinds* of languages to learn, not all verbal.

Such realizations of responsibility for my own fate were discomforting in the extreme, especially since I knew that not only had I chosen that world but it had been chosen *for* me too, because of my culture, my gender, and my family. I would have to live with that paradox and begin to act out of it. Though I was an adult, able therefore (it would seem) to make choices, there were old cultural, familial values I had trouble shaking, ones I lived by, so that experience reaffirmed them.

Both psychological and social causes of powerlessness were to be reckoned with, in other words; and I knew then that these two forces could not be separated from each other: the mental, physical, visceral energy I felt on that tropical island came at a time in my life when I began to feel more power in my social life, more status even with my own children—when, for instance, they would visit my art room and watch me teaching other people's children how to make papier-mâché. Both the energy and the status were grounded in a tuning into the interactional rhythms of that time and place: linguistic ones, definitely, but also others just in the air—the music, the pace, the art, the gestures while talking, the styles of walking and of meeting others, the Latinized versions of 1970s social protests, even the car swervings and horn honkings that would signal a mainland driving style meeting a Puerto Rican one. Shocked by the audacity of drivers there, I learned to meet them on their own ground with my horn in syncopation with theirs.

Whatever the adjustment of life rhythms taking place, first came what felt like a loss of balance and a falling back to kindergarten, to a place of being separated from old ways, of not knowing what is going on and why, and having no say at all in decisions. There was an unmistakable fear and sense of helplessness, succeeded by a speaking up and coming into a new, more stable and socialized place, bringing the old self along but giving it up too. The experience was often exhilarating.

In the mid-1970s I moved with my family back to the States, to the heart of social power there: the Washington, D.C. area. I became a teaching assistant and began to work on my Ph.D. in English at the University of Maryland in College Park. Soon I felt the old syndrome again: being drawn this time to professors I could admire, but being unable to think or talk (and now write) fluently in their presence. Why, I wondered, had I felt strengthened at the margins of some cultures in my life but not these? And though I knew, certainly, that people do revert to old coping styles in new situations, this style lingered too long, dug in its heels. Why was I once again, and over this long stretch, deferring, yessing, and losing my own grounding in the face of some other person's pronouncements?

I began looking now not so much at the governed but at those who govern, the teachers and administrators of universities. A conversational negotiation in the old Puerto Rican days might have worked for me, I realized, because the relationships were more symmetrical between me and my Latin friends, and because the stakes on either side were not so high: neither of our futures depended on our playing the roles right, whether male/female roles or any other dominant/submissive ones. But here in academia it mattered very much that I not jeopardize the degree I wanted so much. When, for instance, I would walk into a faculty office, needing to know something, and when the other across from me was not only different from me in rank and often gender, but was sitting down at his desk while I was standing up, and when he (almost always he) had a strained, quizzical, get-on-with-it look on his face as I groped for words with which to get on with it, I could not feel comfortable or proficient disturbing this universe of meaning and policy. Other teaching assistants, I discovered, had feelings not so different from mine.

The exceptions to the rule of strained communication between TAs and faculty were of course noteworthy, and crossed gender lines often enough. I do not wish to imply that there were not chips on the shoulders of us TAs or no faculty members of both sexes who could ignore the chips, give us warm welcomes, and engage us with respect.

One of those faculty members was our director of freshman English, whose behavior around his "governed" taught me, finally, the lesson I had been trying to learn for twenty-five years: how each side of the force field of governed and governors supports the role of the other. By the time I became his assistant director in the early 1980s, I had already been a supervising teacher for two years, training new teachers of freshman English and trying hard to tell them what to do out of one side of my mouth while intimating they did not have to do so out of the other. The role of authority came uneasily to me, as always, but when I became assistant director the dilemma was worse: Not only did I have to tell many more people than formerly what to do, but for an entire semester I kept forgetting the rules and regulations I needed to know in order to do so.

The long-delayed lesson began to be learned when the director was patient with my questions. Surely, I felt, he should become irritated with me. Next, I watched him closely, day after day, in action with TAs. He listened to their ideas, agreed with them often, disagreed with them just as often, but never did his eyes reveal anger, distrust, irritation, or anything other than straightforward interest. As a result, ideas began flowing through our department, puzzled over, agreed on, argued about; it was such a stimulating time.

The lesson? This man's talk moved with us, in and out of our ideas and his. He did not maintain a constant difference from us through the subtle cues that others might use (averted or irritated looks, perhaps, or formal politeness). He was not feeding us an underlying fear about his status for us to mirror. But then neither did he engage in a circular mutual admiration with people. He did not need to stave off any anxiety about differences that might alienate him from his charges.

That is what it was: There was no anxiety in the air to keep me in my place, and he would not even mirror back to me mine. How easy it is, I had finally realized, for both the governed and the governors to pick up (though barely be aware of) cues about the tensions between them. And feed them right back. The fear and the irritation, I was sure now, were all part of the same worried hanging on to the status quo, an acknowledgement that our social and psychological and therefore semantic moorings are in mortal danger from some action of the other before us, either a removal of support—pulling away—or a swift cut through it—moving toward us. And all of us can smell that terror in the air as well as deny to our last breath that it exists.

The governed—always more agile at picking up cues on which their survival depends—mirror the subliminal message from the governors, and a vicious cycle of mimesis is underway. Each supports the other, needs the other, to keep him and her in their places, with at least the implicit promise, then, of holding off the fall back into kindergarten, where one's resources are not yet mobilized even enough to protest.

And how I had always wanted to keep others in those governing spots, I thought now, to have someone to resist and react to, to ferret out the masked voice the other always thought he or she was hiding, to mirror it back, ironically. But to be so circumspect, so veiled in my mirrorings, that the strong other would not even imagine removing my support system.

The challenge now would be to notice better and to try to lift the bans, perhaps to become more at home with everybody's double voices so that those around me, including my students, might not have to mirror my own second voice, my hidden agendas. I think that what we have always thought to be power is probably actually a holding back—of the energy that can be released in the fields *between* people if we let the oppositions and contradictions and paradoxes come to the surface. I find that very hard to do, but am convinced that it is one key to understanding how writing is at root a tuning into the rhythms of one voice answering another, within and without, not losing itself, not losing the other. That is argument, and that is critical thinking, cutting through the boundaries between people to their similarities, and out of these, tracing out differences that can be lived with.

Old habits can be negotiated and new languages learned

Recently, for instance, a colleague and I were asked to sketch out a new, more rigorous policy for the teaching of business writing at the school where I teach now, Towson State University. When she described to me the way she teaches it and likes teaching it, I at first despaired that we could find any common ground at all; the differences between us seemed so great. I heard her focus on students' investigations of area businesses (at first unfamiliar to them) to differ in key ways from mine on their investigations of their own part-time jobs. But as she talked, the word "situation" kept coming up as a place we might start: She believes as much as I do, I realized, that students should write out of a rhetorical context, in which writer, subject matter, and reader form an interacting system that invigorates writing. I insist that my students find someone (often a boss at work) who needs them to research and report on some organizational problem, and my colleague also insists that her students look into the actual situations of small businesses, from which they write several kinds of problem-solving papers. The differences between our techniques, kinds of papers, and assumptions about the writers still made me feel uneasy (we differed on how personally involved students needed to be); I sensed just a little stirring in the solar plexus when I thought of our job. But on the other hand those differences began exciting me because they forced me, on the waves of scores of deep breaths, to imagine how in the world we could translate our visions into each other. I felt almost as if my whole mind was being twisted and pulled into an uncomfortable place, but a stretching one. I began to hear her better, though, to feel at home in her place and even with the other voices in our meetings joining in, and when she drafted a plan it seemed almost mine as well as hers (she: such a negotiator), almost some of those others' too. I asked for only one additional word and felt content. Since then I have come to share even more of her ideas about business writing.

And business writing anyway! Once I would have thought it the camp of the enemy, so opposed have I always felt to "servicing" entrenched interests that do not (so I have thought) examine their own destructive assumptions and impulses. But following through my own assumptions about politics on any scale, assumptions that tell me that opposing the other in an either/or way is simply imitating his own tactics, I am turning to look the old "enemy" in the eye, entering his camp, listening and answering, and finding common ground between us so that the margins between us change as they could never do if I stayed on my side of the line throwing stones. When I do not model digging in my heels against the other's position, he tends not to dig in his heels against mine, and the "he" here is simply all that has seemed most other and foreign to me at some time in my life. When I began teaching technical writing and business writing, for instance, I felt as if I had entered a gray space of mechanical rules until I found writers in the field like Carolyn Miller, David Dobrin, Michael Halloran, all people deeply involved in humanistic issues within the discipline of technical writing. And I found that the "alien" students who registered for these courses played earth to my sky, kept my ideals grounded, and in turn let some of my ideals into the centers of their very pragmatic, job-oriented lives.

I began, too, to work with friends involved in corporate consulting courses and to do consulting with the General Accounting
Office in Washington. I had to admit very soon that in the middle of
the city that the whole nation seems to perceive as a shapeless
bureaucracy, anguished writers are feeling accountable to the whole
nation, and training departments are stirring up exciting controversies about how best to teach, and assess, and make a difference in
the writing of these evaluators of our federal policies.

The results of my excursions beyond freshman writing are opening my eyes. I have found, for instance, that nearly all the writers I
deal with can be called novice writers, from freshmen to juniors to
many evaluators at the General Accounting Office and corporate
writers beyond. They are novices because they have not yet learned
to stop thinking of their writing as *either* in their own power *or* in
an other's, from the Jimmys who do not want to, or cannot manage
to, write in their own voices, to the students who cannot seem to
observe something or someone outside themselves as falling in a
different conceptual world from themselves. Then there are the
evaluators who feel helpless in the face of their supervisors: as one
of them put it, "I've learned to give my writing away here at GAO; I
have no control over what happens to it up through the review
process."

But old habits can be negotiated, new languages learned. Even
the "weak," as Elizabeth Janeway claims, are not without power to
make changes in their situations (93, 263), especially when they
begin to realize that organizations and communities are not static.
The more marginal any of us is to the political action, the more we
need to find, and often are able to find, meeting grounds that will
decenter the status quo. Students and teachers, evaluators and their
supervisors, staff writers and their bosses, can learn to recognize
that negotiation for the meaning of—and policy for—situations
goes on continually in everyday life, with those who feel peripheral
to the action better able to read meanings into those situations as
well as understand reasons to change them. Both oral and written
interactions implicitly reveal broad ranges of negotiating moves,
from soft compliance with other people's positions to a firm rejection of those positions. Differences in status cannot be eliminated
but they can be mediated more effectively (and often more explicitly) than they usually are. When the other at the center, for in-

stance—teacher, supervisor, reviewer—is not met by ever-so-subtle signs of fear and shrinking, the stage can often be set for a braver entry on both sides into the inevitable conceptual dissonances between the governed and the governing ones. When I would think two years ago about my "visiting" status at Towson, or when my black student Sonya worried about being in an otherwise all-white classroom, or when my working student Tom returned after not showing up in class for two weeks, we all tended to reveal—by word, gesture, and a fearful glance to our governing others—our tendencies to freeze into a helpless and appeasing position or sometimes into a rigid oppositional one. None of us need do that freezing; this book is dedicated to the possibility that change can be negotiated.

Part I establishes a system of values through which teachers of writing might question the gendered roles that too often seem models for student-teacher exchanges. The vision of this section is that the model might be changed if the boundaries between learning and teaching become more permeable. Classroom interactions come alive, and ideas and texts flow more freely when students and teachers of writing integrate each other's functions with an awareness of fit timing, acting as readers and writers of their own rhetorical contexts, of the interactional situations in which texts are produced. Chapter 2 finds novice writers in positions similar to those of women who have felt themselves at the edges of mainstream culture, supporting other people's decisions. It recommends that margins be thought of not as outside edges but as places of rhetorical interactions, where opposing viewpoints can give birth to new ways of thinking about social and cultural contexts. In Chapter 3 are stories about institutional authority and how it is kept in place even by teachers who think they are immune to its power. To change patterns of authorizing and authoring in the academy, we might better learn how to negotiate boundaries than to retreat behind them, where we so often find ourselves teaching with single-minded agendas.

Part II surveys the field of rhetoric and composition through eyes that have seen double visions and ears that have heard double voices in the minds of those who speak and write. The claim here is that when the voices of writers have been understood as questioning and answering each other, the field has been given one of its most useful tools: a means of undercutting hierarchical thinking, using similarities in differences and differences in similarities. Chapter 4 traces a path through the field of composition as it was envisioned in the early and late 1970s by four men with visions that opposed old and deadening ways to teach writing. They can show us a way to livelier classrooms and livelier written texts, even though they do not model for students a way to draw opposing ideas into interactive rhythms. Looking back into the rhetorical tradition, Chapter 5 finds three practices that did focus on the interactions of voices and rhythms: magic's joining of linguistic action with invisible force, mimesis' moving between the possible and the actual, and the mnenomics of Vico's insisting that memory be linked to imagination in the contending voices of stories, ones that resist categorical ends.

Part III moves into the often turbulent waters of reading and writing minds, which belie individualistic models of computer-like operations. The mental act of writing texts, it is claimed, depends not so much on what happens inside heads as on how a writer reads interactive contexts. As we help students become more adept at overcoming disjunctive rhythms between writing and reading, they can begin to integrate grammatical, stylistic, and political currents of thought into their writing. Translucent and doubling minds, it is concluded, are more alert, more attentive, more observantly critical than those confined to single lines of thought. Chapter 6 looks at the needs of writers in terms of models of mind used to describe their activities. What cognitive psychology has given composition studies is seen as less useful to us than a more fluid, metaphorical idea of mind that would let us imagine currents of thought strongly moving with, around, and past obstacles. Chapter 7 brings the activities of reading and writing together in gender-related ways, seeking social and cultural settings that might help writers sense less discordance between the speed of reading and the slowness of writing. And Chapter 8 argues with those who believe talk of grammatical structure does not belong in a composition classroom. It describes classroom methods that can let us metamorphose ideas of form into those of interactive rhythms. Structure acts as an echo of a writer's sense of agency, it is asserted, a silent partner of her voice as a cause of happenings in her life world.

I

BOUNDARIES: WHERE BIRTHING TAKES PLACE

Boundary surfaces, with their rhythmical processes, are birthplaces
of living things . . . be it in cell membranes, surfaces of contact
between cells . . . [or] in the great boundary surfaces between the
current systems of the ocean.

Theodor Schwenk, *Sensitive Chaos*

2

Students: At the Edges Looking In

Rhetoric that pleases

One of my most dispiriting realizations as a writing consultant has been that many organizational settings or corporate cultures have the same kind of mindset toward writing that we composition teachers so often notice in individual students: entire groups in the work world seem more dedicated to learning better ways to save face and avoid conflict about what they write than to learning new ways to understand the conflict and negotiate it. This cultural interest in not making waves sometimes motivates writers more strongly than interest in grappling with and finding patterns in the discovered content, or the data they collect from research. As rhetorical triangles go, this one is lopsided, with the power and purpose a writer senses seemingly resting in the hands of the audience rather than being shared among writer, material, *and* audience. The problem of course is an age-old one, a big clue as to the source of most people's negative image of rhetoric, in which the "audience-pleasing" leg of the rhetorical triangle is seen to have taken over the writer's mind as motivating force, rather than yielding to what Wayne Booth calls "the rhetorician's balance" between writer, audience/reader, and subject-matter interests ("Stance" 78). The problem should not be a surprise, surely, to teachers aware of writing's inevitable political component.

But I *was* surprised, partly because writers with integrity and awareness of the problem were feeling helpless and resigned, partly because I had somehow hoped that their understanding it would lead them to action, that people with some already established ability to think through their writing in innovative ways would of

33

course feel empowered to negotiate meaning with those in the organizational hierarchy above them. What good did it do, I thought (with a touch of professional self-pity), to work with the Jimmys of the world, help students become more active in their writing and think more critically, when out there in the work world they would just get knocked down again, minds contracted into little balls of conformity? And sometimes bitter conformity at that.

My convictions about transgressing cultural limits needed examining anew and more deeply after this discovery, especially since I was urging students to open their minds, notice people and things they had never noticed before, weather the attendant discomfort, and risk that their own minds might change in the process. Now I began to hesitate, wondering whether they could handle opening edges without letting those others they were opening to take over, much as one of my students had described his anxiety at realizing he had almost succumbed to an "alien" religious faith he had let himself hear about. Was I being unrealistic, I wondered, to imagine that writing teachers could or should put issues of power on their agendas, address the inevitable anxieties (or denials) that arise when deadened parts of mind start to wake up as they cross into formerly forbidden territory? Most of the writers I'd met in corporate settings would rather talk about unity and coherence and single-loop learning issues than about ways they might negotiate with their bosses about what message a report *should* convey to readers. And so, too, would most students in my college writing classes rather pull back from confrontation than look it in the face and struggle with it. What business of mine was it anyway even to think of opening multiple Pandora's boxes of emotional resistances in the work world or in my university classes? Whether it was a corporate writer blaming muddled syntax on his boss's interference (a boss he thought "should" quit forcing him to subdue a controversial point), or a junior in Advanced Informational Writing preaching abstract managerial theory to his restaurant-owning uncle (who "should" listen), should I not avoid meddling in these interpersonal affairs, shun the territory of management specialists, family counselors, or therapists?

The dilemma was full of everybody's "shoulds," mine as a writing teacher trying to figure out what I should be doing as a writing teacher, all of us—students and I—so easily tempted into moralizing or centering into stances of rightness against wrong others. The dilemma was full, too, of our using these stances to help us feel more in control, less helpless against vague juggernauts we were not sure how to fight.

The solution to this teaching dilemma would have to go to the heart of both the ethical and political questions, with my steering between them, paying homage to both but not falling into a trap of thinking I could choose to honor one over the other.

Defining ethical teaching on the margins between people

Two bottom lines came quickly to mind. The first was a conviction that I wanted to live my professional life, as much as possible, grounded in the belief that, in Booth's words, "we are [all] made in rhetoric" (*Dogma* 141) and minds are what are made, minds that mix together the values, feelings, and intellects of selves and others. The rhetorical stance, as Booth defined it long ago, is what I wanted for my students, the balanced relationship between the interests and needs of writer, reader, and subject matter ("Stance" 74). "Mutual inquiry" (Booth's phrase [*Dogma* 137]), then, had to be a core principle in my dealing with writing problems, an inquiry that could not flinch at following whatever course our language together—written and oral—laid out before us. And although I had many arguments with many rhetoricians (including Booth), I found that this principle felt ethical to me, leading me to the idea that though cultures and minds do live within their own systems of ideas, only those minds and cultures that stay open to different ones can be fully rhetorical in an ethical way. Tobin Siebers expresses a version of this idea: "ethics . . . denies those systems defined by their exclusions, and it works ideally toward an inclusive community of human beings" (114). He does not mean by "inclusive community" a community with no internal differences, and I do not mean by "open" a necessarily easy or gentle opening, unattended by unbalancing tensions or timely closures. A trust in some kind of change process, then, seemed vital.

The second bottom line that came to mind was that given this belief in mutual inquiry, I would always have to subject *it*—the belief itself—to inquiry among the people involved when I acted in their midst with it: I would need to tell students my operating assumptions, with the knowledge that the asymmetrical political situation between them and me would have to become part of the mutual inquiry, and that I would have to respect the wishes of those who refused to enter into questioning.

Politics and ethics were beginning to come together for me. I was committed in this newly articulated teaching context (how realistically was not yet clear) to the kind of dialogic critical thinking that had long interested me but that I had used only haphazardly till now. The goal seemed deceptively simple: finding more ways for both students and me to say to each other what is on our minds and expecting something useful to come of the saying.

The expecting, of course, still needed some work, given the fact that political forces cannot easily be harnassed by plans and conscious expectations. So the feasibility of taking a stance with the commitment still raised a question: How was it possible to stand in the middle of the commitment, yet still stay open enough to negotiate with positions contrary to it? I sensed that there could be only one answer. It was important to do both of these seemingly opposed things: both take a firm stance and stay open with it. Not an easy attitude to explain to students. Right timing of speaking up and staying silent would have to be involved, and the job became harder when I looked at my own experience and realized I had not always managed these well. This was a good time, then, to reflect on my own and others' feeling of being on the edges looking in, avoiding the conflicts that might emerge while moving in with both stance and openness.

I had not spoken up when I heard a fifth-grade teacher tell how she taught thinking skills for a research paper by having students categorize their questions about animals at a zoo, questions about habitat, eating habits, and other "facts" but never about connections or significance. Their interest in the animals helped capture their interest in the task, she had said. I had wondered how students could think "critically" without questioning the questions, without engaging the value-making parts of their minds, but somehow I did not dare to ask that teacher more about her own classroom culture and tell her about mine and see where we might go with that. Too many doubts stopped me: it was none of my business, my "business" of rhetoric stopped outside my classroom door, and especially with a teacher from the elementary level who might think me brazen or condescending. My silence, though, left us both learning nothing from each other. I risked no political problems and no change of mind either.

I had not spoken up either with Maury, a student I had admired so much for his positive attitude toward writing and his openness to feedback from classmates and me. Eager to revise, a teacher's dream. Curious about how he had come by these work habits, I asked him one day about himself and his values in life. I hoped for an inspiring story. He told his story, and it was founded on a strong religious faith. His energy, it turned out, grew out of contrasting his own good salvational fortune with that of most of the world. I had not felt free to go beyond my weak response, "But what about the rest of the world?" I heard him swallow Muslims and Hindus as antagonists in his system of values, heard him falsify their beliefs in order to center his own, and I only winced. This was not a writing problem, I had thought; it was none of my business.

It haunted me though and I wondered later: Should I silently respect certain areas of people's lives with whom I am talking if I see these are lifelines? Or might the "respect" simply be a retreat from finding ways to speak to those others who pull me out to the edges of my beliefs? How can I then urge students to speak up? Do I, like Maury, write and talk more confidently when I can contrast my "right" beliefs with infidel others, before whom I remain silent? In his rejection of cultures different from his, Maury was, after all, an unbeliever in what I held to be important. But I safely insulated my beliefs from his, not voicing protest at the way he stereotyped others and refused to revise life texts, if not classroom ones.

I am not suggesting that teachers inside and outside their professional lives could possibly become dialogically engaged with all the people who touch their lives. But those of us who have experienced living at the margins of any mainstream culture (women, students, and many minority groups come to mind) need all the practice we can get in learning to take a stance in the middle of others doing the same; shrinking from this practice assumes we cannot learn to do it well with fit timing. It assumes, too, that we have no conviction and vision of strong rhetorical relationship to model for students. Or for corporate writers.

Two cultures, one vision

All three situations I was puzzling over—those of the corporate writers, the fifth-grade teacher, and Maury my student—involved people who seemed to be thickening their own mental boundaries, closing down some life-giving activity, and questioning at the edges of their belief systems. Points of contact with involved others were deadened, and double-loop learning was excluded. The corporate writers appeared to want a voice with their bosses, but they did not have an expectant frame of mind about negotiating boundaries in that world of discourse nor did they imagine the possibility of change. The fifth-grade teacher did not expand critical thinking into a questioning of contexts for the project. Those fifth-graders were being asked to narrow their focus and learn conventional, conflict-free schemes of classifying information. They were not being asked to widen their thinking at the same time, not being encouraged to notice and question some inherent oppositions in the context, not to notice, for instance, restricted movements of the animals as opposed to their own nonconfined ones. (I had heard no hint that this zoo might be experimenting, as some are, with cage-less natural habitats.) Such questions of context, to be sure, might create a sense of disequilibrium in the children, cause some conflict to arise amid their clusters of beliefs.

But should a critical-thinking project not question as many boundary placements as possible, including those between people and animals, homes and zoos, natural habitats and zoos? Gary Larson has done it, and many children appreciate the way his cartoons raise questions about borders between animals and people. Should we not be encouraging questions of context even for fifth-graders? Though change in living arrangements may not be our goal, attitudinal changes that guide writing are. Asking uncomfortable questions and imagining possible answers is an incipient action that generates writing acts, ones that can change attitudes and concepts.

And Maury my student did not question his relationship to Hindus, being content to make a conceptual life apart from them, where strengthening a faith seems to happen through excluding foreign others rather than engaging with their ideas. And I, as part of yet another rhetorical context created around each of these three, participated in the same shutdown through a silence that said I agreed that we, none of us, should rock any boats by starting something new which we may not be able to finish peaceably and fruitfully.

The vision we were all operating by was a single, nondialogic one that involved two cultures: one belonged to those with voices that made policy decisions (bosses, teacher, Maury) central to conceptual or working arrangements; the other involved those who were either the subjects of those decisions (corporate writers, fifth-grade students, or Hindus and Muslims) or the audience who heard the decisions (many others plus me) and remained silent and, in theory, receptive. It takes little imagination to see that the traditional informal cultures of men and women are divided along these political lines and perpetuate the cultural dichotomy not only within gendered settings, but in other settings like the three above that keep central figures conceptually (and emotionally and attitudinally) separate from marginalized ones.

The gendered vision creates a double bind for students who need either to say or write with an authoritative voice. Given their self-esteem problems, they have trouble imagining themselves in the center saying or writing anything someone might want to listen to, so when told to say (or write), they usually try to guess what the teacher wants them to say and write from her position. Or sometimes, like Maury, they simply pontificate from the center, unable to imagine relationships with those in the rhetorical context, either with people they're talking about (subject matter) or people listening (audience). In this vision of the saying and writing world, people either speak up or remain silent, and if either kind should find himself or herself in the wrong compartment, the result is either rhetoric that only pleases (listener types saying to a more powerful audience) or rhetoric that does not even try to please (sayer types unable to listen before they say).

Dead space at the borders

A little like the (at the moment tumbling) Berlin Wall, this picture of two separate communicational roles raises the specter of a guarded limbo for which each side seems to serve as context.

Rather than a marginal space where meetings take place and new interactional life is born, this space often seems to be a deadened one in which neither side dares risk mixing values and ideas, a mix that feels dangerous because it might cause death (of old ways of thinking). On either side of the no man's land are, first, listeners or readers who feel they have no say, so they don't listen well; and second, speakers or writers who don't sense engaged listeners, so they don't say well. Think, for instance, of our own supposed model of communication: speakers reading papers at conferences with only token glances at audiences. When the model is broken and speakers interact with their audiences, real life is sometimes born.

It soon becomes apparent, though, that the two sides of the system cannot avoid mixing with each other, just as the residents of Berlin have found ways to pass that barrier in their midst. True, it is a nonsymmetrical mix, in which the policymaking, patriarchal side has decided on the kind of epistemological borders the system will favor in its cultural doings: categorical walls in which one neatly categorized subculture would appear to authorize the doings of the other. And our classes do indeed become endless simulacra of such gendered roles that keep us from negotiating meaning with the other side we sense in another's power. (Anthony Wilden has a good explanation of how genderized margins function [*Man and Woman* 47–57].)

But the not-so-well-kept secret is that even the centralized policy-makers fear the power of those who receive the policies—women, students—and they know, in their heart-of-hearts, that the borders only play dead and that the "domination" of one side is never as complete as we might think. We all know that there is no such simplified, categorical dualism in any of our lives as the fanciful vision posits, and certainly there are no such rigid roles between men and women. In our own discipline we have now reader-response thinking that gives us writing as reading, reading as writing, softening of borders, questioning of old ways.

But ingrained attitudes die slowly, even when they are incoherent with other attitudes within a single mind; they appear sometimes in odd places of our teaching and learning lives, in the discomfort we might feel, for instance, in our classroom at any minute we find ourselves as silent learners rather than saying teachers. If the silent voices in ourselves are to change their status, begin to believe in a dialogue between sayers and listeners, they will need to raise questions about the status of those genderized margins that separate the two cultures from each other. The questioning begins a double-loop kind of learning, a removal of the learner from her half of the system in which single-loop learning usually takes place, to the loop that surrounds the whole, the surrounding context of relationships in which both cultures are embedded.

We see there that when people cannot feel in charge of those receiving their pronouncements (and they never can entirely), their minds often shrink from braving the turbulence of unpredictable encounters. Instead, their minds are apt to produce the death place between themselves and the receivers, teachers, and learners, giving them a measure of peace and freedom from painful cultural changes. In rejecting a sharing of roles with the other, each side reproduces sameness of role and little real change of mind or attitudes in self or other. This kind of reproduction is sterile, but so common in cultures resisting change that even pedagogical theorists who do advocate change in schools use the word "reproduction" derogatorily to mean reproduction of the same (Henry Giroux, for instance (*Theory* 222–231]).

Sterile reproduction

Carol Cohn has a pointed example of such sterile reproduction in a story she tells of her summer among defense intellectuals in a nuclear weapons workshop. "The bomb project," she says, "is rife with images of male birth" (699): "Teller's baby," "Fat Man," "Little Boy," for instance (the latter two referring to the bombs that destroyed Hiroshima and Nagasaki). Teller sent a telegram to Los Alamos after a successful test in the Marshall Islands announcing the birth of "Mike": "It's a boy," he said (701). The bombs, says Cohn, are never girls.

As the patriarchal culture appropriates reproductive power from the other side, it forgets to appropriate questions of relationship that go with it, and it ends up with the ultimate example of agency, a saying untouched by the input of readers of the human community. As keepers of the communal function of humankind, women (or others marginal to central action) continue in their role of tending the relational context of such texts, keeping things together in the background, acting as support when needed, maintaining silence about the fact that reproduction of something new and lifelike is itself a matter of relationship. As such, it involves not only a central agentic statement of a father/text, but the womb ("real" or metaphoric) as relational context for a new child, which itself could be either male or female so that there will be another round of life after all.

This new little sayer or listener reproduces not just a father's desires and belief systems, but the mother's side as well, writing/recording in its own child-memory her silent readings of all the stories and histories and connections to the rhythms of everyday experiences that support and cocreate with the father. The patriarchal tendency to imagine that those supportive ones at the edges lack cocreative powers is embedded in such visions of birth from Zeus's head as a football team's winning a game (never mind the cheerleaders' role, or others at the edge of the field), an author's authoring (with thanks, to be sure, to the reader at home who read his work and let him create in peace), or a speech writer's timely delivery of a script (with thanks to the wife who took the kids to a motel). We hear from Bakhtin that authoring is answering, and answering is authoring (Holquist 307–319), but surely those readers who send out the questioning desires for answers, and those whose voices and selves enter into the birth of new texts (or new children), contribute some genetic material. All the people and cultural groups within which a writer lives raise questions to which his very self is a desired answer: an author himself is full of all the people and the peopled places, peopled times, and peopled ideas he has lived with.

The division of labor is still too often sensed throughout the larger culture, though, as one in which an active father (writer) produces a line of inheritance (texts that develop a line of thought, with no big changes of direction in his authoring lifetime, and no explicit grounding in experiential, rhetorical contexts). And in the same single-sex model of reproduction, a student writer produces a text out of his own head; it is his text, so other people had better not get involved with its writing, and if he must revise, no drastic changes from new encounters should be expected. Any other kind of reproduction is too anxiety-provoking and threatening to egos.

Reproduction as a private affair

What happens when women break their silence about such matters? Judy Chicago is an artist who designed many startling images of creation and the birth process which, over a five-year period, were translated into needlework images by women nationwide with whom Chicago worked. As described in the book she wrote to record the work, the partnership and group work was a voyage of self-discovery for nearly all involved: never easy, always revelatory, the artistic relationship and the images had a strong impact in the way they transformed the birth experience.

But one needleworker's comment about viewers at the show itself might have prepared me for a review printed in the *Washington Post* in 1985. The needleworker's comment: "Most of the men shook their heads," she said, "but the women ooh-ed and ah-ed" (Chicago 165). I was not prepared, though, for the harsh tone of that *Post* review, for the [male] reviewer's barely restrained censoring of what to me had been a powerful and moving show:

> Somehow she's persuaded hundreds of women, many of them housewives, to view themselves as artists. Somehow she has forced large segments of the public to consider parts of women's bodies, and parts of women's lives, that the public would rather not confront. Chicago's fans adore her. (Richard)

Paul Richard found the show embarrassing and polemical. He calls Chicago the "Werner Erhard of the art world," and also likens her "cult" to that of Scientologists talking "about their E-Meters." Embroidering such images of upheaval "instead of, say, a bunch of flowers may have been a life-enhancing experience," he says. "But it is not easy to see why."

He also thought the exhibit "among the most exhausting shows this city has yet seen," and could not understand how women who worked on the project could claim it changed their lives. "Confronted by these pictures of the agony of labor, one's impulse is to turn away. But Chicago will not let you. . . . Certain moments call for privacy. That of birth may be one."

The puzzle, to Judy Chicago, was that so many people were horrified about her turning moments of creative power into public art. She could not understand, according to a *Post* interview, "why men and women can stomach images of gore and war, examine glossy pages of explicit pornography, but call for smelling salts when they see [pictures] of women giving birth" (Battiata).

Why is birth thought more frightening and more in need of hiding than war? And are there simulacra of this fear?

Boundaries at risk

Many of the images in *The Birth Project* startled because the human form was shown not only altered in shape but opened during birth in some images, and merging with skies, rivers, and animals in others. Richard saw only pain, horror, and agony. He did notice the power of the exhibit but gave that power negative associations. He did not mention anything about new life being associated with the awesome boundary changes in the images.

According to some feminists, men's association of boundary violations with death rather than with death (of old ways) and birth (of new ones) is related to (1) their having to establish early in their lives an identity distinct from their primary caretaker (Chodorow 174–176), or (2) their growing up with relatively impermeable bodily boundaries (compared to women's experiences of such boundary challenges as pregnancy, childbirth, coitus, menstruation, and lactation [Hartsock 294]), or (3) their invading mindset, born at least partly of a cultural connection to early nomads who placed "higher value on the power that takes, rather than gives, life" (Eisler 48; note, however, Jean Elshtain's questioning of the assumption that women themselves are essentially less combative than men [163–193]).

Whatever its origins, the fear of boundary crossings is imitated in a pervasive mindset that believes one either invades or is invaded, acts or is acted on, kills or dies, dies or gives birth, is controlled or controls. Women live in the mindset as much as men do, since it inhabits the culture that dominates our society. To stay alive is to choose to separate oneself into one side or the other of any dichotomous situation and, at the same time, numb the mind to the impossibility of such choosing. And since giving birth involves both bonding and separating, anguish and joy, union and power, turning supposed either/or oppositions into a both-and experience of relation, it is not easy to contemplate. Life-supporting power born at the point of antithetical movements—joining and separating—does not make sense and is frightening to anyone whose survival feels tied to inviolate borders.

Life arising at boundaries

Judy Chicago herself has never given birth to a child; some women who worked on the project had not. Imaginative doublings are more a matter of cultural support or cultural prohibitions than they are copying an "original" experience. In fact, there is a growing interest in some fields in redefining even the boundaries of life: "Life no longer appears as a thin superstructure over a lifeless physical reality," says one systems theorist, "but as an inherent principle of the dynamics of the universe" (Jantsch 19). Many biologists, chemists, and physicists, and sociologists and psychologists—scientists and social scientists—are claiming, in a new interdisciplinary science called "chaos," that lifelike order arises everywhere out of processes that may seem disorderly, but that have "unexpected regularity" (Gleick 114).

In related work growing out of Ilya Prigogine's studies of order and fluctuations, others are finding similar behavior in systems as far-flung as galaxies, clouds, waterfalls, seacoasts, rivers, snowflakes, pendulums, trees, muscles, and cells. They have noticed patterns of unstable boundaries that create turbulences, first a draining of energy into a rhythmic process, then from that process a jelling into physical forms that take on their own life. Patterns of energy flow are being studied in cultural behavior, in political systems, and in brain activity. Even learning is being looked at, for the way it might be enhanced: "States of consciousness that enhance fluctuations produce more insight—more significant change—than our everyday consciousness. New patterns that overcome old conditioning are likelier to emerge from such states" (*Brain/Mind Bulletin* 3). Chaotic and problem-creating beginnings that cause intensified interactions are claimed to be the crucial factor that leads to orderly and fluid change: "Sensitive dependence on initial conditions [turbulent relations with context or environment] serves not to destroy but to create" (Gleick 311).

In other words, something new comes from intense and even chaotic interactions at the edges of life processes. Biological birth may serve as a model for these interactions, with its initial mating between opposites resulting in creation of new life, but creation in all its manifestations is not gender specific. To continue to avoid looking at the wide range of these manifestations, whether we prefer to call them analogies, homologies, metaphors, or "natural" occurrences throughout material, cultural, and psychological lives, is to cut off a major resource for writers that can encourage them to trust in something coming from interaction with others, no matter how intense or even painful the process might be. The "newness," in composition, is definitely not "originality"; that would be either/or thinking all over again (either it is all new or not new at all). Rather, the newness we would hope for in students' thinking is that they newly define themselves in the rhetorical contexts of their writing, redefine their relationships with readers and subject matter. The goal is to help them notice the blinders on their minds' eyes.

People draw back from birth and birth-thinking for many reasons, to be sure, but one major cause must surely be that when the boundary changes are taking place (when a writer, for instance, is forced to throw out pages of material because new data changes the whole picture), there is a fine line between intense sensation and pain, and people want to avoid pain. The process, though, can be as artistic as Judy Chicago's transformations of one kind of life into another: new patterns and rhythms are emerging from old, new balances being created out of beginning imbalances.

What emerges has its own life that cannot ever be totally controlled. "Birth and its subsequent responsibilities," says Chicago, "are a metaphor for being 'caught' by the life process, something most women seem to both crave and fear" (*Birth* 34). And so most writers do too, though the craving is easily numbed by fear (of having their private mind exposed, for instance) if they continue to think in either/or terms.

Instead of listening to other voices carefully—researching and observing with curiosity—students are often protective of the ideas in their writing as they would be of a child they wished not to expose to an unfriendly and harmful world. If the engagement with the authoring process has been intense, the writer bonds strongly with the work just at the time the writing goes out to readers and takes on a life energy of its own. Readers will not always understand it as well as its parent does, yet the primary caretaker can neither give up responsibility for its behavior and reception, nor claim sole ownership. If writers can allow themselves to enter into the birth metaphor, neither claiming ownership of this child nor giving it away, they may begin to understand how their writing is inevitably conceived and authored in a social context with others, interactions with whom raise questions that result in more writing and more answers. Questions and answers together can then give birth to more loops, more ideas. Birthing in any of its forms is a doubling process, a kind of mimesis that pulls differences and likenesses into new patterns.

Little births and little deaths

For writers as for parents, there are multiple births on small and large scales, and dyings included in those births—old hopes, old points, old patterns; all these old parts of the work's personality may need to be sacrificed as new contexts and conditions of its life and readership change. There are small and large openings and closings, beginnings, middles, and ends, and if these can be rhythmically sensed, orchestrated with fit timing, the whole experience of creation can have that elusive and emotionally tinged quality that John Dewey believes to be esthetic completion (38), and Molly Bloom calls "yes I said yes I will yes."

It is not easy: The noes and obstacles keep cropping up as new challenges, and the "other side" is easily shut off. As choices are made and options closed off in any piece of writing, a certain sense of freedom is lost. Though the more hospitably the world receives this production in the world and the more satisfying the work then seems, depression and anxiety often arise when writers cannot feel engaged and in control of their material.

The experience of flow

Psychologist Reed Larson describes a way writers might avoid being governed by debilitating anxiety *or* overarousal during the writing process, as well as avoid governing it so completely that they become bored or underaroused. Drawing on the work of Mihaly Csikszentmihalyi with "flow" activities, those that people found intensely engaging and rewarding, Larson studied the effect of emotion on the writing of "two groups of [adolescent] students: those for whom emotions were clearly disruptive, and those whom emotions appeared to help" (21). Both groups were working on a long research project, and both were matched well in grade point averages and verbal test scores. The difference between the two, says Larson, was "related to the ways these two groups experienced and responded to the assignment" (21) and, finally, to the way they perceived the challenge. Those who developed grandiose schemes and high expectations for themselves became anxious and over-aroused when their skills could not match the challenge: the challenge became an obstacle even to their attention and resulted in "poorly controlled writing" (27).

But those who saw very little challenge in the project became bored: they saw no problems to be solved, no obstacles to overcome, and therefore no excitement in the writing. Their under-arousal decreased their attention too, and resulted in plodding and mechanical writing. Larson concludes that in both cases "attention was severely impaired" (33) and that emotions cannot be separated from cognition in writers; those who are optimally challenged will enjoy writing and produce good writing: as they experience "flow," so the writing they produce will flow for readers, as it did for a third, more engaged group in his study.

A key to students' sensing this satisfaction would seem to be not only the teacher's helping them choose realistic as well as challenging projects, as Larson suggests, but also that teacher's helping them to establish a trust that something will come of strong challenges and turbulent beginnings, that their work will take on an enjoyable and alive flow over and around the obstacles. Deferring to trust in a life process is a powerful deferring that can keep

anxiety levels down, interest and attention levels up, and govern-
ing/governed boundaries in flux.

Politics as art

Psychiatrist Robert Jay Lifton believes that the obsession with
death, war, and killing in our culture is a surface manifestation of a
deeper fear that we have lost the connection between life and death.
Having no major cultural symbols to imagine the connection, we
become psychically numbed and lose our expectations "of vitalizing
experience" (187). Warding off death and death images over and
over relates, he believes, to our experience of "inner death" and
constricted minds. He ties this obsession to the threat of nuclear
war, but it is just as easy to tie it to a centuries-old genderized
mindset that fears breaking down categorical borders between men
and women, beginnings and ends, birth and death, even the
rhythms of art and real-life, everyday conflicts.

Psychologist Mihaly Csikszentmihalyi (141) likens the experience of flow to Dewey's concept of esthetic experience and believes that it is available on an everyday "micro" level to anyone
who begins to notice patterns of small and large takings-in and
givings-out: in social areas such as talking or partying, for instance,
or creative ones, or kinesthetic—walking, or sports.

As a potential flow activity itself, writing is like a complete
breath, one that takes on both artistic and political connotations
when it is partnered with reading: reading the world and making a
mark on it are ways to understand a writer's task, and they necessarily involve listening and saying, "literal" reading and writing,
learning and teaching, patterned rhythms. In a genderized world
these are not neutral activities, but they are doable with a mindset
alert to right timing of questions and answers, of beginnings and
endings, and of speaking up and staying silent. We expect, and
teach our students to expect, anxious moments when we ask questions of old barriers that feel powerful. We expect these moments
are beginning ones, though, and will pass. Private lives have to
become public and social in the process. In a different context (of
reading rather than writing), Madeleine Grumet says this well:

What reading is about, very much like writing, is bridging the gap between private and public worlds. . . . the journey is fraught with danger. To give oneself up to the text is to relinquish the world in order to have the world; it is a birth and a death." ("Bodyreading" 181)

New teachers and political beginnings

Finding a way to take charge of classes without killing student interest (or failing to coach it into being born) is surely one of the most difficult problems for new teachers. And grappling with this concern is only the beginning: students come with their own agendas that challenge ours and call for responses. Because political issues on both teachers' and students' sides are so integrally bound up with every aspect of our classroom lives, and because it is not easy to step outside those issues and take a look at our sometimes death-like grip on destructive habits, I would like now to tell about one experience I had several years ago guiding new teachers of freshman composition into the often anguishing process of grading papers. I will concentrate on the students' side in this chapter, looking especially at one paper that yielded up beliefs about who governs whom in situations involving cultural "centers" and their edges. In Chapter 3 I will return to these teachers and concentrate on our own glued-in-place systems of values that affected the way we taught, deadening parts of our own minds and letting us tolerate our students doing the same to theirs.

At the time the six of us—five new teachers and I—labored over our task, it seemed to me that we were grappling with all the important issues about grading. What we were not yet doing, though, was questioning the way we were buying into the hierarchical system of values we were using—authority/community, and art/nonart, for instance—that structured our academic culture. We had certainly not yet begun to think of student writing as a birthing, patterning, and therefore artistic experience of flow for both writer and reader, and thereby, a method of learning/teaching the art of changing the habitual way in which we all—marginalized students and their marginalized TAs—experienced our places in the academic world. Nor had we any clear idea about the connection between the roles of the governed and those of the governing in academic culture and our own places within the structure.

What we six did have were the habits of mind laid out for us along the way of our own cultural experience, coming from the shaping scenes of newspapers, classrooms, and bookstores and those of "housekeeping" and mothering. Now we came together with yet another cultural agenda: Representing the academic community, we were (however enlightened our methods) going to exercise our authority over the piece of writing we had chosen to look at.

Discouraged and frustrated with the papers that resulted from their first assignment, the five came into their weekly meeting early one October to struggle with the problems of grading. Most seemed to be in a state of mild shock.

Brian, for instance, was still trying to absorb a recent conversation with one of his students.

"I tried to show him spots in his paper that he could rework and improve. You know what he said to me? 'Tell me first what grade it would get now'. I asked him why he needed to know that. 'Because,' he said, 'I want to be sure it'll be worth my time to rewrite it.'" As an experienced journalist, Brian could not understand this failure to take pride in one's writing.

Mary Jane, on the other hand, was bewildered not by agendas unmatched between herself and her students, but simply by "how badly" they wrote. Her long involvement with books and bookstores in the D.C. area had given her a love of words well used and of places aptly described. Why couldn't her students write details and impressions about an intensely observed place, as her assignment sheet had asked? "Either they can't plunge their imaginations into something outside themselves, or they get stuck out there making dead lists of what they see. Either they're telling what they did every minute, or they're totally uninvolved, out of the picture," she complained.

The discussion became heated as the five sent out feelers—or sometimes proclamations—about how they might cure the as-yet-unnamed disease.

"I'm telling them not to use 'I' anymore in their writing."

"We need to make them change their topics sometimes. I told one girl she had to stop writing about her boyfriend."

"They've got to stop boring me."

'There's no *meaning* to what they write."

"Or sometimes *only* meaning—the BIG meaning."

"But they're just babies; they have to learn, after all."

"Hey. We weren't that bad at that age." At twenty-one, Catherine could remember.

"They just want to get the paper over with, get a passing grade. I think we should spend a long time on just one paper, make them write it over and over. *Then* they'll learn craftsmanship."

My own agenda as their supervising teacher, I came to realize some time afterward, had been to initiate them all into the nourishing mother role, warm and soft-edged.

"Use circles of chairs," I had told them. "Spend time with writing and classroom activities that promote community and confidence. Personalize; learn names right away. Don't let people get lost in the big picture. Listen to students, go with their ideas, insist that they hook their own lives to the larger subjects they write about."

My own children were all grown and leaving home, and I could at least recognize that these dictums sounded like those of a mother facing her life's largest paradox: she wants both independence and dependence for her children, wants their strong sense of self to grow out of an equally strong sense of their participation in a small community. It was easy for me to think of my classes as my new families.

But because nourishing mothers have a tendency to ignore their political connections to governing authorities, and because the *way* this either/or twosome (rule or nourish) worked in my own teaching was still fuzzy in my mind, the hidden other of authority erupted in our midst in unexpected and frustrated spurts. One by one, for instance, some of these new teachers had been dropping by my office with messages like these:

"In one class I have chairs in a circle, but my other class works better with its straight rows. I think these students are too immature or too undisciplined to handle the freedom and 'equality' of a circle."

"I'm too young to sit in a circle with them. Standing behind a podium seems good, or separating myself some other way. They respect me more, I think, if I distance myself a little."

Now, this October day, with the fall of certain idealistic hopes, it seemed as if the urgent task was not only grading, and certainly not that establishing of community I had been advising, but the establishing of who is in charge here, who makes the rules in the classroom. If, at this meeting, I could have looked ahead to the next, I would have been even more sure that the issue of authority, not community, was emerging as the more vital one to all five. By that following week it had become explicit.

"You can't give them freedom in their assignments. Freedom is a facade anyway."

"Kids can't stand choices. We're the teachers. They're paying us to know more than they know. They respect authority."

"I need to do something about late papers."

"They want us to stand up and take a position about things like assignments and absences."

"Do doctors say take this pill or that one? Do they say take your choice of three pills? No. All pills are not equally good. Choices like that confuse and frighten a patient." Amy's husband was a doctor.

"Well remember, you do need to stay this side of fascism," cautioned another. We were beginning to need a common enemy.

"But if too much is negotiable you're going to get drained."

These fully ripened worries about control, though, were still a week away, as was Keith's adamant pronouncement that he had *assigned* specific topics to each student rather than leave room for choices. But for the moment, classroom democracy was not yet walking on such shaky legs, and issues of power and negotiation seemed only marginally connected to the larger task of grading.

Or did they?

Brian's Machiavellian student, Mary Jane's either/or papers, and my own growing suspicion that by emphasizing the need for community I had ill prepared these teachers for the rougher edges of teaching—these apparently disparate concerns now seem to me related in a way that touched not only the unnamed "disease," but the subject of politics. Looking back, I can see that the disease was in our not acknowledging the importance of politics. This failure is always a disease, I think, if it is not noticed in the often hidden agendas of teachers and their students, struggling to gain some sense of control over what goes on in classrooms, where every participant wants that same control. Politics can be brought into the open and dealt with and even made invigorating, but because the jockeying for position is so often at the outer margins of everyone's awareness in the academic culture, anxieties are triggered that send us all into our either/or modes—either govern or be governed. Students, used to being governed, cannot imagine their lives to be part of the larger meanings that permeate the school, their work, the nation, or even the universe, for example, and teachers cannot imagine finding student agreement on their own grading procedures, for another. Capabilities seem unable to meet the challenge the other poses (no one mindset or culture on either side can be all governing or all governed) so that vicious cycle of anxiety and rigid line-drawing creates over and over our clinging to old styles of writing (students) and grading (teachers). There is no chance for a common sense of flow between us and them, no heightened attention to the communicating action between us, no smooth line from awareness to satisfying engagement (except for those lucky [for us] few times in every class when a student writer already has the mindset of academic reading/writing).

Grading a cheerleader's search for place

Amy had brought copies that fall day of a paper she was having trouble evaluating. It was written by a black student named Mary, and we all pitched into the task of grading and commenting. We knew little about the student, but we did not think it important then to know anything, since new teachers had enough on their minds simply to master the criteria of excellence in academic prose and to make sure these were grounded in a well-supported central thesis or dominant impression. From later papers we learned that Mary had often sensed herself in a victimized position: treated unfairly by a strict father, for instance, or later by college administrators who would not adjust her dorm rates for the poor condition of her room. Both of her parents "were raised back in the years when times were hard," and sometimes her father's family "would even have to go to the soup line for a meal." She herself liked to have fun and did not want to think about her depressing past and did not "have time to worry about the far future."

Here is the paper:

DESCRIPTION OF A PLACE
A Football Game

I was so excited about going home to my old high school's first football game. I wore my Maryland sweatsuit, ready to see, and ready to be seen.

One of my main focuses was to watch the cheerleaders. I had been a cheerleader for three years, and was the organizer (captain) each year. So I wanted to catch on camera each year's squad.

The atmosphere was really exciting. Everywhere I turned, I would see a poster about the "Eagles," our mascot. The cheerleaders even made a breakthrough for the football players to run through. The crowd started cheering and clapping, getting all hyped up for the kick-off. I got the impression that nothing was going to bring this crowd down and ruin their fun.

The game had gotten off to a bad start because one of our well-known athletes fumbled the ball. But from what I saw, it didn't seem to affect the crowd. They were still ringing their bells, shaking their pom-poms, and yelling for the boys.

The conductor started to wave his hands back and forth. The band was playing the "Fight Song," which is years old, but still has a certain affect [*sic*] on the crowd. Some of the girls on the top bleachers were rockin' with soul. The band was still pitiful just as the years before, but you have to make do with what you got, right?

It seemed that the boys watched the girls more than they watched the game. But they did watch more than the girls, because they hung around the concession stand, and just looked at the guys.

It's almost halftime, and the score is 0–7 in favor of the other team. The atmosphere is beginning to change a bit, almost like a cloud covering the sky. It looks like a repeat of last year. We didn't win many games then either, but this one's not over yet. The crowd looks pretty hopeful like that too.

The third quarter is about to start, and the band just finished their field show. They added a little twist, also a little poppin' and lockin' this year. One of the freshmen, a member of the band, did some breakdancing off of the song, "Ease On Down the Road." The crowd ate it up like free caviar. They loved it totally.

The crowd has dwindled down a bit because the score is now 13–0, and their still hopelessly losing. The cheerleaders are so bored that they are now doing defense cheers, when we have the ball. Finally!! A touchdown. The crowd perked up again and started ringing their bells, screaming, and it was like a real football game was going on.

Well, the end of the fourth quarter came around, and our score never did change. They gave it a good try though.

I asked some people what they thought of the game. One girl answered, "I thought the game wasn't played fairly. The referees weren't good at all."

"The game was exciting at first, then it started to get boring. But I still hung around to talk to everybody," exclaimed Robyn Brown, a senior at F.S.K.

One of the players' parents commented, "The boys hung in there pretty good. The other team was a tough one, but I think that the game could have been called a little better than the referees did."

Then I decided to ask a freshmen. She answered, "I thought it was totally awesome! I love it here at F.S.K. I'll probably come to every football game." A typical reaction of a freshmen.

After the game, I caught everyone going inside to the cafeteria. They had a "Back-to-School Dance." Videos were showing on the walls for every song they played. Everyone was having fun, including me, even though we lost the game.

We don't let everything get us down as long as we have a good outlet. I'll probably go home for the next game, hoping that we'll win the next game. But I think I'll do a little bit more socializing than reporting.

Armed with our primary criterion of smoothly flowing support for a dominant central impression, our group set to work and soon found plenty of reasons that Mary's paper should be given a D or at least a C−. I do not think we were being unusually rigid in this decision (even though, I have come to believe, we were not wisely focused); our avowed purpose was to help new teachers read and be able to rank their students' papers. Nor were we being premature with a grade: Amy had had conferences with Mary, coached her through one revision, and explained to her the difference between narration and description. In terms of that academic culture from which we were operating, this paper did indeed lack unity and coherence on several counts: frequent changes of tense and viewpoint, for instance, along with lack of a center. The closest Mary came to sustaining an underlying concept was her stated desire to see and be seen, found early in the paper and again in the sixth paragraph as an implicit disappointment that guys were looking at other guys. She seemed to be finding a place for herself by reliving life as a cheerleader—almost as if seeing the cheerleaders was also *being* seen.

There was no real sense of place, however, no "dominant impression" as the assignment sheet had asked for. Rather there was an amorphous assumption that the whole situation—cheerleaders, band, game—would feed and sustain a feeling of excitement: "I got the impression that nothing was going to bring this crowd down and ruin their fun." But "nothing" on the scoreboard did indeed bring the crowd down, especially the cheerleader-writer, whose vague center of excitement about seeing and being seen finally dissipated into three depressingly bland and senseless short interviews. A tacked-on ending held a more controlled but condescending interview, a short surge of musical excitement, and a weak complaint about having to report instead of socialize. The center could not hold, and the fault lay outside of Mary's control, in a lost football game and a writing task.

But though we were all surely aware at least implicitly that the governed/governing relation was firmly in place as we assigned that C−/D, we were not *noticing* that relation as active in the way Mary wrote the paper. To be sure her self-critique did acknowledge her own confusion and feeling of helplessness about her work:

> My essay wasn't one of my best. It was alright, but it was hard to be descriptive and not narrative on a football game. I wish I had a better typewriter. It's the first time I've ever used it, so I made a lot of mistakes. I think that I arranged it pretty well, though. It was hard to put things together, but I think I managed. I sort of picked a bad topic, that might be the only thing I would have changed.

Not only a "self-critique," here was what appeared to be Mary's negotiation with Amy, whose comments on the first draft about poor topic and excessive narration she was answering. The reply might be translated this way:

> O.K., so my topic wasn't easy to work with, but I did the best I could. Football games invite narration, after all. I usually write better. Don't blame me for the problems; blame the topic and the typewriter. My job was tougher than that of most people, who start out with better resources. You ought to praise me for not collapsing from lack of nourishment.

And in case none of these perceptions matched her teacher's there were the face-saving hedges: "arranged it *pretty well*, and *sort of* picked a bad topic." The first says "I wasn't so addlebrained as to think I did it all *that* well." The second hedge defends her taste in choosing topics.

Had we let this obviously political move open the door into the whole topic of political moves in our classrooms and their effect on our students' writing, what might we have found? With the paper in front of us, we might have found plenty.

Finding the text embedded in cultural context

We would need first, I think, to have noticed places in Mary's paper that flowed for us as readers, and we would have assumed that she was probably comfortable with the relationship between subject matter, herself, and her reader in these places. There were such places: In fact, the first three paragraphs have a speakable and coherent rhythm, merging effectively with the excited and exciting atmosphere. Again, when the people in the crowd "were still ringing their bells, shaking their pom-poms, and yelling for the boys," the parallel structure of participial phrases gives an upbeat movement, achieved, it seems to me, only two other times, both when there was a rhythmic movement with which Mary could identify: "The girls on the top bleachers were rockin' with soul," and later, the band "added a little twist, also a little poppin' and lockin' this year." And though we in academia would probably cringe at the cliches, one other place moves easefully, I would think, for most readers: "The crowd ate it up like free caviar. They loved it totally." The implicit negotiation (or "argument," if we prefer to keep our minds in the tradition of rhetoric) here in these sections is one that says:

> The people at the game loved the exciting atmosphere as much as I did, and I'm sure you, Amy, will feel the same as you catch the upbeat rhythm of it all that I'm giving you. And I was an important part of this time and place, because I was a cheerleader emeritus who used to help create just such excitement as this.

The problem with the rest of the essay is that its rhythms are fragmented and never build up to points of emphasis, never sustain a thought to a climax over several sentences. Instead, little lists of happenings follow others, not seeming to involve Mary's attention long enough for her to let a reader feel she is controlling or orchestrating their meaning for herself.

Between those fragmented places in the essay, I think, we teachers should have been looking for evidence that the line between awareness and writing action might have broken down, one set of cultural habits disrupted, perhaps, by others not smoothly integrated with the first (even signs of confusion about an academic culture's place in this experienced scene). I would also look for patterns of reaction toward the others in Mary's life whom she perceived as having some authority or power over her, and with whom she had no position, no control, in the situation she was describing. She was, after all, triply marginal to any mainstream culture she may have perceived: black, female, and still a teenager.

If a writer cannot sustain flow, coherence, and a sense of esthetic completeness for a reader, I believe this means the writer senses that her stance within her material and with her reader has broken down and her resources for negotiation of meaning have become scarce. Mary had her emeritus status *and* its attendant climate—excitement—to draw on at first. As her mind became distracted out of that *enabling* cultural scene, it could not seemingly find a new source of flow, and toward the end, we see, it is moving toward the reader as one source of the blame: "I'll probably go home for the next game. . . . But I think I'll do a little bit more socializing than reporting."

So Mary seems to feel at least a little victimized by Amy Academia as some *other* depriving her of fun, but there is one other opposition she sets up in the paper over which she seems not to have control: boy/girl, and in an ironic twist to the team's representing those who lose, the big losers in this paper—in the implicit scene that Mary sets up—are the girls. And they lose to boys. It is this story just below the surface of the paper that I wish now I had urged Amy to pursue in conference with Mary. Amy would not, of course, have superimposed the story onto the paper for Mary; rather, she might simply have begun with any place in the paper that had felt bumpy to her as a reader, and asked Mary if she would tell her more about what was happening there, more about the original experience at the game.

One good place to start would be the two-sentence sixth paragraph: "It seems that the boys watched the girls more than they watched the game. But they did watch more than the girls, because they hung around the concession stand, and just looked at the guys." We six graders got caught in an academic trap here with the word "just": We took it to mean "only" and decided its presence made the last sentence incoherent, since the boys were said *also* to be watching the girls, though *more* than the girls. Now I think that our worrying about the formal incoherence more than the fuller cultural story of her experience sidetracked us, because (1) Mary might have been using the word in a vernacular, culture-specific way unknown to us, and (2) no matter *how* she was using it, finding a spot of incoherence is not helping a writer think more coherently, and especially (3) her major resource in gaining a sense of flow (a sense that a reader would then pick up as flow) would have been a sense of coherence between her own cultural awarenesses and her writing action. Therefore, I would now question her about that boy/girl opposition that she sets up in this paragraph and would hear where the questioning would lead.

The paragraph seems to hold at least these possibilities: the realization in sentence two that boys are watching boys may be a revelation that replaces what Mary had thought before she got a better look at the situation. Or perhaps given the fact that she had come to the game in her Maryland sweatshirt ready not only to see but to be seen, she had *wished* the boys were watching girls rather than whom they were actually watching. In either event, the situation gives her enough pause to set it apart in its own paragraph: she seems to be wondering what she wants, where her interests lie.

They implicitly lie, through much of the paper, in situations that are culturally defined male/female, but that intrinsically marginalize females. A stadium is made for football games; boys play and girls cheer. Boys are physically in the center, girls on the edges or the margins. Boys themselves are on two sides competing with each other for score but at least cooperating by rules which give them a common interest, a sameness beneath their disparities. Girls are only joined together in this scene by their common stake in boys' behavior, simply marginal to the main male activity: It is they, the males, who finally get to control the girls' moods, which stay up with a win and go down with a loss. Girls simply support.

The discernible center of the paper, Mary's desire to see and be seen (i.e., the only repeatedly referred-to or implied element) can be related to the "atmosphere"; exciting at first when seeing and being seen were of a piece with each other and when Mary seemed to reidentify herself with an upbeat cheerleading mood. But it moved through its own crises when Mary's attention left the cheerleaders and the see/seen pair, entering a state of gloom at the end of the game, and finally, picking up again at the dance. Implicit in its ups and downs is the male/female structure: When the atmosphere clouds over (score dropping), or when the male-directed band sounds "pitiful," the only thing that keeps it up is girls (cheerleaders or the girls on the top bleachers) and the yelling crowd, and—at the end—an "outlet" like dancing.

Men and boys have control over the resources—stadium, funding, timing. Mary is not free to act or negotiate in her own interest until the dance comes along, and even then, she is restrained by her English teacher's assignment and the ensuing writing she must do. Since she must do more seeing than being seen, even the traditional resource of the female role—being seen—is scarce. As art historian John Berger describes it, "*men act* and *women appear*. Men look at women. Women watch themselves being looked at. This determines not only most relations between men and women but also the relation of women to themselves" (47).

But as long as Mary can *both* see and be seen, she seems to drink in enough nourishment to give her contentment in her marginal role. By returning to the stadium of her old high school for this highly ritualized event, she immersed herself in a familiar situation whose rhythms and pace she must have known intimately as part of the cheerleading group. And as captain of that team, she had even been in charge of its proper timings, would have needed to be sensitive to apt moments for apt cheers. In short, she would have needed to adapt to *kairos*, the ancient rhetorical principle of opportune timing. Her needs, her interests, her desires, would have been attuned to those of the players on the field, to helping them maintain a mood for their own right timing which would determine that everyone's excitement could stay high. As a cheerleader, she would have needed two-way perceptual movements: to see and be seen, hear and be heard, creating an attunement with rhythms heard and seen and moods felt in muscles and bones. In this rhythmic temporal order Mary's sense of self would have been embedded. The smooth rhythm of short, speakable sentences near the beginning of the paper might be called a resonance with her old position.

But when the point comes at which Mary seems to be correcting her own wrong seeing, not only is her desire to be seen unfulfilled by the boys' gaze, but other sources of excitement in the atmosphere are disappearing too. The boys on the field are losing, and therefore, not doing their best to manage the important atmosphere that she wants to exist. Not only can she not influence the atmosphere in some way by leading its cheers, but she now gives up on seeing those who see. The boys are not looked at again.

The desire for high rhythmic excitement is being thwarted at the crossroads—almost at half time here. In a sense, Mary does not let herself be pulled down with the pervading sense of loss. She distances herself a little by philosophizing ("I'll probably go home for the next game, hoping we'll win the next game"), thinking about the Dance ("we don't let everything get us down as long as we have a good outlet"), praising faintly ("They gave it a good try though"), and condescending openly ("A typical reaction of a freshmen").

Rhythms in prose, claims Paull Baum, are not primarily metrical but rhetorical, that is, more "thought rhythm" than "sound rhythm," and more involved with emphasis and "the alternation and balance of ideas or feelings or syntactical arrangements" (214). A writer's conceptual concerns, in other words, are an integral part of the rhythms of style and arrangement, and if one were to look even deeper beyond the breaks in rhythm in Mary's paper, it seems to me that her first as well as her subsequent papers carried the concepts and broken rhythms attendant upon her feeling consistently deprived of something and consistently disappointed in the others from whom she had hoped for some help in this sorry state of affairs. In this paper the boys could not help her keep her mood where it belonged; in the next, administrators could not get her out of an "overflow" dorm room into a better one; in yet another, her father, who had been "an army man," was now "exercising taking orders" on her. She studied apartheid and concluded a sketchy research paper with a hope that a vague "they" might get rid of it someday like they got rid of slavery. There is at first in this paper a sense of identity with the blacks in South Africa, but then quickly a sense that Mary is looking the other way, ending quickly, needing to distance her attention before it gets involved in this depressing situation.

Mary looked for upbeat regions and places to keep her mind in: she seemed to identify most easily with high school and college cheerleading cultures and with the dance department scene (she had chosen to major in dance). She thought her parents had not "had fun before they made a commitment to each other," but "don't get me wrong, they're still happy though." She cannot identify with her black history, either in Africa or her family home, but something always takes away the fun of the other cultures she aligns herself with. When I saw Mary one day about a year after she had been in Amy's class, she told me that she had not made the cheerleading team she had tried out for, and that she had had to give up her dance major because her family wanted her to be in a more stable field. But oh well, she said, at least she might make better money somewhere else.

Since these patterns of cultural habits seemed ingrained, and since they could have been pretty clear after a couple of papers, what might a teacher, with her own probable academic leanings toward the governing/governed mindset, possibly do to help Mary *meet* and *negotiate* with the challenges at the edges of her awareness rather than give in to them weakly and let them scatter her attention?

Negotiating criteria for grading

Nowadays I would begin by plunging the whole class into the matter of the either/or thinking that disables our enculturated minds as thoroughly as it disables our enculturated society. I would tell about my own tendencies either to give in to what others decide or to turn my back on their political advantages over me. What we all fear, I would say, is losing the support of the other if we rock the boat of our supporting systems, so we either give our decisions (and our writing) away to other people (and their voices and points of view), or we ignore their political power over us and refuse to notice and observe what is going on beyond our own borders in different conceptual countries. In effect, we orphan our writing by killing our own voice in its creation, or we kill off potential cocreators with whom we fear turbulent and nonproductive interactions. I would put my stories of successes and failures on the floor among them and urge them to notice their own. I would tell students how all of our ingrained cultural habits of separatism, death, and destruction can and do appear between the cracks of our writing, disrupting both writer's and reader's sense of flow. And to help them get into a flow experience, I would ask that all papers, all their writing, begin in a felt sense of disequilibrium, a problem of some sort rather than in a "mode." Learning about modes needs to be embedded in finding interests and purposes (as our old friend James McCrimmon knew through the many editions of his book *Writing With a Purpose*) and in birth-thinking that can tolerate and handle obstacles.

I would not put grades on anyone's paper without our mutual agreement on criteria, and I would use our need to find these as a reason to model for a class how to negotiate grading criteria. Rarely do I find nowadays that students cannot come up with these if I simply ask that they equate criteria with readability (which I define to include the rhetorical relation between purpose, reader and writer roles, and the substance of a piece). Since this situation is typically one in which the students are seemingly at a disadvantage in the negotiation process (fewer reading skills, for instance, and seemingly absolute lack of power in the institutionalized decisions about grades), the days given to criteria-making are important ones in any semester's work.

I approach the event by treating it somewhat like a holistic grading session in which evaluators first react to a piece, then rank it among others (in our case, only two others), and finally look for reasons they may have initially reacted the way they did. They work in groups of three or four and I ask them to time their work carefully, keeping up momentum. Comparing one piece to another two helps students learn to discriminate and become more perceptive readers. Though they are working on papers that are past responses to the assignment they now have, and though I have already discussed that assignment with them (which has given them at least implicitly some criteria), I consider that we have joint ownership of the final guidelines, since it is their readings at this point out of which we draw the guidelines. After rankings, disagreements (often strong ones), rearrangements of groups to reflect disagreements, and then criteria making, groups come back together as an assembled class and we hammer out terminology. Usually I need use only theirs, even though sometimes I will say "Do you mean X?" They are always quick to say "no" if they mean Y.

Questioning cultural habits

I nearly always ask students to look at the implied cultural habits at work beneath the surface of any piece of writing they are looking at, to find the way—the style, the rhythms—by which writers either meet challenging others or give up and lose their own rhythms. When students cannot even imagine any arguments against their own position ("the rules in this silly dorm need changing," for instance), we can all know that the rulemakers are just too big a presence to even look at. "Change the topic or look," I insist.

I would want to have asked Mary to look and to ask questions about how those football players experienced the world, or the administrators did, or her father, to imagine ways they felt like she did about obstacles, but acted differently. My purpose would be not that she imagine herself acting like they might, but that she find points of common interest at which to negotiate differences. Thus she might have begun to change her own conceptual position in relation to theirs. My assumption would be that as incipient actions, attitudes need changing before anyone's world can be changed, and someone has to start somewhere.

Mary's essay brought along an entire epistemology with it, or better, an entire pattern of cultural habits that excluded her from governance of her self-perceived marginal life. She lived on the edges of someone else's property, looking in at the others to whom she seemed to lose consistently. Events in their zones belonged to them; she was easily deactivated there, not actively engaged in listening to and observing things there so she might move in herself, taking personal action, speaking up with the trust that something new could come of it, some shaping or creating of new ways to perceive those spaces. That football stadium was an ethical and political space, charged with age-old cultural energies, not even governable by her writing mind. No matter how well we can support a student's rethinking old habits, not matter how much we may all believe with Csikszentmihalyi that experiences of active, engaged flow begin with people's *perception* of how well they control challenges, those perceptions are colored by historical and social contexts in which marginalized people live. The contexts are real force fields of images and mindsets that cannot be changed overnight. We can tell students who sense themselves marginalized that *somebody* once had a hand in creating those fields before the fields were "really" there, and that they, these marginalized students, have a more comprehensive view of center field from the edges than do those at the center. But we need to tell them too that their cultural resources are not yet big ones and their lives not ever entirely under their own control. Change starts with noticing how the whole field operates. That in itself is a big enough job.

Mary had one grand resource that we would have done well to notice: her mind bonded easily with others' and even with what was in the air. The Marys of our classes need our support when we notice this resource, because if they can gather it up along with an ability to separate from others *too*, draw new boundaries (even create stronger patterns in essays), they create bonding power. Birth-thinking can help them do that.

In some dark corridors of the past, writing teachers got in the habit of conveying (perhaps tacitly) to their students that real power in writing belonged only to the elders or the fathers, a logical habit, perhaps, in a field dominated by literature teachers who praise and interpret canonized writers. Certainly this pedagogical position has been negotiated in recent years: Books of student essays are beginning to appear. But it is not easy for teachers to think of student writing as art or literature, not easy for them to believe that they even *should* negotiate politically as a way to help raise the status of student writing, even *should* imagine that barrier between high "art" and low "nonart" broken and students' ethical and political position strengthened. If we can begin seeing the points at which the fluidity of their writing gives in to the obstacles or challenges, we can enter those places with them in a questioning way. We can hope too that whole fields of images and stories will be born from those places of heat and even pain, ready to act as writing resources.

A different culture, a different marginality

There are degrees of marginality, to be sure, and a black female teenager will often have more cultural and historical obstacles embedded in her writing paths than a white female teenager. She will have grown up with different patterns of coping strategies, perhaps, different purposes, different ways of expressing marginality. Here is part of an essay written by Ann Green in a class taught by Betty Townsend at the University of Maryland. Ann was an upper-class white student with more writing experience than Mary had, it should be noted, but with a way to use some resources associated with her own kind of marginal role. Ann had found a comfortable niche in academic culture; many girls growing up in white, middleclass neighborhoods will have found the same. She had also found for herself a little niche on the side of the major events of a hospital. From there she watched very carefully what was happening at the center and at the sides. Her writing shows us one way a writer can find a voice there if she can attune to and create a conceptual lifeline to some centralized others, ones who value sensitive handling of thesis and support. In this case, the other was an academic culture that felt friendly to her in the person of her supportive teacher.

SANCTUARY

One afternoon, at the hospital where I work, I received a phone call from a woman who wanted to notify her doctor and her nurse that she was coming so that they might make her bed ready for her. When I tried to find out which doctor was to admit her and which nurse was expecting her, she grew angry. She asked me if I were deaf or what was the matter with me anyway that I could not understand simple English. I claimed a bad telephone connection and again attempted to clarify the situation. This only provoked her further. She felt each question of mine to be a deliberate and malicious attempt to misunderstand her and confuse her. I was trying to make her sound crazy, and who was I anyway? "A nurse? A supervisor? No?" Well then, what did I know anyway? She hung up.

We had been speaking of different things. I was speaking of

specific doctors and nurses, illnesses of the body, and bed reservations. She was speaking of sanctuary.

When she arrived at the hospital, her Sunday hat and shoes and dress on, her small suitcase rigid in her hand, she was ready for a fight. Either I took her up to her room and the doctor and nurse who were waiting for her or she wanted to see The President of the Hospital. She explained: It was time to rest for awhile. She had decided that she needed to rest. She had held back for as long as she could but now it was time to rest. Her legs were tired. She must speak to a nurse. To a doctor. And she knew, pointing at me, that I was neither because I was not wearing white or a hat. Her legs felt like stones she said. She could not stand up anymore. She sat herself down in a chair and asked me if I didn't understand her yet. This time I said yes, I did, and that I would find her a wheelchair and some doctors and nurses. . . . On my way home that day I saw her standing at the bus-stop—suitcase in hand, legs thin upright stones—after having been denied the bed she was sure was waiting for her because she was so tired and it was so hard to live.

Many others have sought the same bed. . . .

Ann's ability to feel what others feel (phone caller or hospital personnel) and let her own voice show it, creates here a description of how an old woman's needs clash with a large institution's. Ann herself acts as an observer and then as a representative of the hospital, trying to rationalize its policies to the woman, to act as mediator between the social and the personal. Her own marginality to the life of the hospital lets her take on that role and move between the world of another time and place—the woman's—and the businesslike one of the hospital. Even the woman herself, as Ann describes her, is operating under a wished-for, slower rhythm (that of the "bed," the sanctuary), as well as the fast one that pushes her along in a hard life. Her thin legs cannot support that second, insistent one.

Kairos

When writers learn to coordinate the many complex rhythms involved with their subjects, their writing process, and their reader's needs, they are tuning into the opportune timing of *kairos*. They are able then to hear and be heard, see and be seen, know and be understood as knowing, move and be moved by their environment and their readers. *Kairos* is a human time, tied to personal action, different from *chronos* or chronology. It is a kind of time barely acknowledged since ancient times, and according to Elliott Jaques, repressed because of

> the greater ease which we feel with unencumbered chronology as compared with the more anxiety-filled experience of the time which brings human intentions and purposes into sharp focus, with their consequent oscillations between success and failure, catastrophe and renewal, and between life and death. . . . (16)

> In brief, the distinction between these two terms is that of chronological, seriatim time of succession, measurable by clocks or chronometers—*chronos*; and that of seasonal time, the time of episodes with a beginning, a middle, and an end, the human and living time of intentions and goals—*kairos*. (14)

The teaching of writing would do well to acknowledge the importance of timing and rhythms and their home in the circulating minds that are our cultural habits and habitats. Texts always live in writers *and* the other people that touch their lives, and the ensemble created between them grows out of writers both controlling and being controlled, and out of their learning to create new life in the midst of involvement with others. Neither a hard-line attempt to govern those others nor a soft-line giving in to the others' governing will let writers and their readers sense right timing and that sense of ensemble. Opening the borderlines between their stances might.

Both students and teachers of writing can model their interactions on that same sense of double timing that readers and writers need with each other, on the ensemble that plays on the boundaries between people.

3

Teachers: Author(iz)ing Hard and Soft Stories about Academia

The needy writer and the independent writer

Unlike clock time, the human time of beginnings, middles, and ends is not an empty time, nor does it lack the force necessary to reproduce its own multiple cultural rhythms. Full of lives and their many stories that begin, continue through crises, and finally end, *kairos* can weave itself into the way people talk together and—for those five TAs and me—meet together. When it stayed with us in our meetings, we felt high and productive. When it left, we seemed never to come to closure. Week after week during that beginning year of their teaching lives at the university, they came together and threw challenging sparks at each other, so different were their needs and their styles of interaction. But of course so urgent were all our needs to find a workable joint style and joint agenda, that we began living a joint story concerning what we were about, I believing I was orchestrating yet accommodating everybody's interests, they developing habits of talking and thinking in this new little culture that slid into, through, and around my orchestrations: Amy, excited and insistent that her teaching dilemmas be coherently addressed; Brian, brash and full of pronouncements about how real writers write; Catherine, steady-toned and composed in her mediations; Keith, silently smoking one cigarette after another and tapping his foot; and Mary Jane, deceptively soft-spoken when, patience exhausted, she would finally interrupt one of the spiraling arguments and turn our attention to her own unanswered questions.

Four of them wanted help situating themselves among their students; one, Brian, had taught long enough that he already had habitual and for him workable ways to bond with his students and with what he taught them. What he taught them, what we all taught our students, I think we would have agreed, was just as much "content" as was the subject matter of any other course. Maybe it was not facts to memorize, maybe not paradigm-oriented principles and methodologies, and certainly not content that could stay still long enough to be captured in books that might give us true knowledge about it. Rather our content was relation itself—the rhetorical one between the minds of our students, their writing, and us. All of us were concerned about these relationships; though I may describe them with different words now, the sense and the concern were there then, whether in the talk of the new teachers or that of more seasoned ones like Brian and me.

Nowadays I think of all of us teachers of composition as walking through our classroom doors with pockets full of cultural habits born of our meetings with others. I think of our meeting twenty students in those classes with yet other habits, with styles of speaking and writing different from ours, ones born of different lives full of their own habituated structures. We six teachers had twenty plus one "structures" or habits of thinking in any one of our classrooms. To bring new, albeit informal, ones to life from this new pattern of minds, we needed ways to join our differences, to bond old to new and create new habits of thinking and writing. Not an easy job in sixteen weeks, then or now, and never, of course, an unmitigated success for anyone.

So much of the frustration the four newest teachers experienced came from my being unable to give them any sure answers about how to do this, and from their sensing, I am sure now, conflicting advice from us two more experienced teachers among them. Moreover, my hands-off policy in meetings seemed to reflect my classroom style of soft "allowing," a decidedly disconcerting habit for those in the group who would have liked me to tangle with Brian more forcefully and give them some solid answers to their own questions. But I was in my nourish-only habitat in those days, not ready or able to raise questions between our visions.

What happened was that the energy in the group kept oscillating between two of our stories, varieties of which repeated themselves over and over during the year without meeting each other on common ground. Somehow Brian and I must have sensed that we not only had a strong liking for each other, but were locked, too, into a silent mutual questioning about which of these stories, with its attendant theories trailing behind, would "work" in the classroom and in our group story, his about independent writers taking authority for their own writing, mine about needy writers nourished by community. They were single-minded stories, closed off from the foreign-feeling other that I realized later lived in their own midst, second stories on second tracks just below the surfaces of the first, each grounded in the big loop around us both: academic authority. We each distanced ourselves from these seconds, and therefore refused to identify with and accept them as part of our own.

A careful observer, though, might have noticed contradictions in the way we put our two main stories and theories to use in our classrooms (as well as in our group meetings), inconsistencies that would have hinted at hidden agendas, what Argyris and Schön call "theories-in-use," ways of talking that do not match "espoused theories" (6–7). Our playing out the same struggle, the same "argument" that does not recognize the other side, over and over, instantiated death-like reproduction rather than birth-like, sameness rather than difference *and* sameness, just because the two sides were each closed off to the life-giving other at their borders and below their surfaces.

Hard and soft versions of academia

Because Brian's and my stories were not uncommon ones in the department, and because I have seen such sterile oppositional structures capture other groups and whole classrooms too, tying other stories into ours at this point can lead into my point that an unacknowledged other can deaden the spaces between people who are trying to communicate with each other. Political issues were involved—sometimes only tacitly—in all these stories told by teachers, and though politics may seem a marginal part of the day-to-day lives of people playing roles in any academic story, a close look at these teachers' habitual ways of telling at least those stories about life at our university can show otherwise.

Nearly all teachers of freshman English at the University of Maryland were teaching assistants, students themselves, who had often enough felt marginalized in departmental matters. But their political styles and values varied widely. Many, I discovered one day in asking, had not given much thought to the matter of politics at all, though when they had, they had often felt, in the words of one, that "[faculty] don't listen to us in our classes," meaning (I inferred), as another put it, that the research done by graduate students was usually channeled by their teachers into "a canon of ideas we're entitled to operate within."

The other side of feeling unlistened to, though, seemed to be an unsaid that could not even be heard. "I would never dream of letting [my instructor] know what's really on my mind," said yet another. "In seminars silence sits there like a plague. You learn to keep your mouth shut for fear of saying undergraduate things. I even keep my mouth shut at the Xerox machine when [faculty] expects deference. I don't want trouble."

Those who moved most easily through the program "play[ed] the game," with faculty, knowing "it's only temporary." Most TAs realized their own tendency to carefully monitor words and ideas with their professors; many even watched what they said in casual conversations around other TAs with whom they might "lack seniority." Of course such monitoring is not unusual in social situations of any kind; these few examples are simply indicative of some of the tacit negotiating for status—or "survival," as one put it—that went on in at least this program.

Most TAs did not dwell on issues of hierarchy, though, or centrality and marginality, and most had found ways to gather resources into the restraints, opportunities into the challenges, of their long days of teaching, grading, and studying. Many welcomed this life, at least in the beginning years of their graduate careers, welcomed and expected the "toughness" of what they read as an initiation into the academic world. The rewards of good grades, good friends, and appreciative students, and the pleasure of learning to become professionals in a field that most TAs loved, was experienced as a grand opportunity. "It's like joining a religious order," said one happy woman, "renouncing lovers and money for studying dead people in the bowels of the Folger." For her the artistry of these dead people was salvational, letting her "get close to the world" of human truths in an important way: "This major is a way to save your soul." She felt an "awe factor" in learning from teachers whose knowledge earned her respect. She certainly did not think about the department's hierarchy in terms of politics.

Those who felt the power of their professors more negatively were apt to be those who, instead of being warmed by a light from the center, perceived themselves as marginal to those central authorities, moved out to the edge of a negative rather than positive power either by a disappointing grade, or perhaps a realization further along in the program that good performance and loyal commitment to their professors' values were not guaranteeing them a job in a tight market. There were variations on this experience of negative power, or on what one person saw as "going through the program in a little capsule," not touching faculty members or experiencing "bonded energy" with them. But these variations all amounted to feeling let down by the power on which one is dependent for initiation into the profession. The experience would set up an attitude of discouragement, causing people to question the "system."Brian's awareness of himself caught in a power structure, for instance, had been especially acute. To be a writer was important to him; to be a student was not easy, especially when, as he saw it, the ideas of students were not ordinarily respected by professors on a peer level with their own. He felt himself a peer with them not only because of his many years of writing for newspapers, but even more, because he had spent those years using and increasing his knowledge of American literature, reading and researching for interviews with contemporary writers. He wanted, he said, a free exchange of ideas with his professors; he claimed he got not an exchange but condescension when he did not validate the concepts they held. He stirred up issues boldly in his papers, wrote lively and probing essays, neglected to change "different than" into "different from," loved to use one- or two-sentence paragraphs for emphasis, and would not "play the game" to the point of giving up his "journalistic style." He had been trained, he said, to listen *and* challenge in order that his interlocutor clarify his own ideas; he learned best, he believed, if he used this style of interaction in the classes he attended as well as with the people he interviewed for newspapers. The style had not met with unqualified success in academia.

Many TAs—especially women, I think (including myself)—were closer intellectually to a "renouncing" style than to Brian's self-determining one, seeming, at least, to give up many of our old ideas, accommodating ourselves to new ones (especially perhaps in the exams we took, not showing the disagreement that we may almost have forgotten we had). We valued the community there, enough to silence or hide our conflicts of interest. Roger Fisher and William Ury speak of negotiating conflict as a basic everyday experience that people use to get what they want from others; people usually use it, they say, in either a hard way—establishing inflexible positions, or a soft way—yielding to the positions of others (3-14). We renouncers favored the soft way: We had often become acolytes of favorite professors while negotiating softly and tacitly with both them and our students for validation of our work, scholarly in the one case, pedagogical in the other.

Brian's learning style, on the other hand, while it yielded as much to the time-consuming demands of the program as did that of the renouncers, was much more committed to maintaining the central identity—"writer"—that he had spent so many years carefully nurturing. He tended to favor a hard style of negotiation, to be a Noun (Writer) in a rightful place rather than a soft and changeable Verb adapting chameleonlike to the hard central postions of others. Even our group meetings all year seemed either centered on Brian's ideas and on his vibrant, Irish personality, or devoid of his presence altogether.

Two mindsets, one system

But none of us talked in those days of our "hard" or "soft" positions in the department; indeed, we were more apt to play roles (not consciously, to be sure) in an Enlightenment story, in which we would free those below us (our students) from bondage to *our* values and prejudices as well as to those of "the system," differently, of course, from what our teachers were doing to us. Politics was to play a part in our own classrooms only in the mechanics of classroom and assignment management. Insofar as we became involved in the issue of authority as it related to community (as my group did become involved), it was with the assumption that we ourselves were different from most of those who taught us, that we were sanitized of their styles of governing. In other words, we were individuals, separable from the styles with which those above us related to us and we to them. Thinking of our minds as independent before they were parts of this cultural system let us think we were free of its mindsets.

But "sets" they were indeed that we might have found at work in our institutionalized midst, oscillating back and forth as we played out first one and then the other pole of the system in our teaching and learning lives, thinking always that we were in no way like the other we protested against. The other we protested against, though, was inevitably a member of our set or structure, of the cultural system in which we defined ourselves. Brian, for instance, thought of his classroom management as divorced from his adversarial relations to faculty: In his mind, it was he and his students against the system, students thinking their own ideas, not his, not anyone else's. Committed to the belief that students—undergraduate or graduate—were not there to validate the ideas of their teachers, he was upset by what he saw as lack of a university-wide "climate of learning" ("kids partying from Thursday to Sunday")—all caused, in his eyes, by students' realization that they needed to be simply echoes of "complacent professors who are protecting the ideas of dissertations written fifteen or twenty years ago." Even his managing of his classroom reflected his belief in individual rights: Rather than centralizing authority in himself, he distributed it to students working one-on-one with each other or with him.

Had he scratched the surface of his democratic skin, however, he might have found an interest shared with those in the system he so disliked: an interest in maintaining a sense of authoritative self, uncontaminated by the weaknesses of others and unharmed by their strengths. Brian was therefore actually a member of the set or structure that implicitly told stories about independent selves: In such stories, one either maintained one's central, individual self by thinking one's own ideas (in Brian's version, this pole was made up of him and class members) or maintained it by swallowing the opposition (as did senior faculty in this reading). These swallowers were seen as authorities to be avoided, avoided because either they would have power over one, or one would have it himself or herself. This power was unshared.

Richard Sennett claims that in rejecting authorities of any kind, people become tied to the rejected, giving the locus of strength that causes the reaction to a mind outside their own. In effect, "there is alienation from [these authorities], but no freedom from them" (48): minds remain "under the aegis of the existing order" (121). Negating an authority does not remove one from the system in which it is found, in other words, and does not contribute toward changing the system in which there are those at the center and those at the margins of power. In such a system, one can only oscillate between acceptance and rejection, soft and hard stances.

For Brian, for instance, teaching his own classes was framed in terms of rejection of academic authority over his mental space, but acceptance of his students' individual authority over their own mental space in his classroom. I sometimes saw paired-off students there wandering away, physically and mentally, from assigned work, seemingly unable to take charge of themselves without stronger intervention from their teacher.

Many of the community-minded in the department, on the other hand, had not even reached his stage of awareness of power. They had not separated themselves from a vision of relation with what they saw as benign, protective sources. For them, power was sensed as less concrete, vaguer—a distanced and seemingly unaffecting presence in their lives. But their idea of power itself may have had just as negative a connotation as it did for those who rebelled against its closeness, and it could give them faint intimations of uneasiness when the subject came up. For both groups power was imagined as centralized into positions occupied by individuals, and as at least somewhat untrustworthy. "One hopes," said one TA, "for nice people in dragon positions," but the unsharable power of the positions was nevertheless a given. One's future, after all, it would seem, depended on accommodating oneself to those who ruled one's academic destiny, or at least on avoiding scenes where one could not or would not accommodate. Only a few rebels were openly confrontive, with fewer yet using time with their own teachers to openly or frankly assume a give-and-take negotiation of their own perceptions and sentiments about class events.

I was involved in a story much like the stories renouncers told about academic life, one that came in the back door of patriarchal culture by way of a certain limited kind of matriarchy, limited enough that the story participated in the mainstream's allowable issues, those pertinent to the academic scene. I was not telling mine yet either; I was living it out, and was therefore unaware that I was acting out two poles, my soft-stanced mindset and the harder one of the system in which it was embedded. I imagined my position to be a caring one, opposed to the rule-ridden ones I thought so unlike mine. Like Brian, I lived my professional life and argued between those two seemingly separate poles. Hindsight shows me that my long-term teaching habit of seesawing, between the conscious, accepted position and the unconscious, unacceptable one, generated some interesting entanglements with certain students. Ostensibly I wanted to give up authority, help students to be self-starters. Covertly, the institution and I collaborated to see to it that students be quickly notified if that start did not place them in the proper arms of Standard English, focused and controlled. My loyalty to the hard line of that discipline was a reluctant one though, and I had trouble seeing myself in the role of controlling authority or parent.

Controlling mothers

My student Ian did not have that trouble and let me know so not only on his final evaluation form, but in his often-repeated "What *do* you want?" His own barely hidden agenda in his papers almost matched my own on a less sophisticated level: He *seemed* to want freedom, but his texts always returned to the same imprisoning binary opposition: One either controls or is controlled, is free of the other or in his or her thrall. Neither of us was able to notice our hidden agendas, the voice of an unacknowledged other in each of us. It therefore simply operated out of awareness and gave our written and oral actions with each other a certain incoherence. I became for him a controlling mother, a destructive Kali ravaging his mind; he became for me a puzzling case with an unreasonable fear of mothers. In the story we implicitly told together, we played into each other's hands. In neither case were we noticing how different the "real" person before us might be from the scripts we were using, nor was I able, then, to help Ian fill in the gaps in his stories about his own mother.

My initial freewheeling openness to my class's writing in their own "speaking voices" helped to bring a fine sense of rhythm to Ian's writing. This was my early-semester period of the soft line. Even the second paper he wrote—the one that in his eyes brought my liberating reputation to low ebb when he saw its grade (the beginning of my hard line)—had a voice that could be heard. It was in the form of a letter addressed to his mother.

"Mom, I have to be honest," he began, "you put me through hell this last summer. This was no ordinary hell because I could not even fight back. You controlled my life for a summer with this job you got for me. The job was the pits. . . ."

"Is that your thesis?" I had asked him of that statement on his first draft. "Do you want to stress her control over you?"

"No!" And he added his "thesis" later, obligingly but ambiguously, "but maybe you knew something." Unwilling or unable to grapple with his obscure idea of the hard-line, controlling mother (at home or in class), Ian simply "lost" his attention.

I could not, through my reading of his long recital of the job's evils, figure out what his own mother may have known, and when I read the ending of the final draft, I was pretty sure Ian had not figured it out either: "Those days showed me the world as it is and because I know you like I do mom, I can say that that was your purpose when you forced me in that job."

My vivid remembrances of Ian and me struggling over his "thesis" and his "premises" supporting it, as well as my later realization of how enmeshed we both were in ambivalence about legitimate authority (in this case embodied in governing mothers), convince me that with the best of intentions, teachers and students can be pursued by their own hidden agendas, their own ideological struggles with binary oppositions that trap them in ignorance of their life situations and their own particular mixes of cultural habits. Neither of us could imagine that the other—the "not-I"—as controller or governor was legitimately part of ourselves. Ian surely sensed that my own teaching oscillated between nourishing students' own control over their papers and then removing it in the name of lawful higher authority. My two sides never negotiated with each other, never turned round to question what the common ground might be beneath the governor and governed (fear of loss of support, I believe now). Nor was Ian able to imagine himself negotiating between his own mother and himself. Both of us seemed caught, then, in a mental stasis over our attitudes about government and control.

Such ambivalences, such refusals to imagine one's own political undersides, surely create self-fulfilling situations, in the sense that people act by their beliefs, doing their part to create life scripts or life stories that feel coherent *in action* and enable them to function in a turbulence-free and anxiety-free atmosphere.

Ignoring inconsistencies in stories

Csikszentmihalyi's claim that people need to create as much flow as possible in their lives can alert us to their tendency either to ignore inconsistencies in their experience or to rationalize them out of recognizable existence: that is, swallow them up in order to sense that flow.

In the case of Ian and me, a vague enthymemic rationale finally naively relieved my uneasiness, assured me that I was not an acting central authority, that a one-way power belonged to him (not to both of us in a double way) in any conceptual cleanup of that paper. I would have to wash my hands of responsibility, since our talks were getting nowhere. I entered a Pontius Pilate story of sorts, since the tacit negotiation had been ineffective on both our parts.

All actors in such scenes play their parts to tacit expectations, ignoring or playing down unacceptable subplots, creating as few upsets in their respective habits as possible by not noticing inconsistencies. Actors at all levels thus have their positions and their self-esteem validated in everyday life and its oral and written discourses. Since semantic coherence in one's life is a powerful resource with which to carry on, strands of experience felt as alien to one's self-image are simply relegated to some other bin. We might call it a bin of neglected others, of untold stories.

Gates closed to both upheaval and new life

The problem with those untolds is that they have a tendency to enter into interactions in the form of hidden agendas, especially when they are elicited, however unconsciously, by those who are living surface stories so much like these buried ones, as Brian was living my buried attraction to firm, authoritative positioning. Though his ideas about teaching did not at first seem so opposed to mine, I decided when I visited one of his classes that the oppositional ground between us was individual authority versus community bonding, not yet understanding that it was our mutual distrust of institutional authority that contextualized our conflicting pedagogical stories. It was of course easier to see his poles than mine; later I understood better how often the energy in our weekly meetings would gravitate into this implicit confrontation: he with such respect for writers and such disrespect for the tradition of freshman English pedagogy, I strangely attracted to and repelled by his heretical ideas without quite knowing why, yet rarely tangling with him overtly, rather hoping the others would take care of him. That is the common thread I see running through our year's story, and although the other four undoubtedly had agendas that got caught up in these, I do believe that because I had deadened those spaces around my own story that might otherwise have served as gates to his, and because I as the leader of that group stayed safely and "professionally" out of the turbulence, I was never able to help turn the parallel controversies to each other, collect the tumult, and let it bear fruit.

Leaving the divergent stories behind

No wonder I found myself saying to Mary Jane when I talked to her on the phone recently that I had not yet "finished" with that group even now, four years later. My tone puzzled her, I think, but it seems to me that we never got to the punch line that year, that we were all drawn to each other magnetically but could not quite sense our parts in the group story. So it was left unfinished. The five of them still talk to each other, some more regularly than others. Keith went to study in a graduate program in California, Brian is teaching in a community college in Florida, Amy is mothering a new child, and Catherine is still studying and teaching in the program at Maryland.

Mary Jane is working through her own experience of oppositions: She has stopped teaching for now so that she can give all her energy to her studies in the program; teaching was absorbing to her in an all-or-nothing way, she says. She has thought through a chiasmus of sorts: She was being mastered (by her students), she feels, but now she masters (her subject matter). Not an uncommon dilemma for graduate students who tend to bond with their students, this sensing oneself as either governing or being governed is often changed or at least put on a different footing once a teacher/ student graduates and feels more in control of her professional rhetorical triangles. Two legs of those triangles will have been then automatically strengthened: the rhetor's relation to her (graduate) subject matter, and that to her audiences, at least some of whom will come from the "profession" by whom she will be now more respected than formerly.

Life experiences themselves, in other words, can sometimes give a big hand in breaking up the tenacity of an either/or, hierarchical binary opposition, giving people new experiential models to imitate. But the breakup, I have realized, is apt to hold more emotional and ideational turmoil than I once thought: The most profound, double-loop learning experiences never seem to come without struggle. Sometimes it will have been a long-term struggle, and the resolution can then feel like a sudden snap in the world that brings great relief, the end of a dilemma. For me there have been times when the questions have been barely perceived ones at the periphery of awareness. But in one recent professional experience, the question was that same teaching one that had been rumbling in my conscious mind for at least four years and below the surface for much longer: How could I, in a classroom, join shared or multidirectional power with one-way power in a fruitful way?

Chalice and blade

For a long time I had not even wanted to think that one-way power could be legitimate in any way, even though I had that vaguely sensed womanly mindset that I could more easily take directions from someone than give them. In general, though, I saw one-way power as destructively patriarchal, usable to me in a classroom only if I was desperate for a quick fix in matters of attention or policy of some sort with otherwise intractable students. All power should be multidirectional and shared, I thought, as much yours as mine, and though I certainly realized that everybody who lives must act—must be an agent in the world—I somehow pictured, in my own profession, for instance, active speaking or writing blended peacefully or even alternated peacefully with a "passive" listening or reading: in other words, governing and being governed benignly by turns. I left national and local politics in the hands of social scientists who could grapple with the complexities of both informal and formal political networks.

I awakened to the reductive simplicities of this vision only now and then, when it did not accord with observable contradictions. Sometimes I was forced to realize that the world is full of so many more complex ways of being with others than actively or passively, for instance, or peacefully or violently. I began to see that I did not need to choose between these two horns of the dilemma. But a much sharper awakening took place not so long ago during a two-day writing course that my friend Kevin and I taught together to adult learners. As double-loop learning goes, strands of many perplexities and of my own prejudices were brought together and their transformation begun during that course.

We had taught this course together once before, and in the twilight of my attention to its preparation this time were vague memories that Kevin had taught a wonderfully colorful section on grammar the last time, full of metaphors I was hoping to hear again now and remember better: I had especially liked the one about nouns and verbs being the meat and potatoes of any sentence; people shouldn't fill up on empty carbohydrates, he had said; go easy on the modifiers in work-world writing.

I had known Kevin for several years but never well until we lunched together one day during that last course. Hardly time enough to become well acquainted, but after an hour with him I had been strangely moved and disconcerted by his—and I can only call it this—"vision." He is a Stanford graduate, a medievalist and classicist, a Missouri Synod Lutheran, a tall, thin, very straight-standing man with a Paul Hogan kind of stride, full of talk about his family and his involvement with his children's lives, about his carefully thought-out decision to return to his childhood church, and about the wide-ranging ways his religious faith penetrates almost every corner of his life: his work, his recreation, his thinking.

Facts and interesting stories spill from his tongue; love of humor and of showmanship come to him, he says, from his father. He was blessed with two strong parents; from each he took traits he values. He loves and quotes St. Augustine.

All of this came in one lunch that stirred up memories, questions, and attempts on my part to get Kevin straight in my mind, to figure out how his parts could fit together in some one of the categories I had ready. For instance, how could what I remembered from three of my teenage years of Missouri Synod faith (I had chosen that faith myself) fuel such an exuberant, curious, open-minded personality as his? My church had been full of very serious and often dour people, separatist to the core, sure of their rightness and hardly eager to turn with people into talk about beliefs and concerns not their own. Kevin, on the contrary, was making such nonsynodal turns as we talked: I, on the edge of my seat, taking him now and again off to conceptual lands no Lutheran ever stepped foot in, I thought; he, enjoying the trip with me and never trying to send St. Augustine along.

Still, when we would come back to his country a few minutes later, the women and men in his stories seemed so close to staying in God-given places, and St. Augustine to gathering the important issues into coherence. The St. Augustine I remembered was not one I would think could do that, given the sorry role he had assigned women's flesh in the realm of spiritual disasters. Kevin kept creating this conversational world of unmitigated male hegemony, it seemed to me, sending me its rightness in one-way messages, one-way because we were not talking about the same world and mine could not affect his. Yet here I was working out with him some details of my own world and somehow feeling excited and "empowered" by his alien talk. How in the world was he managing to be so, oh, one-way about things and so straight-backed about them, so foreign to what I valued, so parallel to it rather than convergent, yet so relevant and supportive along the way? I had known him long enough to remember that his students in academia often had the same empowered feeling around him that I was having, sensing that they were getting shots of adrenalin from him. I knew that one Jewish girl had gotten a life-sustaining shot: She had decided to become a rabbi because her father and grandfather and Kevin had been such an inspiration in her life.

The question about relevance and foreignness was still with me as I watched Kevin teach the grammar module again on the second morning of the two-day course this time around. And my sense of it was that students here were on the edges of their seats just as I had been with him during our lunch. I watched their attentive eyes, heard him weave into his talk answers to some questions that had been building up in this group, listened as he brought yet more metaphors to his explanations. This time instead of meat and potatoes there was one about that new kind of "lean bacon" being healthier for people than junk food like fried pork rinds (and the junk food creeps in, he said, with empty constructions like "there is" and "it is"). An idea about sentence problems simply being symptoms—like a fever or spots—of a deeper problem in thinking let him address participants' questions about "style," gave him a way to tie it in to their whole way of thinking rather than to surface appearances: Their "sinewy lines of reasoning" would give readers a sense of health both below and on the surface.

The organization that hired us was concerned about the problems its writers were having with their reasoning processes and had recently sent out signals to writing instructors that we should be doing more with these problems in our courses. I got the feeling that Kevin was responding not only to that concern but to at least a dozen others as well, thinking on his feet as he taught, gathering them up, creating metaphors to address them, and knowing exactly when to tie one problem to another, and when to talk and when to listen. He was a master of *kairos*.

This was such artistry, such impeccable interactive teaching that I was deeply moved—and in a grammar module of all things, one in which he had even found time to interrupt the tight schedule with a ten-minute lecture about matters of taste and usage in language history; someone's question had made it relevant, and the participants seemed entranced. ("Mr. Dungey's lectures were interesting," one of these toughened show-me types wrote later on his evaluation form.)

But it was an afternoon happening on the second day that triggered the epiphany, that sent my theories about teaching into turbulent waters. It was just a little event: Participants were revising a long memo they had written the morning before in table groups. We had all just now gotten the originals back from the secretarial staff, neatly typed up and Xeroxed for us, ready to be read anew by the groups and for the first time by Kevin and me. We two, acting as advisors, had divided the four tables between us, read as fast as we could, and were now hustling to finish talking to each of our first groups so that we might put in a few words with the second. We wanted to be able to intervene before it was too late for us to have some input. I noticed that Kevin was finished and on his way.

I heard him say to his second table, "How're you doing?"

"Fine. Not much to revise. We're just about done."

At which Kevin's deep voice resounded through the room, "Not by a long shot you aren't."

Eyes up around the room then quickly back down to work after an almost imperceptible quick laugh. I, back to work too, with not even a fleeting sense that that response of his was not exactly the right thing to say to that table of self-assured writers, three of whom were more senior than most of the people in the room and had been a little more easygoing than we would have liked.

I had, to be sure, an almost passing thought that I would not have pulled that maneuver off so well as he. I even imagined my response in the same situation: I would have said something encouraging first like "Oh" (highly pitched for pleasant surprise). Then, hoping or assuming that I had masked the edge of irony in the tone, I would have added, "Terrific." Then I would have sat down, knowing all along that we would be getting to the clincher in gentle pieces, and asked questions that would draw that clincher out of *them*. I probably would not have been quite sure yet exactly what the clincher was, or where we would have been going with the revision, because my habit is to take cues from the writer and negotiate meaning from two directions. But my initial action would have been to mask my own response for the purpose of bringing the energy toward me from them. It is the kind of masking action Argyris calls "easing-in" (*Reasoning* 61).

The point is not necessarily that my drawing out is not good, or that Kevin did not draw ideas out of his group, but that whatever he did next—and I did not hear it—his first move was one very different from my preferred sytle, one I could only think of as "zapping." My old American Heritage college dictionary labels the word "zap" as "slang," and says it means "to destroy or kill with a burst of gunfire, flame, or electric current," or "to attack (an enemy in warfare) with heavy firepower; strafe or bombard." My newer, unabridged Random House dictionary raises the status of the word to "informal," but still gives it the same sense in its first two meanings: "to kill or shoot," or "to attack, defeat, or destroy with sudden speed or force."

But it is two of the later meanings listed in Random House that interest me in this situation, regardless of which of the many cropping up in recent years may have been at work below the surface of my thoughts that day. "Zap" can mean "to add a sudden infusion of energy," and it can also mean "to move quickly, forcefully, or destructively." I think what was dawning on me when I noticed Kevin making that quick and forceful move was that it is, after all, not only all right, but *good* for teachers of writing to zap their students sometimes, with whatever feels appropriate to zap them with at the time, because the quick movement involved does give them "an infusion of energy," deadening a space in their minds, to be sure, but one that can—under the right conditions—be prepared for new growth.

A space had certainly been deadened in mine, stunned actually, with the sudden zapping of that border between killer energy and birth energy, almost between the two kinds of informal culture I was used to, those that Eisler describes structured by the dominator model of the blade, with "the power to take rather than give life" (xvii) and the partnership model of the chalice, in which "diversity is not equated with either inferiority or superiority" (xvii). I had watched Kevin use the blade—that group's idea was, after all, being dominated by a "superior" rejection of it—and I had seen him act like a partner at other times: he incarnated some of both cultures. My espoused theory was being rattled by a theory-in-use I was seeing, and sent me, as I started reflecting on his action, to a redefinition of where I stood. I had to move from a gross level (blade people are different from chalice people) to a fine-tuning one, observing, thinking, questioning the way I had structured the teaching world. My old values—chalice teaching is good, blade, questionable—were being carried across the Styx.

But the deadened space could not remain without activity for very long because my mind felt crooked; even my ideas about imitation or mimesis were being scrambled when I began to think that I wanted to do some things like Kevin, not all, but some. I was not sure I could zap like that, but surely I could tell lively stories and compose apt metaphors on the spot. And, well, perhaps zap just a little, straight-forwardly and cleanly, not, as I might have done till now, furtively and incoherently. The new pedagogical home felt enlivening and power-giving to me, all the more so, I think, because Kevin's practice had felt so radically different from mine. Now I began to feel a new life in my own practice, born at least partly of killing off some old ways of thinking and feeling before new ones could be born. Sending strongly worded messages out to people had always been frightening to me on some level; I was suddenly associating that activity with a quickening energy. It dawned on me that other people's minds are only hell if one gets stuck there, avoiding relation with them, wanting to master them but never escaping their mastery. *This* situation, I knew, was not like that kind of imprisonment.

Once my mind got moved into that new place, where one-way action (talking at, sharply opposing, pulling off track) is important to the workings of a class even when it may pull students off their own tracks, I began finding new patterns overlaying old ones, and one of the most interesting to me was one I thought I was finding in Kevin's work, in and out of classrooms, and one that gave my own work a turn in focus as I explored the complexities of his.

Two new lunches of conversations from this course were now giving me more thoughts to weave into the intricate network. Kevin had told me that he likes to leave a little gap in any given day's teaching by not being fully prepared, by leaving some room for what might take place spontaneously. He wants to trust what comes in, what happens. He always has two things going on; one is what he is telling his students, the other, what he is showing them: he shows with all those metaphors, for instance, while he is telling them about subjects and predicates. Even his stories, though he tells them, are part of the showing, running along beside the "real" subject matter of a class, relating to it.

He thinks of teaching as midwifing, just as Socrates did in *Theaetetus*, helping students give birth to what is already there in their own minds, incubating; midwives like Socrates may sense it is time to bring on the pain of birth or allay it, and later examine the statements of their patients/students to see whether or not there is life in them. "When you're dealing with people," Kevin said, "power is midwifing, a releasing, not containing. It's letting go of your own personal agendas." I guessed he meant, in this context, giving himself over to student agendas, but that did not seem to be quite it, yet partly it. He added that the agendas he had in mind were "superpersonal" rather than personal, and the offspring, therefore, would be part of "a will stronger than your own."

There we had come full circle, back to the religious faith which seemed to give him both a blade and a chalice. How would I ever be able to feel my way into the center of this system of values that felt still so mostly foreign but also so intriguingly fitting to a teaching system I had been developing for so long?

Centers hold less, I think, for people thinking their way inward from margins, as I was then, but that move inward is an important part of the repertoire of all who wish to change their habit of standing at the edges looking in. We need to create centers in situations like this one, out of things brought along and things found anew. Gathering fragments together into a new life for them is the way of *bricolage* (Lévi-Strauss 3–47) and not incidently, often the way of women, who are used to living in worlds of conflicting demands that fragment their everyday lives, their sense of time, and the kinds of resources they have available. One of their resources is being able to develop a sense of continuity—flow, if you will—out of pieces of time and of materials. It is an ecological resource all of us who are writing teachers might do well to strengthen and model for students, since it encourages a curiosity born of need to know how fragments of ideas might fit together in conceptual worlds that seem so often scattered from each other.

It was not too hard for me, then, to redefine for my own thinking some of Kevin's terminology, yet still believe with him that an overarching spirit or purpose that feels present in one's life can give energy and conviction to one's teaching. I find Hilde Hein's description of spirit as "an active, generative, and generous source. . . . the purposing agent" (149) especially pertinent in this context of blades and chalices, for Kevin's kind of agentic spirit was one I had so often wanted to minimize in my own teaching, with the result that my messages to students have often been less than clear-cut, and therefore, lacking the kind of spirit that can relate hard and soft kinds of energy.

Spirit, energy, purpose

Spirit is energy, too, and I think we have come far enough out of
positivistic circles to be able to use that word "energy" in nonmech-
anistic ways, claiming it simply as a felt experience that seems to
radiate, whether felt in a relation with early morning breezes during
a jog, or in one with people in a good conversation. Personal energy
and social power feel like two sides of the same coin, both rooted in
relation, and if that relation might be conceived of as generative
spirit, there would be no need to argue about whether it is inside or
outside people themselves. How fitting, then, to think with Hein
that "children, the offspring of joint parenthood and like their
parents a complex of physical, mental, and moral being, are a
paradigm spiritual product" (140). That is the vision of spirit I want
to carry into my classes as I urge my students to treat their writing
as offspring of their spirit. Because it is a felt and palpable relation
with someone or something, spirit can never be singular and simply
personal. The more open that relation is to new births and bond-
ings, to intricate and complex movements and patternings, the
more powerful, it seems to me, is anyone's sense of spirit, one that
lives in rhetorical purpose, commitment, and vision.

Kevin's ease with birth-thinking is surely linked to his living out
of relation and trusting the living process that grows out of it. His
superpersonal power is not mine, nor is his idea of life, but in terms
we could probably both be comfortable with, he is able to use both
agentic and communal energies, and use them with the seasonal
time of *kairos*, sensing when each kind is needed in which situations. He can shoot ideas cleanly through, no rough edges left, with
his metaphoric "long shot" projectiles, and he can be a midwife.
And although I cannot say what happened next in that group he
zapped, I can report that a revision was produced, that evaluations
for the course were uniformly positive (I guessed, then, that the
confrontation must have felt timely to that particular group), and
that Kevin did indeed (as I had noticed at other times), have an
unusual ability to both slice into and through issues, and, just when
one might think "Oh *that*'s what he's like," turn direction and
welcome the lively ideas he had just stirred up.

As we parted at the end of that eventful course, I blurted out to him, "You are a wonderful teacher."

He thanked me and replied, "So are you. Maybe not as flamboyant as I am, but . . ."

I thanked him too, and knew exactly what he meant.

Stories

I wonder if Kevin's practice of keeping a little gate open for other people's stories, and especially for those of other teachers and of his students—that edge of unpreparedness—could be one key to his keeping the spirit of relation in his teaching and modeling it for students. Stories are close to experience because they are peopled, and the people come alive as they move through human times together. Stories build community. Every family and every organized group collects its informal stories; Elizabeth Stone claims we can learn about how people structure their lives by listening to these and noticing where values lie, as for instance she has listened in *Black Sheep and Kissing Cousins*. Authoring stories is indeed authorizing certain behavior, as she makes clear: a sending of "messages and instructions" to other group members, offering "blueprints and ideals," issuing "warnings and prohibitions" (5). The stories disappear, she says "when they no longer serve" (5). Stories run through everybody's life whenever they tell about themselves and other people, in their dreams or in their waking life, tying past to future and beginnings to ends. New stories are tied to old in order to accommodate the hundreds of other voices we all meet along the way.

Stories and theories

Between the lines of those stories dwell the theories of action people live by that are reductions of those stories, principles laced with rules and structures pulled out of context. The theories are hard to examine for their geneses and founding life situations unless they can be injected back into the stories from which they have been pulled, to be given there the spirit of relation between all the samenesses and differences that gave them life to begin with.

In the details of the stories, links can be found to other ones, and common ground between them can be made more likely than between the more abstract theories that people espouse. "Among any array of narratives—tales or tellings—in the universe," says Barbara Herrnstein Smith, "there is an unlimited number of potentially perceptible *relations*. . . . of many different kinds and orders. . . . Whenever these potentially perceptible relations become actually perceived, it is by virtue of some set of interests on the part of the perceiver" (221–222). And in those common interests found in shared stories can lie productive dilemmas out of which new practices, new theories-in-use, might begin to grow.

It is not easy for new teachers to decide how they want to teach, much less to match espoused theories with theories-in-use in the classroom or to even recognize when they do not match (as Argyris and Schön note [7]). Theories-in-use are more readily noticed by observers than by oneself, which is one good reason for teachers to get plenty of feedback from others visiting their classes, to have people watch for inconsistencies in behavior that can lead into dilemmas. Multiple kinds of interactions between stories, theories, observations—all of these nourish a sense of curiosity about ways to strike chords between them, to understand better how cultures mix and separate themselves any time they meet in classrooms.

My own dilemmas about being an agent or authority, for instance, surfaced only gradually over the years until they were mirrored to me sharply in Kevin, whose behavior opposed much of what I valued yet at the same time did not oppose at all: It gave me a positive model for what I had felt foreign in my own teaching. That sharp edge had never become so clear before, nor the discrepancy between my espoused theories and theories-in-use. The stories Kevin and I told each other at lunch contributed much, too, to my straightening out many strands of ideas, as did, finally, my sensing a context around us both in the way we thought about peopled times.

One dilemma teachers of composition face when they espouse theories about their own authoritative behavior that are inconsistent with their theories-in-use is that, with the espoused theories, they are authoring a different story—along with its structures—

from the one they are implicitly authorizing in their behavioral world. If, for instance, they engage their students in negotiating grading criteria yet retain fears about losing control, teachers will fall away from the path of *kairos* and lose the sense that they are synchronizing rhythms with their students. They will not time well the giving over of authority or the taking back. If on the other hand teachers decide they want to retain some parts of the teacher-as-gatekeeper story but not all, they need to ferret out of their practices what other stories they are telling along with it, to make sure students are implicitly hearing the one they want them to hear. When conflicting ones are being told, students must surely feel at least a vague discomfort at the margins of their awareness—exactly where they least need it, considering that the best places for them to experience connections to others in their environment lie there. If teachers decide to negotiate some of their authority in this or any other situation, they authorize students' right to author some of that situation. They therefore need to have thought clearly about whether their hearts are willing to legitimize the answering voices of their students, and if there are borders beyond which they are not willing to negotiate with those voices.

Beyond those borders may well be the land of zappings, a clean-cut killing off of certain behaviors and attitudes intolerable to any teacher's theories-in-use. But when that clean cut takes place, teachers had better know in whose name, theory, and story it is done: In other words, who author(ize)s this cut? If it is the institution for which we work and to which we are responsible, can we relate our own system of values to it? Can we fit into that system a student's interests that the student herself may not recognize, as we act almost like Zen masters, faithful to a larger system of values? How can we be sure it is timely and good for the student—are we catching some signal from her at any given time that this message from us is exactly what she needs now? I have no doubt that Kevin's intuitive powers were at work when he sensed the kind of message needed by overconfident senior writers at that moment. And intuition is aided by fearless thinking about one's values and agendas.

I am not claiming that teachers can individualize instruction at all times and vary their tactics accordingly *or* that they should develop a theory-in-use that will be consistent in all cases. Rather, teachers need, I think, a spirit born of many intercultural clashes and resolutions of dilemmas, a spirit that grows stronger and more complex the more meetings it has, and that fosters acts of *kairos* on the borders between choices, when it finds some rhythm, something to be drawn to in foreign-feeling people and ideas. Psychoanalytic theory posits a level of thinking below consciousness in which opposites represent each other in an action called "reversal into the opposite." If brought into awareness, or as psychiatrist Albert Rothenberg recommends, deliberately engaged in, this doubling process of what he calls Janusian thinking, *"actively conceiving two or more opposite or antithetical ideas, images, or concepts simultaneously"* (55), can allow each side to throw light on the other and act as an impetus to creative thinking.

For instance, negotiating seems different from dictating, yet as many social scientists point out, any organized group of people is rife with informal negotiating networks, no matter how "governed" by authority the group is formally. Furthermore, there are as many styles of negotiation as there are people and there are theorists to classify them. A teacher's dictating is simply a hard positional kind of negotiating and needs to be seen in a larger context of whether or not he gets stuck in that position of authority and why. Even negotiating from interests rather than position does not preclude moments of positional dictating from what a teacher sees as larger-than-personal interests. The goal is that both sides win. What they win is the question to be addressed: It may be yet another round of questions to be answered in a new context. Argyris, for instance, claims that neither easing-in nor directive strategies can upset old models of hierarchical, individualized, and single-loop learning models as well as can sharing with learners one's reading of the context of learning (*Reasoning* 147–167). Argyris would have told those senior writers what his reasoning was in insisting they revise, or in, had he chosen to use it, easing-in. Then he would expect a counterreading from the learners.

There is always more to learn.

The discourse of power and authority

Most of us in freshman English at Maryland seemed to see authoritative power as centralized into at least somewhat untrustworthy positions, supporting a point made by Sennett that most people nowadays (since the French Revolution) have a vague sense that the authorities in their lives are not legitimate (48). But the very idea of power being centralized in authoritative positions, legitimate or not, is according to Michel Foucault an anachronistic image, a relic of bygone days, caught up into our cultural memories and more clearly belonging to the times when sovereigns ruled widely in Europe. "Royal power," he says, "has provided the essential focus around which legal thought has been elaborated" (*P/K* 94). Though it still governs the way we talk, claims Foucault, centralized power is not the kind of social control we actually operate under anymore. We are still "under the spell of monarchy" (*History* 88) in our sense of legitimacy, obedience, and prohibitions, but power resides now more in dispersed forces of knowledge and discourse called disciplines—bureaucratic, institutional, or academic ones—than in centralized legal authority.

Today power is more subtle than in the pre-Enlightenment days of monarchy, says Foucault, woven invisibly into our psyches and locally diffused in relations between people. Some people exercise it, to be sure, but they do it in modern secularized versions of pastoral power revealed through "scientific" or acceptable ways to structure talk, which in turn "normalize" the discourse of others. People are then controlled primarily through internalizing the laws and regulations given them by those experts who, by representing the authority of the disciplines, know and can teach the truth for the sake, supposedly, of those they teach. Doctors, counselors, scientists, teachers, and advertisers can, so we are told in our culture, give us better health, proper technique, mental welfare, more money, keeping us all within the acceptable belief systems of modern society. We no longer need to be coerced externally.

More than power *in* people, then, authority may better be thought of as moving *between* them, regulating the way they talk with and relate to each other. The margins between center and edges are no longer easily stabilized, even though power may *feel* outside of us in some other center. It is the discourses we use that attempt the stabilizing, claims Foucault, and discourses can destabilize too.

For composition teachers, a stabilizing discourse would be all the theories or timeless truths that are given us in the name of "knowledge," or "what we know now" about writing. But on the other hand, our best agent for change, fortuitously for our own subject matter, is also discourse, one, however, which might destabilize our tendencies to settle into hard positions of conceptual governance over others or into soft positions of no governance at all.

Once novice writers open their minds to authoritative voices that must be answered (as those must be answered, for instance, that are read for research or persuasive papers), they can easily get swept into a vortex of voices from stories and theories other than their own in which they lose their own discursive way (plagiarizing is just one possibility). A teacher's hard, authoritative stance on such an issue can squelch the possibility of a student's becoming an author and answerer himself (in the double-binding situation of plagiarism, the student who has written a paper in someone else's voice, one he could not or would not answer in his own, is given a failing grade he cannot effectively answer [protest], that says "Next time, answer that other voice!"). But a soft, understanding stance is no better, gives little motivation to author in one's own voice, no guidance in answering the authoritative voices of one's sources.

Rather, both ways of conceiving interaction with students might better be looked at anew and redefined, along with the student's plagiarism which from this different vantage point can be seen as a mental gesture of dependence, a stasis of mind, in which a student is simply leaning up against an idealized self, a strong authority figure (his source), and saying "Drive on." In a radical conceptual convergence between student and teacher, the teacher's stance—hard or soft—itself then becomes implicated in the student's problem, in the sense that the same binary opposition is operative for both student and teacher: hard authoritative position/soft accommodating position (the student softly fitting his own voice into, or against, a central position or voice of strength). The hard and soft positions can then be understood not just as habitual ways of reading social experience, but even more importantly, readings about the way power and authority function in the world of interaction between people, about who gets to use it as a limiting restraint on others and who benefits from it as a liberating resource. Since power is so often perceived as centralized in authority figures and therefore nonnegotiable in academic situations, neither students nor teachers are used to thinking in terms of contextualizing such readings for the purpose of negotiating meanings and thereby the status of participants. (Why *not* open the subject of plagiarism, for instance, to examination of both student's and teacher's hidden agendas, to their theories-in-use and assumptions about a student's time management, his right to secrecy, his loyalty, or the teacher's right to know?)

The problems underlying hard and soft styles of rhetoric or negotiation in the classroom are nearly always sensed as problems of rights or legitimacy, with the people at the center, teachers, thought (by at least hard negotiators) to have certain discursive rights. How complicated it becomes, then, to convince students they can feel confident about themselves as writers in a situation that gives them only limited discursive rights.

But if one understands authoring as answering one's own and others' questions, then authorizing one's own discourse—oral or written—might better be conceived *not* as digging one's heels into a hard or soft position (though there can be room for timely zapping and timely support), but as trying out positions that can be answered by others—that is, negotiated with so that one's next move can be a responsive change. I am not by any means recommending that students be allowed to plagiarize. I *am* suggesting that in order that they develop surer footing in their work, they be guided toward an enabling interpretation of who has a right to speak—and be answered—in what situation. Toward the same end, teachers would do well to examine their own assumptions and theories-in-use and stories about authority, social power, and legitimacy.

As we tell those to each other we might hear some like ours but different, some we might like to imitate somewhat but not entirely. Those matings are the ones that can bear real pedagogical fruit.

II

CURRENTS IN THE TRADITION

The ability to enter into all things and to learn to understand them
. . . these are aims of human striving which we can recognize also in
the qualities of water.

Like water, thought . . . can unite, but also separate.

[In water] there must always be an interplay between at least two
forces in order to create a balancing rhythm.

Theodor Schwenk, *Sensitive Chaos*

4

Four Midwives

Classifying positions

My arguments in Chapters 2 and 3 carried the assumption that the written and oral discourses of both students and teachers might hold more ethical and political force if principles and beliefs opposing their own were welcomed into their minds for generous negotiation. No matter how unsettling the joining might feel at first, I urged, more coherent thinking and greater conviction are born of looking the feared other in the eye and listening to both the familiar-sounding notes in her story and those not so familiar, finding ways to share stories with her and to fine-tune the differences in the overlap.

The borderlines between cultural values, in other words, can best open into fruitful channels of communication if they are both *in* position (so that they are evident when one speaks and writes) and *not* in position (so that the other is not shut out). Now and then there need to be gaps in all of our agendas—teachers and students—so that we leave open the possibility of crossing boundaries and interacting with those of others, in our researched material and in our audience.

Apart from our local scenes, the field of composition studies as a whole has its voices too, and those voices have become so abundant in recent years that the boundaries of the discipline seem to be bulging with new life, just begging to be housed in some kind of orderly fashion. And indeed more and more of the orderly-minded in the field are obliging (Berlin [in "Contemporary Composition"], Kroll, Fulkerson, North, and Woods, for instance), finding ways to put boundaries between groups of their brethren, and being themselves categorized, in turn, by the way they classify the others. Trying to make sense of several taxonomists' rationales, for instance, Ann Ruggles Gere looks at the overlaps in their categories (30–34); and Philip Keith discusses James Berlin's categories, taking him to task for his "overemphasis" on "taxonomy" (91).

There is certainly no question that to be able to classify is to be able to make sense of the world (and our field); without this ability, incoming stimuli would be overwhelming and unassimilable. We cannot do without boundaries that cluster the buzz. But the obvious association with perception should not mislead us into thinking that categorizing is not an interested activity and therefore one with political as well as perceptual edges. At least one of the gatherers, James Berlin, registers full Foucauldian awareness that the way "facts" are selected and shaped in any discourse community is an inescapably ideological activity, that knowledge is always created in conjunction with political agendas (*Rhetoric* 4–5).

But yet another, Stephen North, in his witty and immensely informative book about how knowledge has been created in composition, underplays the role of politics even in the way he sets up his own dividing lines. He creates, for instance, a category called "philosophers," puts people in it, then implies that those people (the "real" ones this time, not the ones he has *created* as philosophers) have trouble staying in it, seeming to want to mix hands-on practitioner status with hands-off philosophical inquiry (96). His own category error seems to escape him, but I would argue that both he and some of the people he complains about may be less to blame for escaping over borders into foreign territory than for failing to notice the political, provisional, and unreliable status of boundary lines in the first place. Two of North's targeted authors, Knoblauch and Brannon, in their book *Rhetorical Traditions and the Teaching of Writing*, seem more adept at taking philosophy into practice (in spite of North's complaint) than at noticing many of the subtle details and rhetorical contexts of the classical world that do not fit into their denigrated category of "ancient rhetoric." I would argue that it is just this deadening of detail or story for the sake of controlling it that threatens to distort the work of boundary lovers who do not *also* sense the life teeming at the boundaries *between* categories.

Aristotle probably had it coming, maker of orderly schemes that he was, but he was not only such a maker, nor were so many of the other rhetorician/categorizers who followed him. There are subtleties in much of the rhetorical tradition that could be construed in different shapes from those we have given them, if our purposes be different. Furthermore, although the field does seem to have given all the modern scheme makers plenty of precedence for their itch, particularizing is as fundamental a process to thinking as is categorizing or schema-making, claims social psychologist Michael Billig; we all have the ability and the need to undercut our own categorical assumptions, with the details and contradictions we meet in everyday life (*Arguing* 120–134). Refusing to notice the details is deadening to both thinker and the people and things thought about.

Once categorized, people and things tend to lose their conceptual complexity and to become stereotyped, says Billig (125), and the infinitely rich life of the mind and its cultural worlds be subdued. Anyone whose talk has ever been interrupted in a group situation with "Do you mean X or Y?" knows how easily he can feel silenced and marginalized on the spot, especially if a frown is sent with the question. I was recently, in such a setting, voicing objections to a proposed plan for a writing workshop when the leader asked "Are you talking about the content or the method?" For some self-defeating reason I fell into her classifying arms by answering, "Method," and realized too late that my whole point, which revolved around the workshop needing to integrate the two into one agenda, was now lost. Speech learns to stumble when it allows itself to be stuffed into someone else's files (a point made implicitly by Foucault [*OT* xviii]), just as classified facts and ideas "learn" to stay in their places, posing little threat of coming alive in the now neat compartments of the stuffers. Compartments lend security to belief systems; unchallenged security kills minds and cultures.

Deadening our historical selves

One compartment many composition theorists would like to safely marginalize is that containing the field's activities during the 1970s, a bygone time thought of now as the "me" decade, divorced from the different concerns of the late 1980s and early 1990s. But the way we have so often filed away some of our old heroes can be deadening to our own minds, to the extent that we have deadened parts of theirs. The 1970s were not only or even primarily a "me" decade; we were all trying to make connections between parts of ourselves *and* between ourselves and the world and people around us. Our selves were often living at the edges of outworn belief systems, exploring ways to create new life stories there, imagining ways the margins between cultures might be redrawn. Ken Macrorie (who began talking to composition teachers in the 1960s), Peter Elbow, William Coles, Jr., and John Schultz were there too, at the edges of old academic habits, and at least three of them (Schultz less than the others) brought ideas into the teaching of composition that have in many ways become centrally established. In fact, these people became such established figures that they eventually warranted compartments in the field (Macrorie and Coles often labeled "expressionists"), and that was the beginning of their gradually becoming marginalized to its central concerns.

I would like to go back into the conceptual life of these theorists, to argue that the "selves" in their work need to be looked at anew so that we as a profession can give ourselves a better historical context for the way we draw *our* selves. All four take us to the edges of institutional life and disciplinary power, where we can look again at the sharp lines academics have so often drawn between their own respectable work and the work of the outside world that may nourish academic research but is considered to live in a different world or place. I will show ways in which these theorists created new kinds of conceptual spaces for writers, spaces that lived beside those of the familiar academic world, coexisting with them, even though not finally converging with them into new, negotiated spaces for writers' minds.

Chapter 5 will pick up the strands of the argument begun here, urging that time and again in the history of rhetoric and composition, what is set out to pasture is all the parts of mind and body that nourish us but that endanger the central body politic—those parts that can be handed over to shepherds with a sigh of relief: sometimes to artists (such as creative writers), sometimes to entertainers, sometimes to dreamers, and often to women.

Midwives of experiential selves

I call these four men midwives because they dared to help bring into the world of composition studies some of those parts of mind lost to us (granted, brought in during the more congenial atmosphere of the 1960s and 1970s) and claim them to be empowering resources for writers. These men helped us all give birth to the idea that categorizing is a deadly practice unless it acknowledges its own trap: the tendency to submerge experiential details that can make the categories come alive. And although I will claim finally that their visions fall short of completing the self's circuit into its social and cultural moorings, they all give us a good look at some places the connection might be made.

Ken Macrorie's Third Way

Not the least of the problems perceived as central in the field of composition studies was taken on by Ken Macrorie in the early 1970s—that of disciplinary power itself. Macrorie did not call it that, of course; I doubt that he had heard then of Michel Foucault's studies of this phenomenon. But coming into print with *Telling Writing* just after waves of campus rebellions had crested, Macrorie said for composition teachers what others were saying for academic institutions in general: We are all alienating those we would presume to teach and something is deeply wrong. The temper of that time was that the institutions in which Americans had invested so much power had misused it by neglecting the rights of persons. What protesters were urging, in Stanley Aronowitz's words, was "an almost religious return to *experience*" and a creation of communities "not primarily of interest (political rationalism) but of *feeling*" (20). With the realization that the individual and his more-than-cognitive self had been forsaken by the institution, came the intention "to restore power to the *person*" (Aronowitz 32). Macrorie's work was probably the best known (and often best loved) of those that brought this kind of revolutionary talk to the teaching of composition.

Telling Writing advised students to speak truths that counted for them in their own authentic voices, honestly and unpretentiously. They were to value their own experience as material for writing; Macrorie praised anyone who could be "faithful to his feelings and true to the world he has experienced or imagined" (13). Speaking for oneself, not for teachers, was important. One was not to place one's "vocabulary on exhibit" (6), not be an image, in other words, for someone else. Macrorie was fighting against the standardization of writing and writers in composition classes, against conventions of form and diction that made most "proper" essays look strangely like one another.

What better spokesman could there have been in composition studies for the nation's waking up to the fact of disciplinary power? Ken Macrorie did not need Michel Foucault to tell him that all the while universities were speaking the liberal democratic talk of freedom through knowledge, they were engaging in the kind of rational discourse that would convince students they could regulate themselves by imitating experts' talk. Young students had until now seemingly been convinced by institutional talk, had *wanted* to become normal and rational (not emotional) and to be guided by academic expertise. Macrorie told teachers of composition, "The professors are failing, everyday, every hour" (*Uptaught* 2). Many teachers were already suspecting an insidious and repressive link between institutional power and professors who imparted knowledge; many were grateful to Macrorie for sharing his indignation and a way to give back some discursive power to individual students, who would find that power, he told them, coming out of their own lives, out of discursive mastery over their own experience. Truth was no longer to be linked to institutional knowledge but to the facts that writers should trust themselves to find "lying all around you every minute of your life" (*Telling* 32).

By 1978, though, Macrorie's ideas were being "rethought" in the pages of *College English* by James Vopat, with complaints that his methods were too individualistic, too prone to the idea "that the personal is more real than the objective" (42). Macrorie did publish a new textbook in 1980 (*Searching Writing*) as well as a collection of interviews with teachers in 1984 (*Twenty Teachers*). And *College English* did run a review article about him in 1982, an intellectual biography by Erika Lindemann, proving his enduring reputation in the field. There are probably few composition teachers who have not been touched in some way by Macrorie—his humane handling of students' experience, his trust in their abilities to give voice to that experience, his care about good writing, *telling* writing, writing that counts for people. But times have changed and so have tempers; institutional worlds are being accommodated in people's lives now more than they are being examined from an opposing position. The oppositional pair that Macrorie uncovered with such discrimination—the after-all-not paternal school versus the repressed student—has lost its hold on the social imagination.

In fact, however, it seems possible that that oppositional pair, rather than having been lost to teachers' minds, has become instead submerged in the same discursive practice from which I would claim it sprang, one that posits people as individual selves, sovereigns over their own affairs, themselves (rather than the king) finders of truth. Macrorie has a special turn-taking, seemingly equalizing, variation on disciplinary discourse, but the talk is nevertheless about individualized mastery, in this case, mastery by the many students with minimum interference from the many professors.

But even further along this Foucauldian line (which finds Macrorie now on one side of it, now on the other), what not-so-kind critics have said about Macrorie's classes is that they breed writing as a form of confessional: One is urged to examine one's personal experience in the writing that is then examined by the teacher, the secular pastor. From this point of view a Macrorie class is a drama of pastoral power: The student warrants secular salvation if she stays with her feelings and is honest and does not try to use big words in order to pretend she is a good girl for daddy, who knows better about those words. There is a sense, then, in which power is not so easily transferred from the teacher as institutional representative to the student as sovereign individual; the sham of academic freedom that Macrorie did indeed expose can come back to haunt him in this other kind of normalizing discourse. In this variant of disciplinary talk, the teacher has not solved the problem of authority in the classroom because the authoritative other—the legal institution as bad—has not been engaged, as the negative partner, in a negotiation that would reveal it as part of the same system that holds the seemingly sovereign student. The negative rebellion stays put, in a way that resembles that in Brian's classes.

The terms themselves need to be rethought, in other words, their meanings negotiated. What *is* the difference between personal power and institutional power? Can they overlap? Do they resemble each other? What *are* facts? Is there falsehood in any truth, fiction in any fact? In what discursive practice is one of these oppositional

terms valued over the other? If the terms vital to Macrorie's thinking themselves go unchallenged, the alien, seemingly dead, institutional voice of the expert might never be found and grappled with
at one's own center, among one's own voices. Instead, it will wait,
and return. Without a look, for instance, at the way in which
today's students become the more compliant alter egos of 1960s and
1970s rebels, without noticing how much they are alike as well as
different from each other, the boundaries of the cultural habits that
house them are not likely to be broken through.

Indeed, it could be said that some of the "rethinking" of Macrorie's views may have been at least partly generated by a more
prevalent desire in the 1980s to accommodate than to rebel against
institutional culture: Macrorie's "natural voice" versus "institu-
tional-Engfish voice" pair does not ring so "true" anymore, now
that natural voices seem themselves shot through with cultural
conditionings. By transferring power and facts from the larger
political/social realm to the personal, Macrorie invites such labels
as "Neo-Platonic," a name given concepts such as his by James
Berlin, with the explanation that in this conceptual category truth is
"finally inexpressible . . . beyond the resources of language," to be
apprehended privately and internally; "writing as a 'personal' activity," as Berlin calls it (771–772). Or, in another categorizing scheme,
William Woods, using categories developed by Barry Kroll and
Richard Fulkerson, calls *Telling Writing* "expressionist," a student-
centered theory

> grounded in a "maturationist" theory of development, the idea that
> humankind has in it the seeds of its perfection, which will flower if
> allowed to grow naturally, uninhibited and unharmed by social or
> environmental constraints. (Woods 397)

Then there is Vopat, who believes that the movement around a self-
center is the biggest problem in Macrorie, a failure to move clearly
beyond a "me" (Vopat 45). In all three versions of his ideas about
teaching, Macrorie is seen as focusing on the individual student,
encouraging writing that aims for a truth not finally affected by
interlocutors, or in Berlin's version, a truth lying in an "inner and
privileged immaterial realm," which metaphors from the sense
world can only approximate.

None of these labels is entirely unfitting, but a close examination of Macrorie's work reveals that the "truths" he wants students to look for live not in an ideal world but in the material one, and often in one of Plato's least-trusted areas: the organic life of the emotions (forces that Macrorie sees as "physical movement" [*Vulnerable* 184]). Moreover, Macrorie is no fan of Plato's teacher Socrates: "Socratic questions are not questions at all," he finds himself agreeing with a speaker, "but subterfuges" (*Uptaught* 105). The kind of mental reality Macrorie presupposes is neither expressionist nor Neoplatonic, though there are half-truths in both descriptions of his work. Both fail to consider that although Macrorie's interpretive framework looks uncomfortably like the hackles-raising negative of the one he would replace, he has spent his career searching for ways to break out of such categories, ones he has felt constricting his teaching of writing.

The term "expressionist" (drawn presumably from the work of James Britton), for instance, in the way Woods uses it, neglects the way Macrorie in recent years has looked for ways to change students' ideas of traditional mental boundaries, to think in terms of a social as well as personal self. (I will discuss this work shortly.) Furthermore, "expressionist" carries with it a negative value nowadays for some people in composition studies: expressive writing as opposed to the more serious expository. To express oneself has been associated with pressing something out from an inside (often, an emotion-full subject presumably needing to release pressure) as opposed to indicating to others something "objective" which is already outside oneself. Jacques Derrida discusses a similar dichotomy between expression and indication, and although he is dealing with a slightly different (Husserlian) notion of expression, he nevertheless finds that neither one of the pair can be logically privileged over the other, because each is found at the other's core (*Speech* 31). To think otherwise is to imagine that one's inside world of concepts does not live also in the outside one and vice versa. I bring this up here in order to emphasize Macrorie's belief that "only when one is struggling with both subjectivity and objectivity is he apt to write live and telling sentences" (*Uptaught* 119), and these would need both to express a self and indicate something to others. To call him an expressionist is to think only of the side of Macrorie that looks for ways to touch base with the subjective self. His work is more complex than "expressionist" would imply; his "expressive" students are also engaged in indication.

Speaking for himself, he is none of the above, but is a "vulnerable teacher" who encourages his students to become vulnerable, to be willing "to admit ignorance or inexperience, while basing one's thought or action on [one's] own experience" (*Vulnerable* Preface iii). This vulnerability, although it is centered on individualized selves, nevertheless opens itself to a tension between those selves, between them and the course, and between ideas that move them toward being social selves. Macrorie's classes begin to penetrate the borders between these oppositions (if not those of his own belief system) in people's experience, and often find ways to mediate between them.

The ground of his teaching came from a turnaround in his academic life, the discovery of a "Third Way" of teaching. It is explained in less than half a page in *Uptaught*:

> In the First Way the teacher hands out a package of information and tests to see whether students can remember its content. The package contains no gifts, and the teacher expects none in return.
> In the Second Way, the teacher provides complete freedom and no direction at all. That way is apt to produce a few splendid, inventive sand castles that are eventually abandoned on a beach strewn with empty beer cans.
> In the Third Way, which I stumbled onto, students operate with freedom and discipline. They are given real choices and encouraged to learn the way of experts. (27)

The Third Way, then, let teachers begin to understand where academia set up its boundaries, and let them begin to challenge its either/ or thinking. He did not bring the two sides together and look at them from a larger context—the underlying system of sovereign thinking—but he did keep them in a liberal balance with each other. In the Third Way the weaker member of an oppositional pair can at least be raised up out of obscurity and silence.

This Way involves a course structured in such a manner that students can go their own way with their writing, with minimal fear of grading reprisal, at the same time that Macrorie as the teacher assumes that both he and they will bring disciplined thinking to that writing. Everyone knows that students cannot both have the freedom to come and go at will in a class (physically and mentally), to say and write anything they wish, and at the same time have a teacher imposing his own will on their activities. The situation is clearly inoperable, impossible to understand by ordinary thinking. One side or the other must be chosen, as a century of oscillation between student-centered and teacher-centered classrooms has shown all Americans.

But Macrorie does not choose; he lets the tensions remain. He does not eliminate the freedom or the discipline, the "subjective" feelings or the "objective" social situation, and because the situation seems strange, because it cannot be focused on as a single dominant point, or ex-plained (laid out flat on a plane), critics usually decide he is on the freedom side, encouraging focus on the student rather than the teacher. It could not be on both, they think. The critical logic has seemed to be this: "Unless the teacher insists on socialization, that is, disciplining of subjective impulses, the student will be stuck in his own center, his *me*. That is the natural direction people take, unless they can find channels to each other under socializing influence." In this logic, teachers become the socializers, the givers of discipline to otherwise self-centered minds.

Macrorie does not believe in this one-way action though, this source of discipline in a single point. Instead he lets the points both work over time. He takes control, gives it up, changes between hard and soft stances. He has a sense of rhythms both long and short: "I want students to learn to move back and forth between people of another time and theirs and illuminate both," he says (*Vulnerable* 18). He shifts roles with them:

> In this new way of teaching I get a sense of power from seeing students exercise their powers, not from my keeping myself up and them down, but rather from my inducing them to make themselves vulnerable to the materials and disciplines to be learned, to me, and to each other. And from my becoming vulnerable to their experience and thoughts. It is not . . . the old power game. (*Vulnerable* 12)

Polarities are highlighted: "Like the best life, the best school combines polarities. Discipline, discipline, discipline; and freedom, freedom, freedom. The wisdom and craft of the past brought up against the pressing present" (*Vulnerable* 13).

Macrorie believes that when people begin paying attention to each other in the classroom, to the movement of spoken and written words, a sense of mind as a social relationship begins to develop, a function of the Moebius Loop that brings the Third Way into his 1980s thinking. He brings the Loop to bear on what he calls loopy learning in *Searching Writing*. He suggests that a strip be cut from the long side of a sheet of typing paper, twisted at one end, and Scotch-taped in order to form a Moebius Strip, by which the outside flows into the inside in a continual reversing movement. The image reveals to him the motion any real learning must take— round a loop where self and others "slide into each other" (though too peacefully, it would seem, too smoothly to be the condition for a big move out of the system into the context. This is not *double* loop learning). Macrorie uses George Herbert Mead's idea of the self as both an *I* and a *me* to hint at how this process takes place. The self that includes both the *I* and the *me*, says Mead, is born in social behavior. It is not to be identified with the boundaries of one's body (Mead 136–138). "The 'I' reacts to the self which arises through the taking of the attitudes of others. Through taking those attitudes we have introduced the 'me' and we react to it as an 'I'" (Mead 174). The *I* behaves on the basis of what others think of my *me*, much as a writer (more consciously) responds to his or her readers. Vopat's worrying about Macrorie's concentration on a personal *me* would be senseless, in Mead's eyes and in the Macrorie vision, since the *me* is the internalized social world.

Macrorie does not detail all of Mead's position, but follows the principle throughout *Searching Writing* that a writer must be able to imagine himself "intensely" in another's position (13, following Percy Bysshe Shelley) as well as his own, as he responds to that other, just as Mead's *I* responds to the voices of his *me*. The principle of the Moebius Loop operates in such interactions:

> Where do we leave off and our words on the page begin? If we write a letter, are we traveling from California to New York to greet our friend? Yes and No. We are the letter and we are ourselves in California—a Moebian loop again. (39)

"The greatest discoveries," says Macrorie, "come to human beings working on the Moebius Strip, both detached and attached" (100). He exhorts writers to meet themselves as subjects on the Strip, to get their *I*s into the search for information that will have a genuine effect on their lives.

Still, the loop has no points of conflict where incoherences might arise, ones that would force those on it to question their own identities; it seems not to embroil itself either in controversy with the voices in the *me*, or to remember Macrorie's own 1970 dictum *not* to perform for others. The *I* on this strip does after all play to the socialized *me*. Nevertheless, there is and has been from the beginning his urging that students not defer to the authority of another, but to take on the role of their own authority. By bringing the social world into one's insides, one can do that and be one's own subject and object all in one. There is not to be the old subject/object separation of oneself from the content of one's world.

Only if writers have a chance to "bring themselves, with their experience and abilities, into the act of reading and discussing the experience of authorities" (13), can they learn anything, including how to write interesting and well-formed papers. Here is Macrorie's summary statement of Third Way teaching implicit in loopy learning:

> The principle reason education doesn't "take" better than it does is that it's a closed loop, with the knowledge and experience of experts on one side and no way for it to flow into or over to the other side, where in darkness—unarticulated, unreflected upon, unused—lie the knowledge and experience of students. The discipline of real learning consists of the Self and The Others flowing into each other. (*Searching* 13)

The Moebius Loop, I think, has been implicit in Macrorie's teaching from the days when he was discovering the Third Way, with information and authority circulating freely. For instance, Macrorie duplicates papers for response in seminars, where he assumes students will help each other as much as the teacher will help them: "In the Third Way, a student gets four times as much evaluation as in a class where he received grades" (*Uptaught* 95). Helping another student helps the helper think about his own work. This method, which has become almost a commonplace for many teachers, was grounded years ago in Macrorie's Third Way discoveries that power could be shared in a writing classroom as a renewable resource.

Even in cases some might deem better held in check authorita-
tively, Macrorie has believed that students need to find and test
their own powers. He describes in *Uptaught* some of his teaching
experiences that could outrage many teachers; students who are
angry, belligerent, or apathetic with him, or who give themselves
undeserved As because he has allowed them to be responsible for
their own grading, or who swear at him. But he has seen no
pedagogical value in squelching conflict, believing it productive of
insights. Most importantly, any actions that take place in either
writing or talking are usually talked about afterward, translated
from one discursive practice into another. Macrorie does not lower
writing standards through this opening of boundaries to each other.
For instance, he assumes that readers and listeners will encourage
"the student to show himself at his strongest" (*Uptaught* 74), later
punctuating the encouragement with possible negative critiques.
Writing gradually becomes more focused, "with freedom enough
within each assignment to allow the student to find what counts for
him. But discipline enough to insure that it usually also counts for
the teacher" (*Uptaught* 179). Writing standards remain high because the student is assumed able to become his own critic through
the loopy learning implied in classroom exchanges.

This looped self-consciousness—out through the class and back
into the *me*—seems to me to be the way Macrorie has been able to
socialize an otherwise closed sovereign self. To be sure, the Meadean vision that Macrorie points to in *Vulnerable Teacher* seems
more stabilized than the way most people experience their others—
as complex, more or less powerful, intimidating, loving, or made of
a thousand variations that can change the way people relate to each
other and define each other and the everyday world. Mead does not
seem to intend that the *I* will need to dance through a moving,
complex, resisting field in which keeping one's footing may be
tricky; the others in his *me* are generalized ones, not involved with
the content of exchanges and power differentials so much as with
the gestures of behavior. And for Macrorie, one's experience is
one's own, a given natural; shared interpretations are about the
language one uses to approximate it. (Here lies a partial rationale
for Berlin's interpretation.)

Nevertheless, "vulnerability" brings students and teachers close
to opening the borders of their own belief systems to others. Mead

insists that one's *I* develops the ability to take on the role of an other, that one can only know one's self, it is implied, by knowing that other. To the extent that Macrorie's classes work on their Meadean Moebius Strip, he and his students, then, are answerable to each other. Macrorie would like to imagine students operating without interactional power imbalances: *that* dream is his tribute to sovereign selves. But he knows that "power remains a prize [teachers] cannot help reaching for" (*Vulnerable* 12): *That* realization is his tribute to selves that will never be stable masters of themselves.

The Two Games of Peter Elbow

Macrorie's Meadean "self" is a reflexive one, one that tends to turn back on itself—no matter how attuned to other voices, other social worlds it becomes—simply because it *is* reflexive. But Macrorie does struggle with the problem of looking outward (explicitly in *Searching Writing*, implicitly earlier), and at least opens the door to solutions through Mead. There is little provision on the Strip, however, for moving that "self" out into an alien other, for giving the force of one's attention over into life beyond the *I/me* circuit. With no gaps, no openings in the smoothly sliding loop, no complex snarls, there are few ways out of this closed classroom system or self-enclosed writing. Peter Elbow's variation on this model gives a way that the direction of attention might stay aimed outside longer. Though I will claim finally that his own vision is also imprisoned in a closed loop, his vision of two games is a good way to define hard and soft discourse, separate them from each other, and look closely at them as "intellectual enterprises."

Elbow has written two books especially for writers, both concerned with power. (A third book, *Embracing Contraries*, covers a wider range of pedagogical issues.) In the 1973 *Writing Without Teachers*, he, like Macrorie, wanted to remove the inhibiting presence of the teacher's authority from classroom interchanges and student writing, and in the 1981 *Writing With Power*, he simply assumed the presence of a teacher and the necessity of coping with that particular more powerful other. In both books, the agenda is clearly a removal of feeling of helplessness in young writers, brought on by their experience of being marginalized from centers of power. In *Writing Without Teachers*, he acknowledges that "this book wouldn't have been possible without the example and support of Ken Macrorie" (x), and there is no doubt that Elbow's division of hard from soft teaching and learning styles has been at least partly inspired by Macrorie's softening the idea of professor into that of teacher.

But what Elbow calls "games" are worked out in a more rigorous conceptual framework of opposing actions than are any of Macrorie's oppositions. They are language games, the one, more dream-like, called the "believing" game, the other, more math-like, called the "doubting" game, and Elbow claims that "there is a constant tug of war" between them: "The history of meaning in a language is the history of this power struggle between dream characteristics and math characteristics" (*WWT* 155). He himself calls them "games" in order to urge that neither one is to be taken as a final decision about the way language works. They may seem like private, one-person intrapsychic activities, and if one thinks of cerebral activities as private, Elbow's versions of the traditional synthetic and analytic ways of thinking do indeed seem little different from those of an individualistic psychology. But Elbow's games do have a rhetorical edge to their structure, in the sense that they assume distinct ways in which people receive the assertions of what other people say or write: "Both games are probably inherently social," says Elbow (*WWT* 175). "Language and reasoning are probably simulations in a single mind of processes first occurring between minds (*WWT* 175).

The two games are ways to read, in the sense that people listen to (or literally read, in the narrower sense) each other's utterances in order to decide whether or not they are true. Granted that "truth" can be a dangerously provocative word, Elbow uses it in this context simply to mean a reading that is correct in terms of what "the speech community builds in or *could build in* without violating its rules" (157). Utterances can have more than one true meaning— some fainter than others. Therefore there can be more than one reading of an utterance, but there will still be some correct readings (the true meanings) and some incorrect (meanings not there).

There are two ways of reading, or seeking truth, says Elbow. The doubting game is the familiar one of logic, the dialectic of proposi- tions that extricates the self (and its values and experiences) and doubts assertions in order to "flush out into the open any hidden errors" (*WWT* 148). The believing game is an *insertion* of self (*WWT* 149), an act of projection into an utterance in order to understand it and experience it similarly to the person whose utterance it is. In essence, the act of mind is a movement of the self *out* of oneself into another's words: "By believing an assertion we can get farther and farther into it" (*WWT* 163), project in the "good" sense, "see more of what's really there by getting more of the self into every bit" (*WWT* 171). The main process of the believing game is moving "out of your own perceptions and thoughts into someone else's" (*WWT* 182). "We are trying to find not errors but truths, and for this it helps to believe" (*WWT* 149). In the doubting game one makes "logical transformations of the assertion," in the believing game, "metaphorical extensions, analogies, associations" (*WWT* 149). A succinct explanation of the two ways to seek truth comes from his 1982 article in *PRE/TEXT*:

> By the doubting game I mean the attempt to assess competing ideas by the method of disconfirmation, that is, by the process of subjecting them to rigorous and methodical doubt and only accepting those which cannot be doubted or which are least dubitable. Think of Descartes.
>
> By the believing game I mean the opposite process. Assessing competing ideas by subjecting them to rigorous methodical belief. In this process we take each idea and not only refrain from doubting it or searching for shortcomings, we specifically take each one in turn and try as hard as we can to believe it or *see it as true*. On the basis of this believing test—this sequence of temporary but genuine acts of assent—we can often see plainly which idea is true or best. ("Preface" 340–341)

The first is a distancing, a moving away from an idea to assess its position in a larger picture; the second moves closer to look at details. Elbow thinks that the believing game helps people understand the truths of words better than the doubting game does, because it deals with "particular, unique things" rather than the "classes of things" of the doubting game, close looks rather than distant. People who play it, therefore, "are particularly good at being many people, being a chameleon, seeing the truth in very different and contradictory propositions or perceptions, making metaphors and building novel models" (*WWT* 164).

Elbow is arguing not that the doubting game be eliminated from writing classes, but that the believing game not be dominated by it. Meaning in language grows out of both kinds of thinking, he claims, and the meaning is not in words but in the people who attribute it to the words (*WWT* 151).

In a 1983 article in *College English*, Elbow explains the concept of the two ways of thinking in terms of good teaching and good writing:

> good writing requires on the one hand the ability to conceive copiously of many possibilities, an ability which is enhanced by a spirit of open accepting generativity; but on the other hand good writing also requires an ability to criticize and reject everything but the best, a very different ability which is enhanced by a tough-minded critical spirit. ("Embracing" 327)

For Elbow, one needs the mental and linguistic freedom to move between the two, a freedom encouraged by the actual physical presence of believing others. The writing self learns to introject those nonthreatening others as helpful readers, to use their permissive mindset to listen more attentively to himself.

Elbow believes that one of the ways writers lose control of their writing in the first place is that they act as critical readers too soon, not giving their words a chance to develop, change, and grow in a natural way before they begin editing and judging, in other words, before they begin controlling (*WWT* 30–35). Letting go of control, or letting the mind work more naturally, Elbow believes, allows writing to have a "sound, a texture, a rhythm—a voice—which is the main source of power in your writing. I don't know how it works, but this voice is the force that will make a reader listen to you." (*WWT* 6). When control can be given up, in other words, when a writer can allow his mind to change when it is warranted by discovered truths (a communicational agenda similar to that of psychologist Carl Rogers, as Young, Becker, and Pike present it [274–290]), voice and power emerge. One must fight "the itch for closure" (*WWT* 176). This itch for a single-minded end to argument is a way to explain or control, to try to close options and find truth free of error. But truth is not certainty, Elbow claims; rather it is "shared, accurate perception" (*WWT* 178), a closure that can come only through patience and reorientation, and above all, that *insertion* of self in another person's viewpoint.

Elbow thinks that giving one's self over to someone else's experiences and viewpoints causes resistance, that it is difficult for people. It requires great energy, attention, and even a kind of inner commitment (*WWT* 149). People fear to play the game, says Elbow, first, because they believe it encourages solipsism. Not so, he claims. It is rather "a tool for *breaking out* of solipsism . . . out of your own perceptions and thoughts into someone else's" (*WWT* 182). It is the doubting game that locks people too often into their own minds, concentrating on defense (one must defend himself against those ideas that conflict with ones he is for). Second, doubters fear groupthink, but are themselves more prone to it, because they require a *disproof* of reigning or majority ideas, a nearly impossible task by doubter's logic, leaving majority opinion, or groupthink, intact, says Elbow. No room for "the little man," or the little ideas that need to be noticed in order that they grow, or the little particulars that might be seen to not fit in those big, dominant ideas if they were to be carefully looked at. Third, doubters think believers are too credulous, but Elbow argues that believing—or attentive listening—is much harder than doubting in our culture; a doubter's propensity to stay with what is easy to believe causes his own stronger credulity (i.e., his own passive and often unconscious identification with the position of the other, I would say).

There, then, is Elbow's entry into the undercurrent of power that begins to surface when one side is not allowed to dominate the other in a single-minded hierarchy. The genderized implications have not escaped him:

> The monopoly of the doubting game tends to reinforce those personal styles which the culture also defines as male: aggressive, thrusting, combative, competitive, and initiatory. A woman tends to be perceived as less feminine if she shines in the doubting game— if she loves to initiate and win arguments and find holes in the other person's position. A man tends to be perceived as less masculine if his intellectual style is *not* that of the doubting game—if he operates by pliancy, absorbency, noninitiation, and nonaggression. Some of our language for the adversary process of the doubting game reveals these associations of gender: "advancing points,"

"making points," "seeing if a point stands up," "finding holes," and "poking holes" in the other person's argument. Both the culture in general and the intellectual community in particular suffer a loss of power from this onesidedness. (*WWT* 180)

Elbow's writer/selves tend to focus on experiencing the other's position, Macrorie's on bringing the other's experience back to the self; but in neither case is there a vision of thinking and writing that would model how directions of thought change, or get stuck, or become stirred as a result of changing political situations in living experience. As a result, the kinds of selves shown by both men seem almost stereotyped, flattened images of students becoming able to see samenesses in the other but not the finely tuned details of sameness *and* difference. To be sure, the selves are welcome antidotes to an institutional emphasis on analysis and difference: these are boundary-crossing selves, bridge-building, empathetic, and synthetic ones, but not ones set up for continual negotiations across lines, not between doubting and believing, not between honest writing and Engfish.

In Elbow's vision, boundaries seem to either break down (in the believing game) or remain standing (in the doubting game, or between the two games). He has never (even under pressure from journal editors [noted by Elbow in a talk at a National Council of Teachers of English workshop, 1982]) found ways to question the boundaries between the two games or between the two ways of thinking related to them that he prescribes to guide both teaching and writing. He does not find the control in the lack of control, or the math-like calculation in the dream, or even the rhetorical figuring in the math-like thinking. Each game seems sufficient unto itself, ready, in Elbow's eyes, only to alternate with the other one, one at a time. Believing, then, will always look like itself with none of the other invading it, doubting, only like *its* self with none of *its* opposite. With no input from the different other, reproduction becomes repetition and sameness of parallel spaces, never meeting in the third and fourth dimensions between them that would round them out and liven them up.

Flattening of details slips easily into that habit of seeing the other as a category, if the provisional and political nature of oppositional thinking is not kept in mind. A counterhabit of noticing details about other people's lives can be encouraged by raising questions at sticky contact points; ancient rhetorical theory erected a theory of questioning called *stasis* at just such points of conflict. But how difficult it is to avoid the flattening can be seen in an article about Elbow written by Ross Winterowd in *PRE/TEXT*, one ostensibly giving Elbow what he has asked for, but, with an edge of irony, giving him instead what Winterowd thinks Elbow needs. Winterowd is "answering" another *PRE/TEXT* article that Elbow himself wrote, in which he reviewed his own ideas about doubting and believing over a period of several years, following their original publication in *Writing Without Teachers*. Elbow ends the *PRE/TEXT* review by opening the subject to others: "I need help in understanding the nature of reasoning. I would be grateful for any other sort of help in my enterprise: reactions, suggestions, criticism, queries, good articles or books" ("Preface" 350–351).

I put Winterowd's "answering" in quotation marks because in order to write his responding article (called "Dear Peter Elbow"), Winterowd has had to slightly miss, or misrepresent, Elbow's point for the purpose of making his own, causing the answer to not touch Elbow's discourse, to run slightly off-center from it, to parallel rather than yield power to it, before swallowing it into his own point. In other words, Winterowd does not *answer* Elbow, does not situate himself in the midst of this other's request for help, but creates a flat image of Elbow (without the substance) that reflects Winterowd's own need, his own argument.

Elbow tells how he "gradually developed the idea of the believing game while teaching writing" ("Preface" 339), how he "stumbled onto a game" (340), and how he believes that people already play it, even play it well. "My claim," he says finally, "is that people—whether they use it or not—seldom *recognize* the capabilities of the believing game for assessing claims and therefore seldom grant it legitimacy" (350). He does not suggest that people have never thought about the game, but that they may not have recognized how one can assess claims with it.

Winterowd responds by praising Elbow's request for communal solutions to his problem of community—believing—and the apt timing of the request. But then Winterowd moves in, like Antony after Brutus, for the kill:

It is always a pleasure to watch original minds at work, and certainly we can see in your isolate cogitations an original mind.

The problem is, of course, that knowledge of a field is never isolate; it involves communion. What troubles me about your 1973 essay is that it does not indicate communion. The whole thrust of the piece is to suggest that you have arrived at some kind of vatic insight and are asking if anyone else has ever thought these thoughts.

Yes, others have. (95–96)

Winterowd now names Wayne Booth, Robert Pirsig, Kenneth Burke, John Searle, and others—including himself—who have written extensively on matters similar to Elbow's believing game. There is an effectiveness in Winterowd's letter because there is, at least on the evidence of the *PRE/TEXT* article, a certain ironic truth to his argument: he shows that on Elbow's own ground of listening carefully to what others have to say, Elbow seems to fall short (the alien other has been found at his own center), to fail to evidence that he has in the past entered a believing game with people who have sought similar ends (Elbow admits that he is "bad at thinking while I look my audience in the eye" [*WWP* 195], and I assume that audience includes those he is answering that have come before him).

On the other hand, Winterowd's ironic fusillade is itself a failure to listen carefully, not only to the *PRE/TEXT* essay, but to the 1973 one as well, and therefore, to the extent that Winterowd talks past Elbow as one of his intended recipients, he talks to a flattened image, as did Narcissus to his own beautiful reflection.

Winterowd misreads Elbow on two counts—perhaps slight, but important for his argument. First, he implies that the "asking" occurs in the original 1973 article. It does not. Rather, in the original there is an acknowledgment of those who have developed forms of the believing game: encounter groups, Quakers, juries, Thomas Kuhn, Michael Polanyi, good literary critics (*WWT* 188–190). Second, even in the 1982 article, Elbow does not ask "if anyone else has *ever* [my italics] thought these thoughts," as Winterowd paraphrases him. As a glance at the passages in question will show, his point is rather that he would like to have input now on the matter of the believing game's ability to assess claims, not on whether it is practiced or thought of. Winterowd's responses, therefore, are ambiguous: *what* they answer is unclear, and therefore they do not *meet* Peter Elbow's point. The power inherent in clashes of voices is not tapped (nor is Winterowd's response then collegial, as he claims [admittedly, he may be claiming with irony]). Meaning is appropriated rather than negotiated, and the other— Elbow—acts only as a reflection of what Winterowd wants him to be rather than a substantial other. Winning against such a flattened image is a hollow victory even though the victory may display surface brilliance. The flow is too glib: not enough challenge.

Granted, finely tuned readings cannot be taken to infinity, and a desire for resolution or endings must sooner or later take over. One must, to be sure, withdraw mental energies into one's own self-concept and self-image to a certain extent, just to exist as an *I* amidst mountains of printed *I*'s. But to the extent that "answers" talk *past* rather than *to* questions, to the extent that details are swallowed in a bid for sovereign, unsharable power, thinking and writing do not generate multidirectional discursive power, but sap/ zap it. Authoring loses the vigor of answering. Such mental movements tend to draw up sides, stereotyping (because not noticing) the others who seem unlike oneself, identifying with those who mirror—and therefore seem to strengthen—one's own best side.

Macrorie, Elbow, and Winterowd might seem strange bedfellows, and indeed they are in most respects. But insofar as they all—in greater or lesser ways—close any part of their own arguments off (and I speak only of Winterowd's present argument, not any other) to the voices of an other in their midst, they play on the field of disciplinary discourse, with its fenced-off properties belonging to the selves who own them (teachers, let us say), but not others (their students, maybe). The owner/selves might be students (as Macrorie and Elbow's students own their own discourse) or players of one game at a time (Elbow's players). Or they may simply be revealed in an argument that erects the fence (Winterowd). But the fences tend to act like mirrors or even Narcissus' pool over time, when they are the outside limit of what one can see, and then finally one sees only one's own—or one's argument's—image. All that is left then is asexual reproduction feeding on itself, and metaphorically speaking, that is a lethal, cancerous kind of reproduction within multicellular beings.

William Coles, Jr., and the last word on what makes writing good

Though Macrorie and Elbow may not have gotten rid of all the mirrors they might have wished, image-conscious selves do concern them, just as they do William Coles, Jr. Like Macrorie and Elbow, Coles places value on the ability of minds to change, and like them, his overall assumption is that mindless writing for (stereotyped) teachers—Macrorie's "Engfish," Elbow's "credulity," Coles' "Theme-writing"—is a conceptual habit in which students tend to give up their own discursive minds to the control of an imagined authority. (For Elbow, to be sure, credulity is only one symptom of the doubting game's monopoly.) Coles' work leads finally to a look at the way people categorize each other in their writing, how they are able to follow along beside the others they are supposedly answering by making images of them that fit their own desires or purposes, that make solutions to their own problems, coherent stories of their own professional lives. To examine Coles' outlook, I want to concentrate especially on a book Coles has co-edited with James Vopat, called *What Makes Writing Good*. Coles' longstanding aversion to "communication," the interactive component of discourse, moves like an alien presence in the territory of this book, controlling a format that is, true to Coles' leanings, ostensibly more concerned with assignments that challenge individual minds than with an answering that communicates between them. But the life here lies in the voices answering others, and in the way the editors have juxtaposed these answers in the most political of arrangements. An understanding of Coles' previous work will help set the stage for these dramatic encounters.

The self that he posits in his work moves away from the one that Macrorie and Elbow draw of a "natural" being imprisoned in the system and needing to free itself from either institutional restraint or its own dominant, controlling side. Rather the self that interests Coles is a "literary" or "artistic" one, and he believes it is only one of at least two selves ("Unpetty" 379), or, in other writings, of many selves. The terms might vary (people, selves), but Coles does envision a mini-pantheon in *The Plural I*: "Would imagining the self as being made up of people," he asks a student, "give you a chance to move in [another] direction . . . ?" (192).

For Coles, writing (as well as learning) is an art, and the styles or voices a student develops are metaphors for his experience and for his selves ("Unpetty" 380). A style cannot grow out of a natural self; a self and the style are "forged" together, when "role collides with role" ("Unpetty" 381). His teaching style, then, is a constructed one, an "amalgam of desire and actuality" ("Unpetty" 381), a self through which and against which students are meant to construct their own styles.

Coles' "art" and "artistic selves" seem to be connected to both metaphor and paradox; his teaching thrives on paradox, and like a harsh Zen master, he enacts quasi koans for his students (one never knows how "intentionally" he does this). He stresses "the notion of invitation" in assignments, for instance (*Teaching* 10), when it is clear from the institutional situation and even the hard-line stance he takes toward students (at least in *The Plural I*) that the "offering you a chance or an opportunity" might be greeted by students as no choice at all. Or he will minimize to his students the part communication need play in writing, connecting it to Themewriting as aiming for a "desired response" ("Freshman" 137), all the while he himself is creating a politically communicative situation by accepting or rejecting students' writing efforts. Coles will tell students that his assignments "are not an argument" or "contain no doctrine" (as he describes in the Teacher's Manual to *What Makes Writing Good* [9]), when even a glance at the text itself reveals, in the very gathering and organizing of forty-eight teachers' assignments, a masterful argument for the need of self-examination. The result for student writers who listen to Coles will surely be at the very least that their writing responses will be thrown off balance. No easy decisions about audience are possible.

What Makes Writing Good is a book of students' essays that their teachers defend as "good writing," and that just happen to fit well in Coles' career-long format of orientation: "Where and how with this problem," he has always asked his students, "do you locate your self?" (*Teaching* 10). He has been able with this book to embrace the contributions within a syllabus that is structurally similar to those described in his past books—*Composing I* and *II* and *The Plural I*—in which students write papers around a semester-long theme or problem (here, good writing; in *Composing I*, teaching and learning; in *The Plural I* and *Composing II*, amateurism and professionalism). These themes are the nominal subjects, but the "real" subject is always "language." Here, in *What Makes Writing Good*, are twelve assignments culminating in one called "Locating the Self," with the student and teacher readings arranged to fit within the framework of each assignment.

Beginning with that basic question, "What makes writing good?" Coles (and I need to add Vopat now, to call this plural *I* the "editors") and Vopat edit a book that becomes "frame embracing frame embracing frame," teachers explaining the meaning of their students' writing, other students (those of Coles and Vopat who used the manuscripts) questioning those meanings in the form of study questions, the editor framing everything in twelve assignments.

This book sprouts an intriguing kind of negotiation for meaning. On the one hand, the editors, being dedicated to art, seem willing to let voices move in paradox with each other, themselves discursively dancing right along with other contributors, questioning their own limits, allowing their stands to be moved by challenges from their own students. But on the other hand, dedicated as Coles is to downplaying the communicational or interactional element in writing, they seem almost unaware of the political undercurrents of so many of the entries. Many teachers, for instance (as I will discuss shortly) discuss their students' writing in terms of their own well-known theories or models, leaving few or no openings for other possible interpretations. Whether they are aware of their students' playing to those theories or whether they are appropriating narcissistically the other into their own self-images, a certain awareness of absent possibilities is being blocked off. Participants negotiate for recognition of each other's identity, in other words, in the midst of what Glaser and Strauss call "awareness" contexts: "the total combination of what each interactant in a situation knows about the identity of the other and his own identity in the eyes of the other. This total awareness is the context within which are guided successive interactions" ("Awareness" 670).

Coles' stand has always seemed to operate in what Glaser and Strauss label a suspicion awareness context (670), one in which he,

Coles, suspects the student of playing to an audience, being an image for an imagined teacher, but in which the students' awareness is closed to this tendency in themselves. Coles' aim has been to encourage students to become as aware as he is of their own image-consciousness, to open their awareness, push them into new mindsets, engage them linguistically with problems outside themselves. What happens in *What Makes Writing Good* is that Coles and Vopat's students take over Coles' role of suspicion, ferreting out from beneath both students' and teachers' discourses what seems "phony"—what has always been called empty rhetoric—on the part of student writers. Teachers praise honesty; responders sometimes cry "fake." Then the editors enter with a chapter called "Masks" and ask implicitly whether an assumed voice, "speaking through a persona of some sort" (218), imitating, might be a way of trying out new roles, *pretending* as a way to sincerely move out of old mental habits. "What value," they have asked in the Preface, "might there be to seeing *all* written discourse as a kind of artfully (or artlessly) worn mask, and in this sense all writing as a kind of creative writing, all telling as a form of storytelling (rather than lying)?" (xi).

A question arises from this idea of masks, about the difference between empty communicating (what has for centuries been the feared negative undercurrent of rhetoric as "mere" rhetoric, that two-legged monster) and full or honest and authentic communication. If all telling is storytelling with a fictional edge for Coles and Vopat, how would they differentiate between "Themewriting" and authentic writing here? Is there an "authentic" self? It is not clear in the new book if the editors are accepting the idea of "final" identity that they bring to the chapter in a quote from Richard Lanham (185): Lanham calls such an identity a mix of static and dynamic selves, which would fit Coles' pluralistic, apolitical vision. And even though the resemblance of metaphor (not complete identity and not complete distinction) has always been important for him, even though he locates the self within a context of "meaningful paradox," the "other" that interests Coles has been nearly always a thematic area of problems and experience rather than an interlocutor. *What Makes Writing Good* lands him in the arms of the problem of his own stance on communication versus the autonomous literary self as the ground of writing: in choosing the self he seems to overlook the possibility of networks of force or political play that would be involved in the many teachers' valuing of "honesty." Having chosen to allow over a hundred voices to talk to each other (with some limits on who answers back), having invited students and teachers to switch roles and struggle with image consciousness, having valued the art that grows out of paradox, he has inevitably brought himself into a negotiating context in which his own student responders claim, implicitly, to understand political motivation of these award-winning essayists better than the essayists' own teachers do.

Teachers praise the essays and defend their own interpretations; some responders question them. Readers' minds begin moving between the different interpretations, noticing the possibility of more perspectives on the originals than doting teachers have seen. The suspicion arises then that some of the sure, confident teachers' voices may be standing guard at the borders of doubt, seeing what they need to see for the sake of their own scholarly images. Image-consciousness is not an inept characterization for such activity, a saving of face when all posts cannot be covered around a fuller, more complex self. Richard Ohmann is one of the few who express any doubts about their interpretation of their students' essays; his ethos invites a friendly participation in negotiating the meaning and complexity of the analyzed text.

The editors open the door to the possibility of unbalancing positions simply by juxtaposing students' answers to teachers' comments and their own study questions. Letting teachers look as image-conscious as students is beginning to upset *that* mindset (the one in which only students were perceived as image-conscious). Letting one's own—Coles' own—linguistic meanings and expertise be questioned open-endedly is doing the same to *that* one (the one that says the artistic self authors its own meanings). The ostensible centerpieces of the book are the student essays chosen by instructors, but the teachers' commentaries that value "honesty" or "sincerity" begin the interesting network of what I am calling negotiating moves. Many of the commentaries fall into this category, and the honesty they praise is seen as a kind of accuracy of perception, or "genuine" understanding about the relationship between the writer and his world.

William Irmscher, for instance, chooses a paper that seems rough-edged mechanically, but in the way his student has looked at death, Irmscher finds a "simple honesty that is quite beyond the capacity of more experienced writers" (18). Janet Kotler's student improves on a previous assignment that the student admits was "trash and I knew it," and out of this increasing awareness of context, the student creates a self-examination that Kotler finds "an honest paper" (24). Susan Miller praises "contextualized honesty" (31), a writer's courageous look at his loss of a leg. Then there is, in the writing of a student who describes the West Texas sky, what Ed Corbett finds a variation of "honest"—the writer has "really *seen* that sky" (44). Janice Lauer takes a slight turn, expanding these intimations of honesty as accurate reading into a "present self" understanding "the past self" (69). Open awareness is the direction, in other words, that these teachers value, an awareness in which the student is aware of his own relations with self and environment and is allowing this awareness to be transparent to the teacher (no one, it might be noticed, is intimating that the teacher's assignment should be included in the open awareness context, or the teachers' own commitments changed because of the papers. The revelations can be only one-way). There are more: James Britton likes his student Maggie's honesty about her relationship to her parents (79). Toby Fulweiler's student reveals that he "understands genuinely" (96). Rosemary Deen is pleased with an "authentic experience" (116); Larry Levy finds "honesty" (126), Erika Lindemann, that her student "tried to tell the truth" (163).

This stake in the honest responses of students to assignments is, I would argue, an intimation that power imbalances are afoot and that the opposite of honesty is possible—a withdrawal from contact of some sort—perhaps lying, cheating, secrecy, even plagiarism, students matching teachers in their ability to choose when and how much to reveal. In any situation there can be subtle variations on kinds of awareness contexts; the forms people usually devalue, including the unsaid or the pretended, can slide more easily than teachers would like into the "masked" that Coles, at least, values. But the point is that what makes writing good for so many of these teachers is something that can only be framed in terms of a suspicion context, a political problem that can, if unaddressed, sap writing power and/or fill it with hidden agendas. It may be too much to say that *these* teachers fear deception or secrecy, but I think *most* teachers do, and certainly the multiple decisions here that good writing involves honesty in some way bespeak a preoccupation. The drive in disciplinary power structures to know all and master the truth includes truth about the self as a thinking being, transparent to self and others. It is to Coles' credit that his love of questioning comes through his own students' voices, raising the possibility that the drive to know, to read "correctly," may not be so simply fulfilled. In the students' answers (and questions) to these teachers, it is not easy to tell which the editors think astute, which wrong-headed. But their opening of teachers' discourse to open-ended inquiry is a refreshing reversal of the usual direction of questions, even though the teachers never get the chance (or the responsibility) of answering back.

Discreetly, in small print, the Coles/Vopat students respond to both the essays and the teachers' commentaries. Can anyone imagine that these students did not have just an inkling of the possibility that their words might find themselves in print? Did they not sense that their own comments might be the last word—at least more final than the words they were commenting on? These students are finding voices that disrupt and disorient the artistic coherence of the original units of essays with their teachers' comments. The responders enter the play by drawing the discourse out of itself, opening the way to negotiated meaning. Readers themselves enter the game by becoming the arbiters.

Listen, for instance, to some of the critiques or questions raised by respondents about what teachers perceived as honest writing. To Kotler's students' intimating that *this* essay is different from the previous one in which she "sleazed through," a student asks:

> Why isn't this just another way of "sleazing through as assignment"? This student must have known what his teacher liked and wanted from him so that's what he gives her. All that stuff about the bad background and his trouble with learning and the parents who don't seem to understand him and what dopes all his other teachers are is a bid for sympathy, really another kind of con. (27)

Another student disagrees, believes it is sincere; and the editors themselves are noncommital as they continue allowing probes.

About the courage of Susan Miller's writer, his "contextualized honesty":

> I wonder how courageous we would find this paper if the writer hadn't *lost* his leg. . . . The writing really isn't very clear. In other words, maybe the people in the class found the writing of this paper powerful and technically good because of the *event*, not because of the writing about it. After all, the writer himself, without his leg, was sitting right there. (32)

About Corbett's belief that his student really *saw* the West Texas sky:

> I think this guy [the student] is putting it on. He wrote this paper out of a Thesaurus, not out of anything he really knew about or saw in the sky in Texas. I don't think his use of words is very precise at all. He isn't really trying to describe anything. He's just trying to show off how smart he is. I couldn't even finish reading this thing. (46)

Or about Britton's Maggie:

> I don't quite see how the writer has achieved this "gain in self-understanding" that's talked about. At the end of the paper particularly, but in other places too, she sounds more confused than anything else. (80)

And finally, a Coles/Vopat student responding to Frank d'Angelo's gentile student's trip to Auschwitz:

> I just read an essay by someone who thinks the Jewish struggle is enthralling. . . .
> My [dad's cousin in Montreal] survived the holocaust but her family didn't. She has a green tattoo on her arm. She wasn't ashamed of it or afraid to look at it. She said she didn't like to cover it up. She didn't look enthralled though. (87)

I sense here a felt resource: Being Jewish gives the writer more contextual power with which to write about Auschwitz; the "some-one" in this response seems not to have the benefit of being an insider to the struggle.

I think it possible that some students notice an interactional component that teachers often seem to miss; it is a resource for them, an awareness of a possible way to negotiate for meaning from a weaker conceptual position. The teachers have minimized the interactional element between themselves and their students; the responders often play the part of those who understand that the true identity of the writers, their peers, needs to include this element or even to foreground it. In other words, these responders are accusing student writers of what Coles has spent his career arguing against: image-conscious rhetoric, aimed to please. And they are accusing the instructors of those student essayists of being deceived by this rhetoric.

Coles' own students show me that a writer needs to consider both interactional and conceptual functions, or what the tradition of rhetoric sees as the rhetorical triangle: relation between the writer, subject matter, and audience. It does not matter whether or not their debunkings are thought "valid" or not; what matters is that they understand the effect power differentials *can* have.

The theoretical or philosophical stance of the teachers has not, in most cases, appeared changed by whatever their students have written. Rather, what they praise in student writers seems to reflect their already decided stands: d'Angelo likes archetypal symbols, for instance, Ira Schor, social issues. I am not suggesting any teacher should give up his or her pedagogical belief system in order to listen to his conceptually weaker students. But how do they become stronger? Some negotiating for meaning, two-way listening, two-way open awareness contexts, would seem necessary.

Where do the editors stand? They are fleet-footed in this book, posing study questions after their students' comments but not giving away their own stances on the original essays. Coles' approval of masks seems a move away from his earlier ideas that students should "belong to themselves" (*Teaching* 80), not imitate the styles of others. In this book he and Vopat let teachers speak for their student essayists, pulling those voices into their own, but then let *those* voices be pulled off-center by others. Disunity arises, opening in the reader a desire for reconciliation of voices amidst each other. Contexts are questioned: who is aware of whose identity? Whose voice is whose? Individual voices—including Coles' own— are tempered by others; the field of negotiation becomes the reader's mind, withdrawing commitment here, moving in there, trying to find a comfortable home in the journey from the beginning—moving beyond limits—to the end—locating the self.

It is an Odyssean journey, an individual quest for self that finally saves that seemingly self-sufficient self from intersecting other selves. Here the salvation comes from a parallel structure of sorts: there are silences between selves and others which only the reader and the book's structure connect. Parataxis rescues teachers from having to answer their respondents; the last word could be said to be the structure (Coles and Vopat's twelve sequenced assignments) that lets the editors gather everyone's meaning into their own. From its "Movement Beyond Limits" (Chapter 2) to its raising the possibility of feigning identities in order to gain (discursive) power, *What Makes Writing Good* lets readers begin to think about the effect of power on movements of mind, just as does the *Odyssey*. Coles himself, in fact, is not unskilled in masking his own political identity (becoming Noman) and in having (perhaps therefore) the last word.

But it is just such a textual world of centralized power that raises ethical questions for a writing classroom today. Does hiding political agendas keep power in teachers' hands? Is there an ethical difference between using violence as one-way action (against suitors) and authority as one-way interpretation toward students? What kinds of awareness contexts must both students and teachers have in order that students gain more negotiating power? It seems to me that *What Makes Writing Good* brings to its readers some potent instances of a tacit negotiation for meaning, one Charles Taylor would probably call "bound up . . . with the distinct identity and autonomy of the parties" (44). Minds do not intersect openly so much as they hide their agendas, but the agendas are a fertile rhetorical field for composition classes to explore. This book's voices show student readers how the meaning of "good" is negotiated in individualized (parallel) situations. It does not matter which comments about student intentions are "right": Readers learn about the dance simply from watching it done.

Image and discourse in the work of John Schultz

But if the people or the selves in the negotiating stories are to face each other when they speak—if they are to meet in nonparallel lines—they need ways to imagine those interactions. John Schultz grapples with the meeting of image and discourse in a more socialized classroom than that offered in Coles' work.

Schultz directly addresses the problem of interaction that Coles leaves amorphous, positing a link between thinking, imagining, telling, and persuading. He sets up a classroom situation that does not seem at first sight to be concerned with matters of power and negotiation. But his important contribution to the decentralizing of classroom authority is that he finds ways to activate not only connections between students' senses—sight, hearing, kinesthesia— but to connect the activated senses to both oral and written interactions in the classroom. He seems to set up an intense circuit of linguistic energy, moving around the room and stimulating writers to put the experience in writing.

Seeing-in-the-mind, as Schultz describes it, is a coordination of mental or discursive movements with a sense of bodily gesture directed to an immediate audience. He believes that anyone who is seeing in the way he describes is experiencing what he calls an "urgent sense of address" that will result in tellings that keep both writers and readers (or speakers and listeners) connected with each other. Each teller becomes, in effect, the mediator (or the margin) *between* the words and images *and* the listeners in the classroom. The felt resonance between inside activity and outside response (more mental and discursive activity) is assumed to activate and enliven the writing and telling voice.

The classroom scene is planned in the following way, as Schultz describes it in both his text, *Writing from Start to Finish*, and its *Teacher's Manual*, as well as in an article he has written about this "Story Workshop" method. The teacher acts as director, facing a semicircle of students, coaching them, for instance, to recall and retell especially clear images from a particular reading, their own experience, or their own writing. Students begin their tellings to one person in the group and gradually add others. These people respond in a friendly but demanding way, asking for qualities of aliveness in the telling. Because Schultz believes that writing is an all-at-once activity involving "content, seeing-in-the-mind, audience, intention, the relationship of speech to writing, and form" (*Writing* 5), he will need to find a convincing way to establish the possibility that people *can* integrate all these activities experientially. Moreover he needs to establish that such an integration can call forth the aliveness he is looking for in writing without bypassing some troublesome differences between speech and writing. I believe he succeeds in the first effort, but only partly in the second.

First the integration. Schultz argues that the physicalness of voice and gesture involvement gives the important dynamic quality to oral telling that is transferred to writing, giving it pace and direction. He is not negating the differences between writing and speech; rather, he is claiming that there is a radical perception beneath both, leading to that urgent sense of address, connected to the seeing-in-the-mind that includes, almost breathlessly,

> visualization, conceptualization, symbolization, perception from the other senses, empathy, sense for points of view, the capacity for making concepts and the connections between concepts, and for pictorial seeing in the mind as clearly and with as much impact as one sees in a vivid dream. With seeing-in-the-mind, we conceive and anticipate the spatial and time and other relationships that we need and desire so urgently to communicate to other human beings. (*Writing* 2)

Why use the word "seeing" when so much more is involved? Schultz uses it the way people do in everyday conversation, as a stand-in for "understanding," but he means it in a way that stresses physical involvement, images sensed more fully than simply visually, with kinesthetic, even visceral functions at work. He begins with how-to telling, recommending that students tell about something they know how to do that involves whole-body attention (cross-country skiing, for instance), that automatically activates gestures as incipient verbs, and then the verbs themselves. Because there is no single word in English for this complex mental, emotional, and perceptual movement, and because images are involved, "seeing" seems an apt word. There will be a magnetic pull "upon language and gesture," claims Schultz, "with an urgency of sense of address and a pressure for precision to express perceptions of how things work" (*Writing* 3) as long as the person doing the oral telling maintains his or her "seeing." I have seen this circular stimulation work with groups of students, listeners responding with heightened attention to tellers whose voices are responding to the moving images they are experiencing. Writing that comes out of the telling has usually been lively and rhythmic, even with nonnative students.

Schultz's idea is that without their imaginative connections, thoughts are dead in writing or telling, and audience connections weak. "In Story Workshop classroom methods," he claims,

> the structured activities of oral reading, oral telling, immediate audience focusing, listening, inclass writing, out of class writing, out of class reading, internal listening and rewriting are powerfully integrated. (*Teachers Manual* 8)

All classroom coaching is aimed at a realization of seeing and urgency: "See it now," the director might say. "Tell it as if it's happening right now." Students who develop this ability can "feel" verbs in gesture and can sense pronouns in eye contact, Schultz believes; the voice that pulls the whole movement together is

> more than speech. Voice is gesture got into writing, voice is culture (including the personal background of the writer), voice contains the powers of the unconscious and the conscious and the possibility of style. Voice is also the movement of a telling/writing through time, everything that connects words and perceptions, the economy of which is to use what it needs and to leave out what it does not need. Voice is the articulation of all perceptions in verbal expression, written and oral, including the so-called nonverbal which we want to get into writing too. (*Writing* 85)

The teacher's primary goal is stirring up attention to the magnetic pull on listeners and readers that comes through the seeing; for Schultz, there is no learning the rudiments of writing separated from its fire. Bland instructions are useless. He assumes that if there is enough stirring, the rest will follow, not only the urgency to communicate, but the forms and precision needed to communicate in writing.

It is at this juncture between oral and written forms that problems with Schultz's vision can occur, I think. In fact, at the point of its greatest effectiveness in helping students sense the power of their own discourse comes the vision's greatest weakness: its failure to allow writing to move into the center of life from its position on the margins of oral language.

Although Schultz is careful to acknowledge the differences between writing and speech, he does set up the one to lean on the other, a derivative of it. He believes that after the two became (long ago) directly connected in phonetic writing, "the written language becomes a secondary form of the spoken, a kind of 'sustained speech'" (*Writing* 13). This belief has fueled a good deal of work in studies of literacy (e.g., Pattison [195–196] contrasts "spoken vitality" to a presumably alienated language embedded in written works), but it is a belief that fits too easily and too neatly into those same old debilitating compartmentalizing habits: One side of an oppositional pair is stuck with imitating its master (oral discourse) if it wants peace in the family and the radiated benefits of that governing/governed relationship.

Furthermore, to believe that speech has more life than writing is to miss an important and vitalizing component of writing: From at least one point of view, writing is an act of incarnation that embodies the past as well as the present, traces of a lived time that was always partly dying, disappearing time, being born again in a mark made on the living present-becoming-dead-past. This is the perspective Derrida takes (*Of Grammatology* 68–71), and it is one that can get us away from the deadening habit of thinking writing to be less "natural" than speech.

Derrida's model is Freud's idea of memory as a physical movement inscribing in an organism a trace of temporal experience. From this point of view, all writing is a physical gesture of making a dividing mark, inscribing a boundary, cutting a line through a space (an act, therefore, of defining, of deciding where the cut goes, creating one category split off from another). This system of traces and relations between "the psyche, society, the world" (*Writing* 227) is an "interruption and restoration of contact between the various depths of psychical levels: the remarkably heterogeneous temporal fabric of psychical work itself" (*Writing* 225).

Inscription, then, is deeply implied in the mind's work, and certainly no simple derivative of speech and its associated sounds. In fact, only because we imagine inscription to represent the sounds of a phonetic alphabet, claims Derrida, have we failed to understand writing's closer connections to earlier ideographic alphabets, those of "the mute signifier," more involved with "a fundamental synesthesia" (*Of Grammatology* 89) and its rhythms, less tied than the phonetic to a sequential and linear unfolding through time into units of words and sentences. Not even the triumph of the phonetic model in the West has been able to suppress traces of ideographic writing, for instance, in the silences of punctuation. Ideographic inscription spaces out time just as the memory does.

Here is Derrida's line of reasoning. Language needs to be understood as a "species of writing" (*Of Grammatology* 8), he says, because the unit of writing (what he calls a "grapheme") exceeds and surrounds the unit of language (the phoneme). The study of language is based on sound and the possibility of its continual presence (what Derrida calls logocentrism), whereas the study of writing must include not only sound but the silent physical gestures of "pictographic or ideographic inscription" (*Of Grammatology* 9) as well. The systems of notation that we have always thought to be the essence of writing (and thought derivative of language) are themselves derived from the activities or gestures that give rise to such systems out of differences in the forces of psychic life:

> We say "writing" for all that gives rise to an inscription in general, whether it is literal or not and even if what it distributes in space is alien to the order of the voice: cinematography, choreography, of course, but also pictorial, musical, sculptural "writing.". . . All this to describe not only the system of notation secondarily connected with these activities but the essence and the content of these activities themselves. It is also in this sense that the contemporary biologist speaks of writing and *program* in relation to the most elementary processes of information within the living cell. (*Of Grammatology* 9)

It is not surprising that the kind of rhetorical gesture Derrida describes as writing (the link he posits between mind, society, and world doubles the familiar rhetorical one between writer, reader, and subject matter) bears a resemblance to the move from text to relational context of Argyris and Schön's double-loop learning: Derrida has used some of Gregory Bateson's work in his own (as have Argyris and Schön), as one of his translators points out (*Of Grammatology* 322).

Derrida's revision of what the act of writing can be not only opens it to a vast historical context (to be discussed in the next chapter), but to a more enlivening point than speech: to the point of conflict between life and death: the dying of the present moment into history, where the impetus arises to record new experience into the layers of signs laid down in memory. The present keeps disappearing into the act of writing/recording, new thoughts into old systems of records.

Writers need to grapple with the (more complicated than "recursive") spacing of time before they can transfer Schultz's insights most usefully into writing, and the spacing includes the empty spaces on the page as well as in the conscious mind. It is darkness and death as well as light and life. I think that writers' experience of the mind drifting off during writing, the anxiety writing creates and the extreme attention it needs in order to rescue it from "forgetting," all are related to the difference between the speech one can more easily control than the writing that gets away from one.

Speech's greater ease in staying with a single line of thought suggests a picture of birth as part of a hereditary line: one topic rather naturally, usually, grows out of another when conversational partners are attuned to each other and the situation; they inherit lines of thought in the shared rhythms of turn-taking. Writing is related to a more complex kind of birth-thinking: multiply demanding, full of fragmented and fragmenting rhythms and pacings, necessitating an ability to think of ten things at once in the midst of (mental) turbulence, without being sure of the outcome. Writing, for most people, involves more pain than does talking, but insofar as its palpable results record new patterns of mental and social complexities, it involves some pleasures that speech never can. Writers cannot experience a simple gliding from the attention generated by oral forms (as Schultz would wish) to those of writing, because writing is not only phonetic, not only present to the ear. It is a present negotiation between an inherited past and a possible future.

If writers can learn to situate themselves in the more-than-linguistic, history- and rhythm-ridden contexts of their work, they can begin to draw on resources of mind that may till now have felt marginal to their own thinking. To some of those resources in our own professional history I now turn.

5

Peripheral Visions from Rhetoric's Past

Opening and closing borders

Creating paths to what so many of us thought of as more responsive and truthful lives was a preoccupation of the 1970s, and Macrorie, Elbow, Coles, and to a certain extent, Schultz became spokesmen for all the composition teachers who hoped they might help people write along those paths. Alienated from many of our national institutions, we heard those voices promise us that writing could come alive in more authentic selves if we could just resist—and help students resist—the pressures of deadening conventions.

But the preoccupation faded into other concerns; perhaps we found the search for authenticity to be never-ending, or perhaps it simply went underground as the economy did somersaults that brought us to attention before the limits to growth: Economic, professional, or psychological, the limits seemed to stimulate our interest in limit itself, in the rules and conventions we had wanted to fight but we now found defining our lives and selves. We gave hard looks at the cognitive structures we thought ruling our minds and at the cultural ones gathering us into disciplinary communities. We looked for ways to model the disciplinized selves we were cultivating, and found Myers-Briggs tests to tell us how psychological traits determined our personalities, or role theories to show us the social scripts that staged our identities, or Foucauldian theory to let us see how determined by language we were. We became answers to our own 1970s selves, embodied arguments for the 1980s closure we had earlier neglected: teachers should learn rules of the social, psychological, disciplinary, or linguistic game, not worry about open and authentic selves.

Borderline selves

Oscillating between two sides of any argument in liberal or Enlightenment fashion, though, is a less effective model for our teaching selves than attending the margin between contending forces might be, contextualizing the whole in order that we poise ourselves for action at the point of contact, hold potential energy in contingent selves. From places of contingency we can notice how both openings and closings of trends and arguments occur, how currents or thought come together before one current takes charge of the other; there we find the critical junctures that precede moments of decision, almost like openings in the rhythms of a turning jump rope, where the marginalized ones, teachers or students, can enter the rhetorical game.

Contingent selves would live less inside people than be "forged on the borderline" of inner discourse and outer. That borderline, says George Dillon ("My Words" 71), drawing on the work of Bakhtin, is where one can find one's own language. In other words, contingent selves are rhetorical ones, made in dialogues and questions and answers between people, with what is "inside" acknowledged to be already thoroughly socialized through enculturation. Furthermore, searching and probing selves, stationed as they are on cutting/ writing edges, learn how to spot hierarchical structures in social interactions. They develop peripheral vision: are able to focus on the central points of arguments, but to hear second or third voices, perhaps forgotten edges, as well. If we teachers are to develop and model such rhetorical habits, we need the habit of noticing the ways currents double over each other in any mainstream thought, ways they are sensitive to each other's movements, joining in, separating out, creating new streams of thought from meetings at boundaries.

Edges of tradition

Argument itself has its historical undersides, currents of neglected rhetorical life running beneath and beside mainstream currents. I will talk about three of them here—the magical, the mimetic, and the mnemonic—three signifying practices that did not, as argu-

ments-turned-exposition sometimes do, lose sight of themselves as
sites of contending forces. Such sites can entrance attention, give
people a sense of challenge not yet overcome, and waken parts of
mind often deadened in our students, change just a little their ways
of relating to the arguments in their writing.

These practices have probably been part all along of what Michael Polanyi would call our tacit knowledge (34–35), working
subliminally when we talk and write to each other, but being closed
out of sight and mind (and therefore out of competent, confident
use) because they do not fit easily into our ordinary everyday
thought. But they belong in our peripheral vision at least, from
where we can draw these almost forgotten resources into focus now
and then.

All three have gone through many cultural transformations in
and out of the rhetorical tradition, but the kind of mindset they
encourage raises uncomfortable questions for hierarchical thinking:
They are not commonly stressed as helpful to any kind of thinking
that tends to set up one valued term in oppositional structures, such
as reality over appearance, or substance over image, or signified
over signifier, or symbolized over symbol. Foucault would tell us
that knowledge based on hierarchical valuings is never innocent,
the categories always political. This chapter is meant to show how
certain often devalued moments of our own professional history
have scrambled, in their time, the rhetorical hierarchy we now
accept as almost commonplace. (Conventions and rules of argument, for instance, are usually more esteemed than what can
happen beyond conventional values, or one's writing mind is
thought to reside in the brain, separate from and superior to, more
human than, one's body, which is not supposed to "think.")

What brings magic, mimesis, and mnemonics together is that all
three have set up cultural, semiotic systems that have valued linguistic
and social power arising from the mind's participation in the happenings of the world—sometimes the social world, sometimes the physical, sometimes both—a world somehow *like* the mind, though with
unquestionable differences too. By bypassing certain cultural hierarchies that we accept as natural (subject and object, for instance, or
rationality and irrationality, or body and mind), these practices have
drawn attention to the way couplings themselves might occur, and to
means by which rhythmic resonances might be set up rather than

structures of domination. And most importantly, the doublings involved were thought to capture and entrance the attention, create a spellbinding alertness to the task at hand.

These mental and cultural practices have been rhetorical in the sense that they have posited social effects resulting from language use; insofar as they have threatened existing political structures, they have found themselves on the fringes of respectability, hidden, made occult. But their mindsets linger today just behind our more "rational" thinking, often acting as hidden attracters and persuaders. How they arose in the first place, how they changed over time, and how they faded can give today's teachers of writing hints for how we might penetrate their mystery and adapt them for our own use.

Magic between visible and invisible worlds

Daniel O'Keefe has made an exhaustive study of magic from a sociological point of view, and can suggest to us why it was associated with rhetoric in the first place. Simply put, both are forms of social action that achieve their effects primarily through words, and both traditions have often gained new life during times of political and social unrest, when old cultural habits and old systems of governance were breaking up. Pythagorean magic and Gorgian rhetoric, for instance, were flourishing in the fifth-century B.C. Grecian world, during the time when tyrants were being overthrown. And both Christian oratory and Chaldean magic spread throughout fourth-century A.D. Mediterranean communities, as civil wars were threatening the fabric of everyday life and Germanic tribes were pushing their way toward Rome from the frontiers of the Empire. At such times as these the position of the individual in society is altered, whether broadened or narrowed, and that alteration is unnerving enough that she looks for new ways to connect herself to others and to the world around her. John Ward claims that the link between rhetoric and magic is in their appeal "to individuals and classes located outside or on the margins of the intellectual or political establishment or centre of power" (47).

Magic aims to make or change something (O'Keefe 27) through its assumptions that action will follow from one's using language, and that one breaks the social framework that *is* by changing the "state of attention that sustains it" (96). In other words, according to O'Keefe, "the normal cognitive frame" is itself a social construction, and the practice of magic is simply an acknowledgement that through language, through the words and sentences that embody concepts and images, that construction can be altered. The magician introduces the possible, the absent power into the present reality, and shifts the framework. She thinks of herself as a mediator between the actual visible world and the possible invisible one, unifying and controlling their interaction. Magic is a practice that sees itself moving "with the rhythm of the world" (to be sure, a socially mediated world) rather than "merely attempting to coerce it" (O'Keefe 66); there is the sense of a double vibration, or ensemble, articulating two worlds that might otherwise be discordant.

In the process of mediating, the magician creates a self dwelling on the edge between worlds. "The manifest function of magic in man's development," says O'Keefe, "has been to serve as the midwife of the self and as co-founder of the individual" (15). The mind moves from passivity into activity, and into "an assault on the objective frame of reference of the paramount reality" (137). Magic is a way to manipulate symbols, he claims (40), in which "the quality in the words passes into their objective" (41). The power moving through words and mental images makes a real change in how people can handle their own and others' attention; the attention *acts*, often making verbal or imaginal "doubles" of whomever or whatever is to be acted upon or affected in some way (41). Model-making becomes a "guide to action" (41).

The making would, we can infer, be a conscious one, different from the unconscious use we make of symbols in our ordinary life; symbolic words used in magic are thought to purposefully set off action at points of contact with objects or people. The words we use in our everyday conversations are seldom given such motivating power: They are not *believed* to have it. In contrast to the word's pointing to the "real" thing beyond (as it is supposed to do in our mainstream culture), the magic signifier is thought to take on a rhythmic vibration with its signified, causing something to happen where they meet; greater life, more energy, more power.

Even so, claims O'Keefe, we should think of a continuum rather than a break between the way meanings are made in everyday life and in more esoteric thinking, because there is a weak and a strong sense of magic: "Most social speech is magical" in the weak sense, he says (84); even the unstated part of every communication—"'I am he who says this by right of who I am'" (83)—is magical thinking in a weak sense. Strong magic simply marshals more power over one's own and others' attention than weak, having more conviction behind it, perhaps, or a more coherent vision that gives more force to what is communicated. Magic's main purpose in the way it models symbol power is, believes O'Keefe, "to save [oneself] not from physical death but from *psychic* death" (213).

From the many stories that come down to us about "magic" we can picture the kind of perception involved: One moves into a sense of active self by sensing one's body and mind acting together (alike in every way needed for action), one's self acting *with* natural forces and *with* the movement of other body-minds, and one's words becoming as alive as one's self. Magic is a boundary-breaking practice. It becomes unbelievable, maligned and often degenerate in ages that have supposed those boundaries to be unmovable rather than flexible. At such times it suffers from poor self-image and is apt to put forth grandiose claims, unsupportable in communities whose belief systems have no common grounds with its own. Its claims become inarguable, then, unreasonable and unnegotiable.

In the light of its function during breakups of old cultural habits, magic's living alongside rhetoric in the lives of some Greeks, in the fifth century B.C., seems understandable. In the Greek colony of Akragas on the southern coast of Sicily, for instance, Empedocles was born into a wealthy family and a privileged youth but later became involved in political upheavals surrounding tyrannical rule. Aristotle was said to have thought him the father of rhetoric (de Romilly 94); stories of his life show that he was also a poet, a magician, a philosopher, a doctor, and a politician (Laín Entralgo 82), a combination not so unbelievable if one considers that in that century categories were drawn differently from those nowadays. Reason, for instance, had not yet had its Plato and Aristotle, and the only body separate from the Greek mind or soul had until recently been a dead one (Snell 16–17); philosophers would be as apt to think of the bodily effect of words, then, as would poets believe their work philosophical. Empedocles, in fact, believed that it was the blood encircling people's hearts that "is their thought" (Kirk and Raven 344).

He was interested in how cultural forces could affect natural ones, especially how the words of ritual poetry could influence nature's healing powers (Dodds 145–146). He himself was one of those he described as having an interest in reaching "out with all his mind" to "every particular thing that exists" (Wheelwright 143). Empedocles' life gives testimony to rhetoric's roots in the hope that language can "magically" make a wedge between the governed and the governing and upset the balance. Between the disrupting strife and the uniting love that he thought permeated every being in the universe, he placed the healing power of words and story-poems. And between the ruling tyrants and the people of his home, he placed his own words, which helped overthrow the tyrants.

Is the wedge of any concern to us, especially since his story does not end in success? After all, he was exiled by the tyrants' immediate descendants and, so tradition has it (without suggesting cause and effect), ended his days by throwing himself into Mt. Etna. His story here, though, is not meant to be one that says "magic works," but rather one whose details might play on the edges of the belief systems of both teachers and students, to raise a question about the hard and fast divisions we usually make between real power— material, influential, causal power—and the words we write or speak. Sensing the words—the signifiers—to be as palpable as what they signify raises the importance and interest of what words we use where and when. (Since the seventeenth century, we have tried in the broad reaches of Western culture to think of words as *not* palpable, *not* visible, only see-throughs to "reality.") Moreover, there is a link to mental images in the story of magic and rhetoric, in how much more strongly anyone's attention is captured or en-tranced if images and the imagination are involved.

When on this hot day in July, I read, for instance, that Empedo-cles "enjoyed strolling . . . in the silver-green shade of olive groves" (Martí-Ibáñez), I become more entranced with him *and* his ideas than I would without the details, and entrancement can lead to wonder/questions and finally to a reverie in which I identify with him in his walk and hence his thoughts. And since I can scarcely think of starting a day of writing without my short run at dawn, I like reading in the same source about ancient philosophers being peripatetic, "as if walking stimulated their thoughts" (18). I become hooked on the image of refreshing walks, and my mind then begins playing over some of the differences *and* the similarities between us: the place, the time, the genders. This kind of mind's work is minimized so often in our teaching of writing, but images in stories of all kinds have more place in our classes than we have imagined, I think, waking all of us up into implicit arguments, serving as what O'Keefe might call "weak" magic. Good storytellers today need to depend on images, repetition, emphases, and rhythms as much as in times gone by. The judicious use of these attention-gatherers is more likely to signal occasions from which change of mind can be born than is the kind of theoretical thought embedded in the rules of argument, themselves more akin to the separations of the blade that categorize and conquer living details if allowed to reign unchecked.

The point becomes more explicit with Empedocles' pupil Gorgias: Jacqueline de Romilly notes in *Magic and Rhetoric in Ancient Greece* that Gorgias' association with Empedocles puts him into the heart of magic, manifested in his work with ritual formulae, rhythmic utterance, and incantation. It was from such association of magic and rhetoric that de Romilly suggests Plato may have thought rhetoric to be a *psychagogia*, a word "first used for the magic ritual summoning the dead" (15), and later becoming a little less potent as an "action of speech on the soul" (14). Either way, *psychagogia* became associated with awakening minds from their sleep, with a rhetor's persuading them through the power of rhythmic and repetitive words and images to follow his thoughts, an experience any of us with 8:00 A.M. classes might appreciate.

Gorgias believed, as did Empedocles, that the world is not composed of single truths but of double, antithetical ones that give the world its life (and rhetoric, many of its compelling figures), and that since truth cannot be one pole or the other, it cannot avoid "deception" or "illusion," since its task is to reveal the what-is in the what-is-not. For him then, right decisions could not be dictated by abstract, absolute truths, but by a vigilant awareness of the tumultuous play of antitheses in everyday life, and of the *kairos*—fit timing—of action in their midst (Untersteiner 182). Such an idea encourages the thought that even stories which we might believe to be fiction have their place in the course of learning, that attention to the possibilities in the actualities (or vice versa) may act on students' minds at exactly the right moments for them to turn off onto a new angle. We need to be alert to such moments, I would think. They might be magical ones.

Aristotle and feminists

Although Aristotle's *Rhetoric* seemed to centralize his ideas about argument and the means of persuasion, there are undercurrents that flow to the surface in some surprising and seldom acknowledged ways. They lead us into the idea of mimesis and into a signifying practice not so far afield as we might guess from the magic of some of Aristotle's predecessors. But Aristotle was no magician, and it must be admitted that when we begin to look at the work of this man who was born about one hundred years after Empedocles and Gorgias, the stories are gone and the theories are in place. Moreover, for anyone interested in tapping his work for writing classes, especially anyone whose thinking is moving through feminist ideas toward a breaking up of counterreproductive hierarchies, Aristotle's vision presents a big problem. It is grounded in sexism.

More and more feminists are noticing just how much so, and that noticing calls for a lengthy detour at this point before his rhetorical work can be put in any kind of perspective. Having remarked that J. H. Randall (242) claims that all of Aristotle's philosophy grows out of his interest in "biological investigations," Linda Lange notes that whether or not this claim is true, Aristotle does weave his ideas about sex difference throughout his work in a consistent way: "the important Aristotelian distinctions between 'form' and 'matter,' 'mover' and 'moved,' 'actuality' and 'potentiality,' are all used by Aristotle to distinguish male and female" (2). And in each case, the term which is weighted as causally important, from the universe as a whole to its smallest part, is associated with the male, in the same way that Aristotle finds in his discussion of biology that the male is clearly "the real parent" (Lange 11, drawing on *Generation of Animals*). "Aristotle simply accepted," says Lange, "the 'observation' of his time and place that women are inferior" (13).

Gerda Lerner, in language stronger than Lange's, concludes that "Aristotle's world-view is both hierarchical and dichotomized. Soul rules over body; rational thought over emotion; humans over animals; male over female; masters over slaves; and Greeks over barbarians" (208). Furthermore, "The fact that sex dominance antedates class dominance and lies at its foundation is both implicit and explicit in Aristotle's philosophy" (209).

As if these claims are not enough to keep us from imagining that any part of Aristotle's work could be coherent with an ethical system of teaching, we need to carry the line of reasoning into the *Rhetoric*, and say that if this dominance permeates Aristotle's works, it must permeate the *Rhetoric*. And even though we do not often examine it closely for its associations with other works of his, and even though Daniel Graham claims it to be part of Aristotle's early rather than later conceptual system, of the logical treatises rather than metaphysical ones (16), the *Rhetoric* is unquestionably part of a system that shares terms and biases with the later works, those in which the objectionable talk about gender occurs. If we want to use Aristotle's ideas about rhetoric at all, it would seem, we would certainly need to blind ourselves to these connections.

Well, yes. We would need to. We would need to if we were to adopt the separatist inclinations of those men we are claiming to be different from. We would need to if we believed that the best way to change the social structure is to argue as Gerda Lerner does that women "must, as far as possible, leave patriarchal thought behind" (227). We have, she says, already gone through the stage in which "thinking women have refurbished the idea systems created by men, engaging in a dialogue with the great male minds in their heads" (227). No matter how useful it has seemed, by "accepting such dialogue" we have remained "within the boundaries or the question-setting defined by the 'great men'" (227). And within those boundaries, those systems, we are marginal and "the source of new insight is closed to [us]" (227).

I want to gather the strands of this book here into its strongest point: The route to the source of power that women have always been closest to (but that men, I am claiming, can literally imagine themselves into) is to refuse either/or thinking and acclaim the absolute necessity (in this case, for our pedagogy in composition classes) of facing the feared other (the powerful other who seems as if he will swallow our identity), and willingly enter into a conceptual turmoil with him in which questions and answers might appear on either side, but in which the birth of an "aha" is trusted. Although

I want to claim that linguistic fearlessness at this time and in this academic place is increasingly possible, I do not want to claim that it was possible in earlier years or is now in many places in the world, or is even outside the academic climate that women *like* Gerda Lerner have been preparing for the rest of us. Such women, who have been willing to develop their rhetorical power by taking separatist stances, have created a space for yet a different kind of thinking, a kind that may be able to meet the patriarchs anew. There is room now for trust that we might be able to gather enough face-to-face strength to replace deference to patriarchal boundaries with some shared upsetting of them.

Because I think that all of us of both sexes are already inscribed through and through with complex gender roles, and because I agree with Sandra Harding and Merrill Hintikka that "women's experience systematically differs from the male experience upon which knowledge claims have been grounded" (x), I believe one of women's complex tasks must be to find the rhetorical voice to inscribe their experience in larger systems, painstakingly extending at least that one basic experience of birthing into corners of life that the separative death experience seems to have conquered. What we need for the task, more than having experienced physical birthing (Phyllis Schlaffly, after all, is probably a mother), is having begun to attune our minds to a network of birthing signs and symbols, especially those that model the outrageousness yet presence of antithetical truths in our lives. There are plenty, from moments when we both love and hate a task at hand, to moments when we are quite sure we are thinking with our bodies.

We can all be political and ethical artists in the sense that Judy Chicago is, by participating in the artistic practice of finding patterns of likenesses in differences, differences in likenesses, ourselves in some other person, he in us. Learning is a pattern-making activity, says educator Leslie Hart (168), and those who have felt marginalized have, I think, an urgent need to translate from one area of life to another, one group of people to other groups, those patterns of conflict resolution (*not* surrender) that are our *strengths*. Birthing we women do well. We have never been so good at separating, just because thousands of years of experience have left it our second-best option. When I read about the network of birth imagery used by Pentagon officials, I know beyond a doubt that women desperately need to bring more and more of their own versions of birth imagery into public dialogue with such chilling appropriations of creation power for destructive purposes.

Beyond negotiation

In Southeast Asia, so a story goes, there has been a history of colonization, and during times when the conquerors had swords and the conquered did not, the latter, at a great disadvantage of course, had no choice in a fight but to learn to be more clever than their opponents. This is how the martial arts were born: by using all his powers of mind and body to "read" the attacker's intents, the one being attacked developed a great sensitivity to what might be called fields of energy in such moments of intense opposition. By aligning himself with the directional force of his opponent, he was able to use the attacker's own energy to defeat him. Later, so a further story goes, cultures became mixed, and the old conquerors—the Japanese, it so happens—themselves perfected even further the techniques of those they had conquered (a happening with questions, surely, about who won and who lost). This is how aikido was born, and as a conflict resolution technique used at one time in its own history to fight insurmountable odds, aikido might give women a technique to use in the enemy's camp when they sense themselves too overpowered (physically or conceptually) to attempt negotiation. Aikido has many techniques, not only one, but there is one that seems especially apropos in this context. Often instead of fighting, or fleeing, or just simply taking no action (appropriate in certain circumstances), experts in the art of aikido will blend with their opponents' force and then *redirect* it.

In some ways, this is what must happen in order that a child be conceived and born: Opposite kinds of energy must merge and be redirected into a new life.

But blending may be a more useful metaphor for anyone sensing a more destructive attack from a strong other than a birthing image can give. One thing that blenders often need to do, once they have sensed the opponent's movement of thought, is move just slightly out of the line of attack, so that the blow falls elsewhere. Feminists themselves have not been without a similar strategy: as they have noticed that discourse of our mainstream culture is neither gender-less nor innocent, they have removed themselves from the position of the universal "he," leaving their own place there empty. Arguments directed toward that place—toward the woman in the universal "he" spot—have begun to fall flat in the past few years because there is no one there to receive them, no one to receive admonitions that women should "stay there." It could be claimed that the change has come about because women themselves have waged a good argument against the not-innocent habit of including them in the category of mankind, and surely that is true too. But I think there is some side-stepping involved that has been effective, even though our former blending into that universal category was an unconsciously submissive one rather than a consciously directed and purposeful preparation for the next step.

But, you might say, look what is left to do. We have barely made a dent in the cultural habits and signifying practices of this nation. Right. But might we not notice how dents are made in this blending and side-stepping practice in aikido, how "progress" in eliminating old habits might take place?

One of the primary beliefs in the culture of aikido is that one shares spirit or energy with others (and this includes mental energy) but must take charge of one's own energy, practice changing directions with it, keep it gathered together to face challenges from any source, be able to move off the challenging path with it if necessary. The belief is that the opponent within oneself is as formidable or more so than the one to be faced, and that practice gathering one's own spirit (or in the context I have been using, one's belief system, concepts, and signifying practices) into a sense of purpose and direction prepares one for threats from any direction. When the blows from outside come, "no matter how hard and swift," in George Leonard's words, there is a sense that one is a "moving center that holds all opposites in perfect tension" (99), one's own self and the opposition's. At that point of blending the slight shift takes place and the attacker—who will continue on his path—will sooner or later fall on his own, because the attacked one is no longer opposing the attack. Thus, aikido's form of argument.

Blending with Aristotle

Feminists who create separate histories create separate paths, but the histories will finally need to blend with those we sense as other, blend and be redirected, where men's and women's histories may be slightly phased, slightly decentered from each other, but share a text that can be read doubly, with their undercurrents sometimes showing up as our main currents, and vice versa. Aristotle is a formidable foe to feminists, but we need, with our lately garnered strength of purpose, to blend with that enormous text of his that has left so many traces on all of our histories. To keep a strong sense of purpose, we need the both-and ability to let his work resonate with our own experience, trying to dismantle the hierarchies by first blending with the oppositional energies, then doubling the centers and letting the texts undo their own pretensions (a strategy in both aikido and deconstruction).

But given the possibility that this opponent might after all turn out to have a second, less formidable voice, we might wish not to hold a funeral until we are sure something new might not be born of the whole affair of our meeting. And as it turns out, there is a discernible countervoice that Aristotle himself uses when he discusses mimesis, one that begrudgingly connects itself to his other concepts, but one that not only has some overlaps with the culture of aikido, but has some salvageable rhetorical use too. I will first explain and connect with some of his other works Aristotle's ideas in the *Rhetoric* about mimesis, and then tell how they doubled over on—and thus helped me understand better—one student's work in an advanced composition class.

Mimetic rhythms in the work of Aristotle

There are, as Derrida points out, a chain of concepts in Aristotle's works that relate to mimesis as a kind of imitation, and they are all governed by "the value of truth" (*Margins* 237): metaphors, likenesses, meaning, voice, imitations—all are given value in Aristotle as they were in Plato and would be by philosophers for the next two and a half millenia, given value attached to how well they could be shown to reveal truth. Yet another chain of concepts associated with truth itself can be found in Aristotle, but for the mimesis of the *Rhetoric*, these seem less relevant to the present context than two further sets of associations, ones that can be read pedagogically rather than philosophically. Mimesis is associated (1) with learning and learning with pleasure (1371b), and (2) with style, given an impulse by poets because their words were imitations (1404a).

Yet to open Aristotelian doors into these mimetic matters of learning and style is to find a surprising path, one that leads us to the margins of Aristotle's thought and of his time, backward into an older set of beliefs that are also central to his own. Not even this philosophical giant could deaden with categories what still existed in the Greek air of the fourth century and what has so often been killed in ours: a vibrant sense of movement and rhythm that cuts across boundaries between bodies and minds and language and worlds. It is this part of the *Rhetoric* that we have not often opened up (especially as it might relate to the subject of argument), but that touches many of the experiences we would probably call women's, and many we would want our students to have.

Aristotle would prefer not needing to deal with matters of style and delivery—matters of the "how" rather than the "what" of logic. But because not everyone is capable of following "a lengthy chain of argument," he says (1357a), and because the facts alone do not persuade, "we must pay attention to [opinion]" (1404a). Therefore a rhetor needs not only to consider the character of the rhetor, his ethos, but the experience and emotions of the audience as well, its pathos. And finally, in the last book of the *Rhetoric*, he reluctantly tackles the "how," as one finally turns to pesty necessities one would rather keep marginal to one's enterprise: Style is rightly considered vulgar, he says, but since hearers are corrupted, "we must pay attention to it" (1404a).

Aristotle tells us now that words are imitations, and that prose style should not imitate that of the poets. But earlier in the *Rhetoric*, he has said more about imitation, raising questions about how these stylistic matters might connect with ones about learning and even about mimesis itself. At the earlier point we can understand him well enough when he lets mimesis be an occasion for a spectator's drawing inferences about nature from a work of art, and thus learning something (1371b). But when Aristotle finds that "the imitation and the object imitated are identical" (1371b), modern readers can have real trouble finding any connection between the two activities. What *does* he mean by mimesis?

What he does *not* tell us about mimesis is what a fierce debate the whole idea had aroused only a few years earlier, when Plato had condemned and tamed mimesis in his discussion of its use among poets (*Republic*, Book 10), made it a mere sensory shadow of more enlightened, more rational mental practices. But Eric Havelock tells why Plato needed to tame it; mimesis, he says, had been "the name of the active personal identification by which [an] audience sympathises with" a poetry performance; "It is the name of our submission to the spell" (26). The Greek mind till now, says Havelock, considered the poetic occasion the educational one, a way to gain an encyclopedia of knowledge through rhythmic and sensory identification with the poet's words. Minds "imitated" the movements, sweeps, and rhythms that the poet repeated over and over, both the poet (or rhapsode) and audience remembering through the spell of the narrative. Plato wanted to call this narrative spell "opinion," says Havelock (250); after him, philosophy needed to create new mental channels of learning, abstract ones that would "throw off the spell of material things" and give allegiance to "an abstract reasoning power which knows identities which are unchanging" (250).

But Aristotle was too much the faithful observer not to recognize the importance of the psychological phenomenon of mimesis. Havelock's explanation gives a context for the words about mimesis in the *Rhetoric*; Aristotle himself expands in other works. He claims in the *Politics* that listening to the rhythms and harmonies of an imitation causes a participation in the feelings being imitated, and thereby an actual change in ethos, all the habits that go to make up a person's character (1340a). And in the *Poetics* he tells us that rhythm, language, and harmony are the means of imitation, that dancers use rhythm but no harmony, and that they thereby imitate character and emotions and actions of living persons (1447a–1448a). Mimesis is a natural way to learn, he claims.

The experience of rhythmic identification was obviously more common in fourth-century Greece than now, and seemingly therefore more dangerous to a philosophical project of rechanneling perceptions into channels of mental abstraction. Aristotle tried to subordinate the whole topic, but though he seems to bury it within his larger system, inferences about its place in the human world and even the cosmos can be drawn. He notices, for instance, how we measure time by psychic changes (*Phys.* 218b), and how we perceive time and motion together, bodily, through number (219a, 219b). He associates our experience of number—*arhythmos*—with rhythm—*rhythmos*, and claims that one could know nothing unless all things were limited by number, and within the context of number, prose by its rhythms. "Prose must be rhythmical," he says (*Rhet.* 1408b), and here, in spite of its intellectual self, rhetoric is thus plunged directly to the core of the knowable through the door of rhythm, without which we could not know anything through the language of prose. And words are rhythmic imitations which *become* what they imitate, an idea which had not then yet reduced the power of words to the pointers of post-Renaissance thinking.

Furthermore, although the matters of this last book in the *Rhetoric* are ostensibly stylistic ones, of the giving voice to prior thought that is the presumed principle at their core, there is a real sense in Aristotle's statement about numbers and rhythm that nothing can be even thought without rhythmic form, and that therefore, the rhythm of words imitating the world is more basic to the way people think than is a kind of thought divorced from it.

Such may have been the belief of early Greek culture, of those rhapsodes and the people who listened to them. Havelock describes Plato's struggle for intellectual control of cultural indoctrination, as the rhythmic participations of didactic oral poetry were being gradually replaced by an "alphabetic technology" (294). Cultural control over education was passing from the poets to the philosophers, with value given to the powers of abstract intellect. One need not share Havelock's oral bias in order to agree with his idea that there were social reasons for denying the importance of the spellbinding oral rhythms of fourth-century Greece. The older and powerful social cohesion was being devalued, and rhythmic participation in all the invoked rhythms of everyday life—breathing, heartbeats, talking, ocean waves, currents of rivers—discouraged. But even Aristotle could not entirely tame these rhythms or the mimesis by which they were discerned. They form an undercurrent in his *Rhetoric* that refuses to disappear.

John Jones claims that Aristotle's idea of mimesis is one that supports "the gradual emergence of personality" in the way it channels patterns of action (38). The word "ethos"—character— itself has etymological roots in the idea of habit; if personality is not thought of as any more "inner" than character, then, both might be understood as one's habitual actions, mental, physical, linguistic, the cultural rhythms one participates in or imitates (Hall's idea of informal cultures as rooted in rhythms is similar). Character implicitly inhabits style in the advice given in the *Rhetoric*, and style and substance made to entail one another, even though Aristotle does not explicitly make it so.

But if imitation of cultural rhythms and actions might be seen as a way into developing an ethos or a voice in writing (or in Aristotelian language, an ethical proof), how can one ever break out of old habits of imitation, if the environment, or the life situation, does not itself change?

Aristotle in the world of business

This problem was a particularly acute one with one student's project in an advanced composition class I taught two years ago. I had asked people in the class to spend their semester studying any subculture they might choose, and about halfway through the course, they were to begin noticing, exploring, and asking questions (of themselves and those in the culture) about how conflicts between members (or between members and outsiders) were handled; resolved, for instance, or perhaps ignored, or even cemented into place somehow.

Lynn's project was centered in her own work situation in a hardware store. The people involved were (1) an absentee owner, Mr. Title, who both did and did not want a hand in the business, (2) a manager, Mrs. Worth, to whom he had supposedly delegated authority, and (3) two or three clerks, including Lisa. Sales were down, creditors clamoring for their money, bankruptcy approaching, and morale bad. Mr. Title dropped in at unexpected times and often countermanded financial decisions Mrs. Worth had made.

Conflicts in the store would usually arise between creditors and Mrs. Worth and, though unvoiced, between Mrs. Worth and

Mr. Title. Lynn noticed that although Mrs. Worth would side with
Mr. Title on the phone with creditors, she and the clerks would feel
squeezed between Mr. Title and the creditors when talking among
themselves.

Lynn chose to investigate the effect on the business of the owner's
ambivalent hands-on, hands-off policy, and to include any questions about conflicts and any study of changes within that framework. But papers about the conflict lacked life and point, and the
choice of classmates as audience was not working. Two of the
papers, especially, seemed to go nowhere, repeating and repeating
information, garbling sentence structure. Here is a section from one
of them, typical in its soporific effect:

> The third and final division consists of the largest number of
> creditors. Those being the creditors, usually current suppliers, who
> know you are doing your best. The talk between employees about
> these creditors is usually friendlier than about previously men-
> tioned creditors.

As we began to talk about purpose more emphatically, it became
clear that no writing purpose could come close to the most important
one in Lynn's work situation: stay harmonized with Mrs. Worth.
Lynn's mind, as it turned out, had become so attuned with
Mrs. Worth's that it was difficult for her not to receive all her
"education" about the impending bankruptcy from a mirroring of
poor Mrs. Worth's embattled position. These two supported each
other in mutual sympathy against the owner and creditors, and
gathered the other clerks into their story of woe. Within this little
group of blurred discursive boundaries (no inclusion of outside viewpoints), mutual support (spell of involvement with each other) was
possible but change of mind/attitude/action impossible with the
continual mirroring of each others' arguments. The story and Lynn's
drafts became dull for classmates and me, their sense of impotence
reflected in our reading. Her style of conflict resolution seemed
reflected in her writing, and I became surer than ever that "knowledge" which refuses to hear from opposing sides loses its vigor, no
matter how right (and here, quite righteous) it might seem.

I began to sympathize with Plato, even though his new Forms had
their own problems with sameness of viewpoint, unchanging models
that they were.

But Aristotle himself, with his disconcerting practice of acknowledging the unstoppable motions and rhythms of life in the cosmos even while capturing them in hierarchies, has a word to say in this matter that might help minds elude the dangers of endless repetition, use the brightening power of mimesis in a different way. We need to remember that mimesis is a pleasure, as he says in the *Rhetoric*, and pleasure itself "is a certain movement of the [mind], a sudden and perceptible settling down into its natural state, and pain the opposite" (1369b). I am reminded here of Csikzentmihalyi's comparing the experience of flow, with its overcoming of difficult challenges and its arriving in pleasure, to Dewey's idea of a "completed experience," one that becomes aesthetic just because it runs a course through a destabilizing beginning, through a middle of struggle or pain, to an emotionally satisfying conclusion (Dewey 35–45). Pleasure, says Aristotle, is not an end in itself, not a state that can be maintained, but an activity—an *energeia* (*Nic. Eth.* 1153a)—and activities are always end results of a certain power for change called potentiality (*Gen. An.* liv); therefore pleasure cannot be an uninterrupted ongoing affair. It is a completion of a life activity (*Nic. Eth.* 1175a), a coming from a state of being *un*settled.

The more Lynn tried to be like Mrs. Worth, I think, the less pleasure she experienced, because she was stuck in a circle that had no end. (Certainly in writing about the whole affair she seemed to be experiencing a deadness.) The class and I began searching for any places in her writing that might seem to be breaks in the harmony of viewpoints, give a hint about where life in this little subculture might still lie. (For "Culture that reproduces itself as a series of endless mirrorings is literally the death of culture," say semioticians MacCannell and MacCannell; "it conserves itself as is" [28].)

Though no one found such breaks, I backed up one day and decided that the real break was one we had been sensing all along, that we readers never ourselves felt pleasure in the reading because it was missing Mr. Title's voice. The papers were all centering on his guilt for the impending doom, and because Lynn was not willing to talk to him about the whole situation there seemed no way to bring him to life.

But poor no-voiced Mr. Title finally had his say one day when we moved into a new segment of assignments and I asked her to imagine him as a reader of the magazine she had decided to write for. (I urged all students to believe that the value in this part of the semester was more in the sending than the publishing; simply the possibility of appearing in print was a good enough motivator for the writing.) Somehow this challenge was just enough less overwhelming than having to talk to the real Mr. Title that Lynn woke up into a new spell of involvement. Shifting her gears, turning her attention to engagement with a less formidable challenge than the man himself (to a magically created double, a symbol or sign of Mr. Title), she was able to imagine his answers to her questions and questions for her answers. She found a well-defined readership for *Nation's Business* in *Writer's Market*, and began imagining herself communicating with him through an article.

Lynn's final paper was written with this readership in mind—her boss as she imagined him. There was challenge enough that she kept getting pulled off-center, but not so much that she could not pull her energies together. She analyzed one of the articles carefully, and together we noticed the force of its rhythms. (I especially asked her to try to sense this force.) The article she wrote imitated its structure *as* force. Its style was crisply authoritative, based on her own expertise as one who had experienced the questions and found the energy to answer (1) readers and writers she had listened to in the magazine, and (2) classmates and me. We sent the article to *Nation's Business* along with a query letter, and though I never heard from her after the end of the semester about its status, I assumed I would have if any action had been taken. I did not mind. I hope she did not either, because she had waked herself up with that activity that I, at least, felt good thinking of as mimesis. I knew she had felt pleasure after finishing the article: her eyes were brighter, her walk lighter, and her tone in talk with the whole class more confident and relieved.

Here is part of it:

STRAIGHTENING THINGS OUT

If you are the owner of your own company, the passing of decision-making authority to a manager may be a difficult task indeed; however, if it is to be done, it should be done on a complete scale. You should hand over the authority and then step back and allow

your manager to manage the company. Since looks can be deceiv-
ing, and this handing over of authority may look easy, perhaps this
delegation is not all it is cracked up to be. In fact, the business
where I work has fallen prey to the owner's inability to delegate
authority then step back, and his failure to communicate between
himself and his manager.

Lynn then details the problem, says that "Although this business
may appear to be beyond help, there are several steps that could
help it, as well as other small companies undergoing change," gives
six sensible steps, and concludes by saying, "If none of these suggestions work for you, perhaps a 'heart-to-heart' talk between yourself
and your manager is in order to straighten the problems out."

Writing as imitation of forces

I had moved a little off-center myself from my semester-long engagement with Aristotle's mimesis, drawing at the end on its exten-
sion in Derrida's work. His belief that no mimesis can be simply a
repetition or re-presentation of something that has been totally
present cuts through the possibility that there can be identities
between things (*Disseminations* 186–193). There are always differences in the similarities, openings in the doublings, gaps in the
articulations. No pleasure can be a completion and fullness because
every action of doubling presumes a making-absent of what is
doubled (*Margins* 237–241), and therefore a lack of fullness. Derrida reminded me to take Aristotle's interest in movement and
rhythm one step further, beyond the idea of form, into form unfro-
zen and therefore force. Lynn did feel that language in her magazine as force, I think; her article seemed to me to imitate words as
forces.
  Philosophy conceived apart from poetics "is the twilight of
forces," says Derrida (*Writing* 28), and what he values—and I want
to value with my students—is sensing the intensity and force in that
larger sense of writing he describes. He tells of Nietzsche's unhappi-
ness with the necessity of sitting down in order to write, with having
to bend over "when letters are no longer figures of fire in the
heavens" (*Writing* 29). Images of writing in contexts other than

bending over desks are ways into students' imaginations that help them begin to sense the mental force connected with the whole concept.

Ernst Curtius describes the movement of Islam into medieval Andalusia, for instance, and the flowering there of an Islamic and Spanish notion of inscription that pervaded the rhetoric of its poetry. He cites examples of this deeply ingrained sense of writing as more than sound, as a participating too in the Sufic love of contrast between light and dark. An impressing on the mind, for instance, is said in one poem to be an "engraving on the corner of the eye" (342). Or in another there is a "script of swords" (342), and in yet another, blood perfuming what was written in sand (342). As the writing imagery became more profuse in the Spanish Renaissance, swallows wrote deeds, songs were written with feathers from Cupid's arrow, the sea wrote letters with foam, dawn with dew on the flowers, the ploughman with his plow (343–344). For Calderon, the whole cosmos was a book. The northern European tradition of rhetoric left behind the rich imaginal world of the Mediterranean and the Islamic idea of writing as flickering light/dark contrasts. But that writing is not very different in kind from the grammatology Derrida speaks of, a writing that claims the importance of absence, death, and mental unconsciousness/darkness in order that light might even be known.

Vico's Mnemonics

As one last historical moment that lets light and dark flicker together beneath a victorious light/point in an argument, I look at one corner of the rhetorical tradition of mnemonics, with the idea that practice creating unfamiliar images in their minds might help our student writers with one of their hardest tasks, putting their minds in the place of an other.

Although mnemonics, or the art of memory (inventing combinations of familiar places and unfamiliar images in one's mind) was known even before the time of Quintilian (who gave the clearest description of it, according to Yates [3]), the eighteenth-century Italian philosopher and rhetorician Giambattista Vico turned the concept into a path that can brighten writing minds and connect these currents of the rhetorical tradition to some psychological underpinnings I introduce in the next chapter.

For Vico, memory is not simply a remembrance of one's experience, stored as units in the head as in a container (as some current models in cognitive psychology would seem to have it), but rather a power not only to remember, but to imitate and change things as well:

> Memory is the same as imagination, which for that reason is called *memoria* in Latin. . . . [It] has three different aspects: memory when it remembers things, imagination when it alters or imitates them, and invention when it gives them a new turn or puts them into proper arrangement and relationship. (313–314)

Instead of being involved with a same-for-all structure, in other words, Vico's "memory" is a force, a rhetorical activity whose powers range widely across traditional provinces of rhetoric: invention, arrangement, style.

But Vico himself does not categorize rhetorical provinces in the traditional categories above, and according to Donald Verene, Vico's idea of memory and its imagination are antithetical to the mental activity of categorizing:

> Categorical thought has no place for the memory and the narrative. The category invites us to create ultimate singles, unequivocal grounds for thought and being. Memory and imagination can treat oppositions as composed of dramatic forces, the principles of which can be captured in narration. The categorical mentality, the logical mentality, is shameless in its reductionism. The category actually robs us of our memory and of any actual sense of drama of time or place. ("Categories" 201–202)

Of course no mind can think without using categories, but in establishing the idea of memory as grounded in the imagination of time and place, Vico, according to Verene, is urging a mental functioning that avoids imposing its own categories on others and thereby escapes the conceits of cultural arrogance ("Categories" 197).

Vico's recommendation also necessitates a remembering, imagining, and narrating of one's historical and social links to life in other people, other minds, other times and places. The inventive memory can achieve this end partly because, as Verene points out, "narration is the language of oppositions of which there is no dialectical or categorical resolution" (*Vico's Science* 166).

Moreover, the ancient idea of *topoi*, topics or images of places in the mind from which further images and ideas arise, formed for Vico a basis for all three of the memory's powers—the remembering, the imagining, and the inventing—and there was no radical split between the way a person was considered to recall and the way he or she created, as there is, for instance in modern cognitive models. For Vico, thought and discourse should begin in the *topics* that people share rather than in the first truths that Descartes wished to establish (Grassi 38–45). But although Vico adopted the Aristotelian idea of topics as middle terms or lines of reasoning for arguments (*Study Methods* 15), his own bore differences from the enthymemic premises in Aristotle's *Rhetoric* (which were arguments from existing decisions, for instance, or from consequences, or from previous mistakes [*Rhetoric* 1396–1402]). Vico's topics were more concrete; he called them "sensory topics" (*New Science* 166). Verene labels them "Vico's theater" (*Vico's Science* 192), an age-old collection of stories and myths from countless cultures and places. These peopled "commonplaces" in all our lives, believed Vico, make "minds inventive" (*New Science* 167), able to connect present concrete moments with past ones because the topics are metaphors of shared, universal experiences.

The connections generate arguments, rhetorical language that lets us communicate with others out of common memories and images, rather than, as Descartes would have it, out of deductive first principles. For Descartes, the first principle was an abstract *I* as subject, thinking itself formally, not situationally or concretely, but separated from the object of its knowledge in order to think clearly about it. For Vico, this separation made no sense: people could know only their own cultural creations, and those, through the thinking done in the memory and its imagination (Verene, *Vico's Science* 55, 57) that yield up not certain and categorical knowledge, but multiple dramatic, concrete, particular situations. The direction of knowledge is thereby reversed from a collection of many signifiers (in this case memories or minds) representing a single or single-minded truth as signified (the model of both rational and empirical traditions) to the images and particulars themselves (here the cultural creations of multiple minds), ordinarily thought marginal to, or simply representative of, the concept.

Rhythms of argument

Any time and place has patterns of awareness that permeate its cultures, and the three I have talked about here are, to be sure, ones especially fitted to times and places not ours. Our own students, in fact, are certainly attuned to different rhythms, different perceptual channels, different signifying practices from those we as writing teachers value most; computers and television, so we hear, have written rhythms in their minds in ways our book-oriented thinking often cannot fathom.

But peoples of any age, I think, especially those with as much reason as we in this country at this time to raise our antennae into the social and cultural dissonances around us, need as many resources as possible to perceive and write with multiple cultural inputs. Flexibility is the key, ability to use myriad parts of mind at appropriate times, and if we writing teachers can do just a little shaking of the thinking in our classes, just a little changing of minds that creates a space for new options in the forging of selves, that may be enough.

The three practices discussed in this chapter are spellbinding ones, ways to change the quality of attention at the point of interaction of voices before one of the voices claims victory over the other, stops participating in its rhythms. The kind of argument we so often teach our students (or think we should be teaching) serves us all better as the skin of a rhetorical onion than its psychological core. The many layers that can be peeled off are stories of interactional disequilibrium belied by the final smooth surface of reasoned, that is, governing, conclusions. And although any argument paper might give the warrantable steps its writer wants the reader to take toward that governing idea, writers themselves, we all know, rarely (ever?) reach home through warrantable steps. The recommended structure assumes an already decided issue.

But getting to the decision is what argument is, and it is not only a coming home into settlement (i.e., "after these premises arranged this way, I give you this claim"). It is not just the end of the story ("given these conditions we are content to bring this adventure in thinking to a halt"). It is not even, as J. Anthony Blair and Ralph Johnson point out, "'a set of statements some of which (the premises) are offered in support of another (the conclusion)'" (46). Rather, argument needs to be thought of first as it has often been thought of since it took shape in Aristotle's dialectic, say Blair and Johnson as "a human practice, an exchange between two or more individuals in which the process of interaction shapes the product" (46). As such, they claim, it is a matter of questions and answers, to be understood further "against the background of the question already asked and the answers already given" (45).

What we might hope is that students will neither give up on seemingly unanswerable questions and decide not to care, nor answer questions so definitively that they close their minds to the social and cultural complexities involved. I have a student now, for instance, who wants to be a music critic, who has decided no music composed in the nineteenth century or beyond can be "great," and who cares so much about his hard-earned decisions that it is hard for him to hear other voices in matters about music. I wish more students cared as passionately, that they would raise questions that would hold them as spellbound as he was until he found his answers, that they would have such conviction as he, the "comprehensive vision" that Chaim Perelman believes always grounds argument (33).

Yet my student's conviction is a closed one: he has argued with himself and others and settled into his answer, wanting others to settle there with him, unable to imagine that his own social, psychological, and cultural context still grounds his own beliefs as much as that of others grounds theirs. To such students as he—rare as they are in their caring attitude—I bring rules of argument; to those who seem to care little about issues, I bring practices that might draw them into entrancement. To all I bring this conviction: both rules and wonder grow out of interactive contexts that raise questions at points of conflict and require trust that answers will come out of those questioned contexts.

Of course there will always be writing that needs no long-term entrancement or no arguments at all—small, on-the-spot assignments, technical descriptions and instructions of many kinds—plenty of the work our students do will never need such involvement. But the most expository of all writing will have its buried arguments worth drawing attention to, and the more seemingly straightforward writing jobs we can urge enchantment with, the more engaged and thoughtful about strands of hidden arguments will be the work.

Hubert Dreyfus claims that one major difference between expert and novice performers is that the experts have a "compelling sense of the issue" ("Expert Systems" 33); they are able to grasp matters as a whole through intuition: "One takes the whole constellation of a situation, correlates it, and out of that correlation emerges the correct response. . . . The expert is simply not following any rules" (935). He is a "fast player," "spellbound" by a barely conscious involvement in an activity, being gripped "holographically" by three-dimensional, holistic memories of whole situations (30, 34). Argument itself, claims William Brown, is well served with a holographic metaphor, with the kind of thought that sees not so much the parts in the whole as the whole of the argument in the parts, "visualized in an overall flow" (96) that yields up "similarities among conventional differences and differences among conventional similarities" (95). The "unblinding" that brings this holistic vision comes, says Brown, with shifts of attention when points of stasis arise in the thinking process (97–99). Getting stuck, in other words, should be welcomed for its forthcoming gifts.

Arguing responsively and responsibly, then, is as much a matter of speeds of intuitive thinking, gripping of the imagination, involvement of memory, and quality of attention, as it is learning the rules that might serve as checks on the logic. Writers need minds that are resilient, able to move both fast and slowly, changing pace as the situation asks. Issues are ridden with the human times and rhythms of cultural habits. The many ideological worlds they bring with them ask arguers to keep their antennae up and their minds fleet. The tradition of rhetoric, as we have seen, is not without resources for this demanding interactive task. It is not, as Susan Jarratt points out, a monolithic tradition, not one with a discernible line of inherited, unidirectional thought. Rather it is a history full of subtle and often oppositional complexities, one that calls for our "confounding categories" (Jarratt 16). It is just the kind of history we might have hoped for to overlay, translucently and holographically, the rhetorical lives of ourselves and our students.

III

VORTICES: WHERE TURBULENCE ARISES

If water flows quickly over many small obstacles, such as pebbles, so many small trains of vortices are formed that they result in turbulence. Turbulence also arises if there is a great difference of speed in the water, say between the edge and the middle of the stream.

Theodor Schwenk, *Sensitive Chaos*

6

Writers' Minds: Which System?

Minds and metaphors

Most of my students who have thought at all about their own minds and the way they think, I have found, have a fairly bland, academically influenced idea about how those minds operate. Upper-class people may have taken a psychology course or two and are often ready, when I ask them what they think those minds of theirs *are*, anyway, with a tale about something that processes information and represents it (a few years ago I would hear more often about stimuli and responses), or now and then, about something that lets the student exist because it—the mind—thinks. Of course it could be said that I am trying to trap people by framing my question in terms of an entity or noun, since I want to lead them from here into a place where mind is decidedly not a thing. (Like many of us who teach composition, I look for more rhetorically enabling images of thinking than that of the mind as what Richard Rorty calls "a self-contained sphere of inquiry" [126].) But I like best to start with concepts my students are familiar with, and they do after all think of themselves as "having" minds (and I do not mind the few humorists who claim not to have them).

I look on our now-and-again interchanges about minds in all my writing classes as an important part of a semester's writing, and that is why I spend a few minutes talking to students about their minds on the second or third day of class, when the initial shuffling of courses is just about finished and we are getting ready to settle down into the semester's work. I would like them to begin supplementing the picture so many have of little calculators in their brains; a more dynamic vision of mental possibilities might change their images of machine-like heads. I tell them some metaphors I use for my own thinking and urge them to negotiate with these. The agenda is a double one: first, the idea of metaphor gives the talk an informal tone that lets people hold on to whatever other beliefs about mind they may have, and second, thinking through metaphors or figures starts us all off on a semester-long journey toward a habit I hope they might develop or strengthen, one of looking through one idea or image to another, getting used to raising questions where concepts meet.

But before I return to that class and those metaphors later in this chapter, I need to establish the exigency of holding the discussions with my students in the first place. Why confuse those who have spent time memorizing definitions in psychology courses? Why ask for figuration when after all, psychologists have spent thousands of hours and many more thousands of dollars in research funds learning how the mind *really* works?

My rationale is this, and it has been implicit in the pedagogy I have been advocating all along. All of us in Western culture are heirs to over two hundred years of thinking ourselves into individual minds separate from our bodies. Moreover, as Rorty points out, such separatist ideas about mind have become linked to a large cluster of concepts that privilege positivism, foundational knowledge, and true belief. Novice writers need all the ways they can find to sense their own minds linked to those of others, and our Cartesian inheritance is a negative image for such purposes. Whether our students have learned in other classes or simply from a pervasive culture that the brain is where thinking takes place, we teachers can bring their minds into a stimulating and often fruitful debate with themselves by suggesting that "mind" *can* be a metaphor for what it does and thinks; and if we think of it as an object to be studied by psychologists, it is indeed that. The mind will imitate the model as much as the model imitates it. For writing, it is helpful to model how it might be *possible* to think rather than how we already know people *actually* think. We can help students feel less marginal to "knowledge," less passive in absorbing what others tell them is true about themselves, if we raise possibilities and encourage vision(s).

Knowledge and paradigms in composition studies

To that end I hope some students may begin to think of "calculator" as a metaphor no different from any other we might all choose to use; my reasons for that hope are as tied to my stance within composition studies as they are to my stance with my students, to the way I have come to understand the cognitive models my own profession has been giving me over the past few years, in its journals, in books, at conferences. Emphasis in recent Conferences on College Composition and Communication seems to be shifting somewhat away from cognitive issues to social ones, bespeaking less interest in a wholesale importing of cognitive psychology into composition studies. But cognitive psychology has by no means disappeared from our midst, and some of the assumptions about mind that have already been imported could use a close look. An article published some time ago in *College English* can act as an entry into a few of the problems cognitive science raises for our field.

Clinton S. Burhans, Jr., undertook the task of surveying the state of the discipline in the lead article of the November 1983 issue of *College English*. Soon after he moves into his analysis of composition's situation, he begins to use a word that has appeared often in the field over the last few years: "knowledge." Three hundred and fifty years after Descartes told us that mind as subject can know everything else as object if only objects are conceived clearly and distinctly enough, there is no lack in Burhans' article of Cartesian confidence that objective certainty about a matter is possible, that limits can be definitely drawn, frames set in place. Knowledge about writing is "emerging" (647), we are learning more and more about it through studies and research, and what is learned by researchers is generalizable. The truth about the matter does not seem to change; rather the knower himself draws methodically closer and closer to it. Burhans concludes that if there is

> no particular method or technique [which] will by itself solve the problems of teaching writing . . . there is certainly a right way to teach writing in terms of the requisite framework of knowledge and

experience. Teaching writing, like teaching anything else, must begin with knowledge of what writing is and how writers go about writing. (653)

Though Burhans here dilutes with individual "experience" the article's main implication that the entire field needs to move as a moth to light, the emphasis is still on the sense that there is a single rightful light for the moths to draw toward.

In other words, rather than mediating or negotiating moves *between* people (and a moving and changing light in their field of activity), there is a knowable center, objective knowledge, *outside* each person, around which gather the needy ones to absorb what they can. And the teacher is its representative. Teaching "must begin," must have a center, in what the teacher knows; individual students are not part of that center. They are the plural writers who need to learn about themselves as writers from the teacher's knowledge. But whether the central light is located in or around a teacher, researcher, Cartesian subject, monarch, or God—all dispensing truth, and all (except God) having learned it themselves in orbit around one who knows—the structure is one that is mentally contagious, and insidious in its effect on active learning of writing. It encourages a mindset of passive absorption. It is a framework easily transferable between journal articles, institutions, classrooms, lives, and writing, based on an artificial separation of and tension between subject and object roles that cannot be maintained in the social and psychological context of real life.

Since only objects can be known clearly and distinctly in such a model, other knowers must themselves be objectified, distanced from oneself in order to be known. As the father of this dichotomy, Descartes not only associated knowledge with power, but believed that by "knowing" properly, we could "make ourselves masters and possessors of nature" (45). That belief fuels modern academia as much as any other institution, and Burhans seems to be attempting not a breaking of the framework, but a reversal of power in the by-now-familiar English department political battles.

Let us see how his subtle moves reveal this kind of power struggle in the profession itself. He first expresses concern about the number of English departments across the country that are still apparently teaching writing by outmoded, ineffectual methods. Examining "a

representative and statistically significant sampling" of college catalogs, he discovered that very little learned about writing from
studies and research over the past twenty years is reflected in course
descriptions, writing requirements, or departmental structures. The
scholarly work, the lively exchange of ideas, and the excitement
generated in conferences and journals, in other words, has not, he
believes, been translated into action. Burhans realizes the possibility, of course, that catalogs may not indicate subtle changes in
departmental policies or in individual teachers' undercutting of
official accounts. Nevertheless, he is sure that senior staff at least
approves the material that appears in catalogs, and that its intentions are represented accurately enough to support his findings.
Thus far his tone seems reasonable. But then he uses his word of
power: "knowledge." What the findings show, he claims, is a good
deal of talk about the importance of writing, but very little understanding of the knowledge we have accumulated about how to
teach it.

What is this knowledge Burhans speaks of? It can best be understood by contrasting it to the old "cluster of concepts and methods"
he calls "traditional" (641), the school rhetoric Richard Young has
labeled (borrowing the term from Daniel Fogarty) the "current-
traditional" paradigm ("Paradigms" 30). Late nineteenth- and early
twentieth-century pedagogical systems gave the paradigm its
atomic complexion, its modal classification (with exposition separated from argument, for instance) and its divisions into teachable
units of word, sentence, and paragraph. Concentration is on usage
and style. Most catalog descriptions still fit these guidelines, says
Burhans, and the sad truth is that a current-traditional class format
simply does not give any reliable help in improving writing. He is
probably right, but how does he support his claim? Burhans labels
the cluster of ideas and methods behind it "myths": "beliefs accepted uncritically" (650), that is, presumably, untested by the
empirical methods of research, which are supposed value-free and
therefore valid support for knowledge.

To the traditional he contrasts the contemporary, another cluster
of ideas and methods, but this time one that constitutes "knowledge" rather than myth. The listing of traits belonging to it is
Maxine Hairston's from an article in *College Composition and
Communication* called "The Winds of Change: Thomas Kuhn and

the Revolution in the Teaching of Writing"; the listing includes the interests generated from two decades of professional work and study. I quote Burhans, who includes only ten of the original twelve points:

1. It [the cluster of ideas and methods] focuses on the writing process; instructors intervene in students' writing during the process.

2. It teaches strategies for invention and discovery; instructors help students to generate content and discover purpose.

3. It is rhetorically based; audience, purpose, and occasion figure prominently in the assignment of writing tasks.

4. It views writing as a recursive rather than a linear process; prewriting, writing, and revision are activities that overlap and intertwine.

5. It is holistic, viewing writing as an activity that involves the intuitive and non-rational as well as the rational faculties.

6. It emphasizes that writing is a way of learning and developing as well as a communication skill.

7. It includes a variety of writing modes, expressive as well as expository.

8. It is informed by other disciplines, especially cognitive psychology and linguistics.

9. It is based on linguistic research and research into the composing process.

10. It stresses the principle that writing teachers should be people who write.

This seemingly admirable agenda is a mixture of old and new material, weak claims and strong. Its suggestions look reasonable at first glance, and most are indeed useful prescriptions. But beneath the surface is a complex network of assumptions that needs examination. The writing "process" is of course the primary focus, with its "recursive" qualities and its drawing together of rhetorical principles (invention, primarily), cognitive studies, and linguistic research. Hairston further defines the process as a "disciplined creative activity that can be analyzed and described; its practitioners believe that writing can be taught" (86). This claim is the recent strong voice of the profession believing in knowable heuristic structures, an answer to charges that writing teachers do not teach because they lack control over what students learn.

Hairston's list calls the paradigm "holistic," since the creative process it stresses makes room for intuitive as well as rational parts of mind, and she links the process to cognitive development by noting the connection between writing and learning. Holism here reveals no social influence, no relation of writing to what takes place beyond individuals. The system closes within the person. Coherent with this individualistic slant is the separation of expressive writing from expository (that of orientation to a subject from that to an object). And despite a mention of rhetoric and audience, the list seems more oriented toward one-way communication from writer to audience than three-way action between reader and writer over a subject that comes alive between them. (The Greeks would seem to have honored this three-way connection when they used the stem *akro-* in their words for "hearer," "lecturer," and "thing listened to" or "lecture," joining all three concepts into one connoting points touching or silence breaking [Liddell and Scott 49, 56–58].)

There are ghosts of many voices in Hairston's list, and their many networks of interests and orientations, from Janet Emig's in developmental psychology to Linda Flower's in protocol analysis. The clear note in all the voices, however, is an interest in the mind as it creates, as it thinks in writing, and there is an unmistakable tone of cognitive psychology in that interest.

Cognitive science and its truths

Cognitive psychology is often associated with or even called cognitive science, to underline its gathering of several disciplines under one umbrella, labeled by psychologist Robert Solso as including in its "domain" studies of perception, attention, memory, imagery, language, thinking and development, and artificial intelligence (47). Cognitivists tend to speak of behaviorism in the past tense; they believe that it failed "to account for the diversity of human behavior" (Solso 13); its banning of the word "mind" from its explanatory vocabularly has been dramatically reversed by what some call the cognitive revolution of the last twenty-five years. Heavily committed to understanding how minds (both human and artificial) represent the world and process information, cognitive psychology is "the study of knowledge" (Solso 20). It was born in the 1950s from such developmentalists as Jean Piaget and Jerome Bruner, and such linguists as Noam Chomsky, though people from wide-ranging fields have shared in its growth—mathematicians and philosophers, for instance (Solso 445–447).

"Structure" has been a key word from the beginning, stimulated not least by Chomsky's emphasis on innate language patterns, and Piaget's on genetic epistemology (psychological processes linked to logical organization) (Piaget xlii–lxi). This interest in synchronic, nontemporal structure pervades not only the subject matter of cognitive psychology, but its formal presentations as well: cognitive models (metaphors or schemes representing mental components, storage systems, and objective processes as stages rather than concrete movements) can sometimes resemble the S-R (stimulus-response) models familiar from behaviorist days, as Solso admits (17), or in their more elaborate forms, become labyrinths of boxes and arrows. The boxes, it must surely be noted, often seem related to another familiar family—the software that embodies programmable sequences. The analogy is not lost on cognitivists, some of whose favorite metaphors are proportional: software is to mental process as hardware is to brain. Active mental processes are said to be part of the "cognitive system" along with the static structures, to be sure (Solso 9), but in this generalizable system of individualized internal operations, there is no opening to destabilizing influences of others, no room for the "contents" and concrete particulars of everyday life to make a difference in the way this system works. It is effectively closed.

What this boils down to for writing teachers is an emphasis on the active mental processes formally related to static structures as containers (Solso 9) as these appear in the creation and organization of papers, and as they appear in the language of those papers. The cognitive model has fueled a good deal of research in areas ranging through linguistics, rhetoric, psychology, and even sociology. Regardless of the field, cognitivist presuppositions are seldom absent from articles about the way *the* mind works (in its language or in composing, for instance), cleansed of its particular concerns and stabilized into a uniform structure for whatever group of subjects the research involves.

Burhans does not mention cognitive psychology by name in his own "fruitful areas of concern" (his follow-up of Hairston's list), nor does his "emerging knowledge" category cover the same kind of knowing as the mental process referred to by the cognitivists (their kind is simply cognitive content; his implies truth, facts). Nor can his own important work with prewriting in a precognitive era be forgotten. But his concerns are all those that have been looked at through cognitivist glasses; even inventional rhetoric can be given over easily to a cognitivist's viewpoint.

Furthermore, it seems hard to believe that for Burhans there is not a slight slippage from one kind of knowing to another, giving more force to each: He who knows how cognitive content is effectively processed is doubly in league with true knowledge: knowledge of the way knowledge arises in cognition. Cognitive psychology has become a politically powerful discipline in the last few years, one that still gives promise of shoring up composition's status against its reputation for impotence in English department politics. Burhans' frequent use of the term "emerging knowledge," his coupling of it with "intellectual integrity" (653), and his demotion of one of literature's favorite technical terms, "myth," to the popular status of falsehood (opposing, presumably, knowledge as truth), speak for years of collective frustration and humiliation in the colony of composition studies, and a readiness for revolt. This revolt becomes a contagious structure, spreading itself beyond simple anger at an old paradigm.

When "knowledge" becomes a power word against "myth," as in Burhans' hands, it is a signal that Cartesian sovereignty, the power of the knowing mind to exist independently of world or context, is lurking in the wings, along with a way to reverse old structures of domination by stripping them of legitimacy in one's own world of knowledge. The identity of those Burhans opposes implicitly or explicitly, though, does not stay stable. His argument moves in against education and against English departments with the declaration that they have been avoiding a writing commitment, and that English departments need to center themselves around reading and writing because their time "may be running short" (656). No suggestion here of negotiation, rather of a dominant center in a discipline (reading and writing) of which Burhans is of course a part. The mental war for control seems imminent or present, not only against the old paradigm in composition (weak because not controllable), but against the English departments over which composition is beginning to hope for some power. With his insistent repetition of the phrase "emerging knowledge," Burhans does not let them forget it.

The word he is *not* using is "paradigm," nor is he mentioning the connection between his "emerging knowledge" and Thomas Kuhn. Robert Connors, in an earlier lead article of *College English*, objected strongly to a trend he saw in composition to adapt Kuhn's theory of periodic paradigm change to its own discipline. Social scientists had already argued about its applicability outside natural sciences, but it is an attractive concept, as Connors points out, and Maxine Hairston is not the only composition scholar to see a shift of paradigm coming in the discipline. However, Connors effectively argues that Kuhnian paradigms are concepts for true sciences only, applicable to fields that "result in clear-cut progress" (10) in solving puzzles through empiricist methods. Within composition, he claims, the best-known examples of experimental studies are the protocol analyses of Linda Flower and John Hayes, and the work done in sentence combining (the two areas highlighted by Burhans, incidently, to be included in "composing processes"), but Connors is adamant not only that composition's problems are not science's puzzles, but that even for the problems we do have, there has been no clear cumulative progress, no new paradigm to replace a former nonexistent one, no "explanatory structure to guide further research" (8).

Then why does Burhans so strongly hint that we are accumulating knowledge, that there is an emerging certainty countering what he clearly sees as old falsehoods? The question becomes even more insistent when it is noticed how carefully and explicitly he avoids using that word "paradigm," mentioning Connors' "persuasive warning" about its inappropriateness (Burhans 650). But strangely, his reasoning for refusal of the term does not follow that of Connors: Burhans just notes that we do not have two discrete methodological paradigms; rather we have simply the "truth" that "the emerging understanding of writing and the teaching of writing is developing slowly and cumulatively" (650). Connors' main points seem to have slipped by Burhans. Connors says we are not a science; Burhans does not claim we are. But he believes knowledge is on his side and myth on the other, a claim literary scholars would rarely dare to make so forcefully about their own biases. Burhans has begun to speak the language of what Wayne Booth calls "modern dogma" (in *Modern Dogma and the Rhetoric of Assent*), a scientism that Burhans would probably call functionalism (the new method works, he would say), but which comes perilously close to Booth's "dogma": "My side obtains knowledge of facts, yours asserts mere value" (Booth 17).

I am not claiming that Connors does not leave a way open for Burhans; Connors does, after all, hedge on the question of knowledge, speaking of an "epistemology of psychological research" (11), and of not cutting off "our discipline from verifiable knowledge" or "the search for consensually-arrived at truth" (19). Nor am I claiming that the old current-traditional way is better, or a way to knowledge—above all I do not wish to claim that. What I do want to argue is that those at the margins of power—as composition teachers have been—are as apt as those at the center to behave in the same win/lose manner as their "opponents" when the time comes that they have the chance—or hope for the chance. This opposition, though, is a counterproductive move because it infects teaching minds with a contagious disease; no matter how unique the current situation appears, Clifford Burhans may simply be revealing the widespread tendency to use the weapons of knowledge, truth, certainty, and the power of right on one's side against others. Those others may be paradigms or strong English departments in which former paradigms had no muscle. But what is important is the tenacious mental structure of subject trying to control knowable object, to gain status by distancing itself from an opposition, claiming an unsharable *right*.

Composition studies are more than ever in search of a conceptual home, and if Burhans' important article is any indication, seem close to staging their own revolutionary war with English departments (or depending on your outlook, a civil war). The rationale for the war is knowledge of a different language (based on social science research models) from that of English departments and the power that language brings its users. Whether or not the language brings more skill to composition students is highly questionable.

If there is to be room for more than one "consensually arrived at" truth, for a pattern of teaching methods rather than a single one based on knowledge derived from knowing others as objects, it is important to examine the "mind" being given to composition by the cognitivists. The emerging knowledge that composition scholars are accumulating may not be an unmixed blessing as a guide to everyone's teaching or everyone's critical thinking. Cognitive psychology does not, without a needed critical look, make us better teachers.

Cognitive minds

Robert de Beaugrande, as an especially eloquent believer in cognitive science's promised gifts to composition studies (though his recent book on literary theory indicates something of his wide range of interests), illustrates the peculiarly calculative, machinelike quality of the cognitivist's "mind" in "Psychology and Composition: Past, Present, and Future." De Beaugrande believes that "a general science of cognition and communication should be antecedent to a science of language," and that "the latter should in turn be antecedent to the disciplines that deal with reading and writing skills" (211). The science about mind that is to ground these studies should be neither a positivistic behaviorism that neglects internal organization nor a Chomskyan mentalism that ignores actual use, the "operational criteria" that might connect writing processes to empiricism. Rather we should take the best of mentalism and behaviorism, he believes, and allow empirical evidence to support theory. Cognitive science is the crossroads of these renovated disciplines, says de Beaugrande, who condemns behaviorism less than many cognitivists do.

De Beaugrande sees both "cognitive processing" and "social behavior" acting in mental events, but when he discusses humans as "information processing systems" who develop under constraints arising from "the requirement of self-organization" (231), social behavior slips into the background. The human intelligence that needs to be studied through experiment is said to be (in a quote from D. Norman) "real or imaginary, concrete or abstract, human or machine" (231), and when de Beaugrande quotes P. H. Winston's dictum that we should "describe the objects in a domain in a way that uncovers useful constraints on how the objects interact with one another" (211), it is apparent that the mind that produces discourse has become objectified. And although de Beaugrande does not wish to have cognitive science associated with positivism, there is at least a residue of that positivism in his belief that legitimate knowledge is empirical, derived through collecting value-free data about objects, which are in turn separated from and represented by experimenters as subjects.

But when minds become objects of study, the richness of situational knowledge is apt to be ignored, since empirical research moves inductively toward typifying situations, generalizing from data to gain knowledge of how minds work. The atypical detail, the individual story that draws attention away from research agendas is not easily noticed, that which appears rule-like, more valued. The cognitive scientist is he who understands the rules of mental functioning, which itself becomes theoretically programmable and interchangeable with that of computers in the burgeoning field of computer simulation.

Protesting the model

Since digital computers are thought by many cognitivists (not all) to be able in theory to simulate mental operations (if not now, later), it is important to understand what Hubert Dreyfus calls the assumptions made in such comparisons. The first is the mechanistic assumption that sees intelligent human thought and language as the kind of interdependent processes that depend on a "repertoire of mechanisms" (*Computers* 56). Underneath this assumption lies a second, the metaphysical one that understands situational background as also objective, knowable through a structured description. Dreyfus argues against this assumption:

> My thesis, which owes a lot to Wittgenstein, is that whenever human behavior is analyzed in terms of rules, these rules must always contain a *ceteris paribus* condition, i.e., they apply "everything else being equal," and what "everything else" and "equal" means in any specific situation can never be fully spelled out without a regress. Moreover, this *ceteris paribus* points to a background of practices which are the condition of the possibility of all rulelike activity. . . . In explaining our actions we must always

> sooner or later fall back on our everyday practices . . . our sense of
> what we *are*, which is according to this argument, necessarily, on
> pain of regress, something we can never explicitly *know.*
> (*Computers* 56–57)

The situational context, in other words, can never be abstracted
exhaustively, defined rigidly enough to allow human mental process to be compared to that of a programmable computer. There is
no evidence, according to Dreyfus, "that whatever orderly behavior
people engage in can in principle be formalized and processed by
digital computers" (*Computers* 136–137).

A third unfounded assumption for Dreyfus, the biological,
equates brains and digital computers, and a fourth, the psychological, claims there is an information-processing level of mind that is
context-free, comparing, classifying, and searching in an objective
way. Dreyfus protests, first, that the technical, mathematical definition of information is here being confused with the idea of information as ordinary everyday exchange. Everyday information is always full of meaning, based on meaningful experience. Experience
cannot be "analyzed into isolable, atomic, alternative choices"
(*Computers* 165), subject to "heuristic rules in a sequence of unconscious operations" (*Computers* 189). Such rules would separate
mental processes from the necessary connection with a time-bound
individual life situation that can never be completely known.

The implications of all four of these cognitivist assumptions for a
writer's mind are obvious. From a cognitive standpoint, mental
development can be described in a series of universalizable steps,
separate from historical circumstance. The writing process becomes
primarily calculative because known and programmable (and
therefore teachable, as teaching is defined by its control over
"knowns"). The mind is stripped of its forces and its nonformaliza-
ble properties, and of the mutable context in which it operates. Its
process is not affected by *what* it thinks; rather it remains a constant.

Even a look at the way the mind posited by cognitive science
changes periodically, as research interests (and funds?) in the field
of Artificial Intelligence move into new areas, must give us all
pause: when computers are needed most to process information our

minds are modeled as information processors. When built-in expertise is needed (and when Japan seems to be making strides in this direction), we are treated to talk about our minds as expert systems (vs. novice). Puzzlement over our minds' decisionmaking capacities just happens to occur about the time that AI people are puzzling about this matter in machines (that are undoubtedly needed on a market somewhere), and now that the revolution in parallel distributed processing has taken place, our minds are seen as neural nets. Dreyfus and his brother Stuart survey recent controversies over this new model and conclude that

> human beings are much more holistic than neural nets. Intelligence has to be motivated by purposes in the organism and goals picked up by the organism from an ongoing culture. If the minimum unit of analysis is that of a whole organism geared into a whole cultural world, neural nets as well as symbolically programmed computers still have a very long way to go. ("Making a Mind" 39)

There have been other protests against modeling thinking on such desiccated structures as these. Examining Linda Flower's *Problem-Solving Strategies for Writing*, for instance, Anthony Petrosky objects to its "narrow notions of mind that smack of logical positivism" (234). John Clifford, reviewing Gregg and Steinberg's *Cognitive Processes in Writing*, ironically calls cognitivists our "newest rescuers" and claims that "all models of the mind are partial, tentative" (101). Erwin Steinberg himself sees "dangers of uncritical acceptance" of current writing models, and believes we need "to be modest about what we 'know'" (158). Even cognitive psychologists find problems in their own field: Donald Norman, for instance, believes cognitive scientists have neglected to imagine humans fully, failed to see them as animate, emotional organisms, "multi-minded" and socially interactive in ways artificial devices can never be (266, 280). Picking up the social theme, Lester Faigley argues that writing processes "can be understood only from the perspective of a society rather than a single individual" (535), and both David Bartholomae (146) and Patricia Bizzell ("Composing Processes" 59) state that writing ability is as much a matter of mastering discourse conventions as it is of learning cognitive strategies.

Inside minds and inside cultures

I would like to pick up now on a recommendation of Bizzell (in a review article of Gregg's book) as a way back to the importance of introducing alternate images of mind to students. In rejecting the cognitivist "quest for certainty" that looks for "one universal model of the composing process" ("Cognition" 235), Bizzell recommends that we balance the work of this "inner-directed" school with that of the more social "outer-directed" one, itself honoring context and community.

Certainly her recommendation is a sound one, but the dichotomy between inner and outer points up the very problem with words and the images they evoke that makes revisioning mind so difficult yet so important. The word "inner," here, in its contrast to "outer," sets up a kind of push-pull picture of oscillating, shared control, not exactly a dynamic one for any teacher to use who wants students to sense writing as mind-changing. (The outer world of such a model is itself too often seen as a disciplinary one that leaves the students' worlds behind, as Nicholas Coles and Susan Wall point out [299]). Furthermore, "inner" is used in such a way that there seems no question about there being a mind inside a person. Stephen Toulmin notices how culturally pervasive is the assumption that because cerebral processes occur in our brains, the life of the mind must reside there too (5). When we confuse these two activities, he claims, we create a needless imprisonment of our thinking, which is never as private and as "opaque" as we might imagine, though we might try to make it so. And though Toulmin is not trying to draw mind and culture together as I am, he does put into question the painfully concealing way in which we all in this culture tend to think of our minds as internal to our own heads, not living a life among others.

Given the way most of our students come to our classes unaware of the effect of their political relations on their writing, every possible image, story, metaphor, or theory we can weave into our thinking and talking about the mind's life in culture will be useful to raise needed questions about mental boundaries and therefore contexts of writing.

One of the groups of words that needs stretching and remolding for this purpose is the "inner" group: internal, inside, in. For instance, when Burhans and Hairston say that contemporary ideas about composition are holistic, it is not clear what kind of internal relations they have in mind (the word "holism" by definition assumes internal relations between parts). To be internally related is to have parts of a whole or a field that are *necessarily* moved by changes in other parts. (E.g., in a semantic field in which one is a female, the state of being married and of being a wife are internally related because if one meaning were to change the other would have to.) Since the minds that cognitivists posit are not internally related to other minds or their environments (they are more like atoms finding channels to other atoms), the ideas those minds have (about composition or anything else) are not as likely to be holistic as those of minds imagined embedded in larger systems, in which changes in one end of an interaction must change the other. A cultural system's "inner" is almost holographic, with many connected mental "inners" reflecting the whole.

Figuring worlds

If a group of people—a class, for instance—can be envisioned as being part of a culture (even an emerging one), the internal relations that move within that culture *as* system give a reason for writing *to* someone else there *about* something in the first place. One of the most useful discussions I have found for helping me bridge the gap between minds inside skins and minds internally related inside such cultures comes from Robert Romanyshyn's book *Psychological Life: From Science to Metaphor.* I sometimes use Romanyshyn's images in talk with students about how we will figure out and tell stories about the other people embedded in our writing. They may read their own minds' work differently from the way I read mine *or* theirs; I might ask for their readings, too, as a way to begin negotiating the stories we tell each other.

Romanyshyn believes, as do George Lakoff and Mark Johnson in *Metaphors We Live By,* that the world we can know in any way is shot through and through with metaphor. For Romanyshyn, psychological life *is* the metaphorizing of the world, a collecting of oneself and others into worlds of stories we all create by making doubles of what we find, reflecting—psychologically reflecting—over and over, figuring and refiguring. We are each made up, he thinks, of the many figures in the many tales we make about ourselves and others and those they make of us: we figure our worlds by peopling them with figures, and that is how we know the world (even the "inanimate" world is figured in answer to the way other people have figured it). This psychological activity is an undercurrent of daily life, says Romanyshyn, a usually out-of-awareness background of the "fixed, habitual, taken-for-granted character of events and things" (169); unconsciousness is simply an "absence of a reflection" on that activity. "Psychological life . . . must always be recovered from forgetfulness," he says, "from its hiddenness in habit and routine" (19). Its figures will appear and disappear from awareness and be lived out in relations between people, even in one person's smile being picked up by another's quickening stride:

> The transgression of boundaries between me and you, this mutual impregnation of styles of conduct, this relation of mirroring, is an essential and primary reality of human life. . . . this recovery forces us to reconsider the notions of behavior and experience. (64)

Recovering and negotiating the figures and stories we make might be seen as a way into the life of the mind(s) we share with others, into the sense of agency that can lead students from an awareness of thinking to an awareness of action. The recovery is a recipe for double-loop learning, any learning, that is, that takes learners out of a specific learning task into its context, which can then embed the task in a new way. For instance, from giving an uncle advice in a report, a student writer might move into an understanding of how he and the uncle figure each other [out] in the situation that grounds the report. Once figured, the situation needs refiguring to include that figuring, a little difference, perhaps, in the advice that is given and the *way* it is given, different ideas more attuned with what the uncle can hear, different words, different rhythms of syntax. Something new, in other words, can be born, some newness of relationship in the writing. Argyris and Schön have yet another angle:

> Interactions between [participants] may need to be understood in terms of mutually interacting fantasies of self, other, action, and

situation. One's own action has not only the meaning one intends it to have, under one's theory-in-use, but the meaning it is given by the other under his theory-in-use. And one's action's effects on the behavioral world must be a function of those mutual . . . interpretations. (207).

Negotiating metaphors

With the hope, then, that in the next fifteen weeks the students in front of me might write with some understanding not only of the contexts they write within but of the way that writing can change these contexts and even help them refigure other writing projects, I encourage them to begin negotiating ways to think of their own minds as active, interactive, and influential in setting up the worlds they live in. Giving them my own favorite images of writing minds, I start with Achilles' shield, just because it is such a bright and easy image to remember, and because it illustrates my first belief so well: minds are whatever is in them. Hephaestus the god of craft and fire made the shield for Achilles, asked to do so by Achilles' mother Thetis, who knew it would be used in her son's last battle. Hephaestus comforted her with the hope that his work would protect Achilles from a painful death, and then he created a shield of silver, gold, tin, and bronze, a glittering circle divided into concentric regions: earth in the middle, the heavens around it, and finally the river Oceanus at the edge. At its core were scenes of life and death, marriage and strife, vineyards, workers, cattle and sheep, potters working, dancers dancing.

This work of art then, I tell my students, can be seen as a metaphor for the life of a Greek mind, a figuring of the world Achilles lived in, and thus an emblem of the mental life that signified his being alive. The battle into which Achilles carried the shield might be seen simply as strifeful life, beyond which lay, as for everyone, death. And every student may have a mind full of just such scenes, a cosmos of sorts in which everything lives that is thought or even has been thought and forgotten. Minds are simply figures, like this, of experience.

But is this particular mind/shield an emblem of only Achilles' mind? No, actually it has elements of what many Greeks of those days probably thought about, and certainly Hephaestus himself had this life in *his* mind. Are these overlaps unusual? No again. Overlaps exist today too: memories we share with families, or friends, or people at work, or in the dorm. We share memories with many people, and they resemble ours in many ways. Americans have George Washington, for instance, chemists have elements, Towson students have their Union. No minds are ever exactly like ours, but people we come together with day after day never have minds altogether different from ours; the clusters of similarities are cultures, and everybody lives in many, many of them—groups that share certain kinds of language, beliefs, ways of thinking.

I draw on the chalkboard a small circle with concentric regions of life (a self in the middle and an ocean at the edge) to represent one mind, and I draw overlapping circles to show how people share some of their thinking habits and memories, gather so much of their lives from other mental lives—our traditions, and customs—all the many cultures we share with others. We can imagine those circles as the river Oceanus flooding the whole picture, giving life to people in it because they are strong and will swim or even surf with and against the cultural currents, not drown in them. We and our whole world of minds and cultures are somehow living and moving with the flow of water over the shield now, just as Homer described life actually being *lived* on the shield, in fluid images moving with each other.

I ask students to imagine as many scenes in their own lives as they can, as vividly as possible, and to then try seeing them through currents of moving water. I would like them simply to have the experience, for now, of seeing some part of their lives being moved and changed with the rhythm of currents. Later in the semester I will want to relate different experiences of rhythm to syntax. Now I am experimenting with double vision, seeing through, sensing more than one thing happening at a time. Life moves, minds move, cultures interact and so, I think, do we all, always affecting each other's minds and cultures.

And now I tell my second belief about minds, one that turns a little away from the first: minds can be thought of after all as quite a bit more than "whatever is in them"; in fact, they can shape life, just as water does. Minds are doers, creating the interchanges of everyday life, where people talk to each other about their lives, tell stories about them—*not* "fictional" ones, but ones through which their lives take on meaning. I put people in my stories, I say, and see them differently from what others might: they become figures in my stories, shaped by my mind. Stories are the way people experience their lives; even when they seem not to be telling them, listeners can usually "read between the lines" of what talkers say, registering on some level implicit stories, talkers' ideas about and attitudes toward their listeners and toward what they are talking about.

People may not think much of the time about "stories." Lives seem "real." But out on the edges of their minds, almost like the periphery of their vision where they can barely make things out, in deep waters, there are plenty of stories, lots of life that sometimes gets noticed, sometimes not. It can be seen as making a kind of background for everyday thinking, and sometimes even as interrupting it; when a break in thought comes in talking *or* in writing, for instance, just behind it might be a trail to an old story, tugging on the attention, keeping it from tending the business at hand.

I tell however much of this mind-vision I can in five or at most ten minutes, then ask students to respond to it in another five minutes or so of writing, accepting what they can, rejecting all that feels incoherent with what they can imagine as their own minds at their most active. The responses vary widely, but in nearly all cases, students begin to wonder about and reflect on the life of their minds. Last semester, for instance, Jon may still have thought of his mind as a processor, but he added "emotion" to the "information" it processed, and thought he was better at mechanical than analytical problems. And began wondering why. Rachel's mind "works even while I sleep," Venus's, "in a remote corner of my brain which allows me to be creative." Some could use my water image: "I picture my mind as a swirling whirlpool that takes everything in . . . reforms it and then spreads it around"; some would rather have "a piece of tinted glass" so that only *some* things can be seen; some refused the image altogether, one person adding indignantly: "The mind is a private affair only to be shared with a select few of my choosing. I do not like your idea about the mind and sharing." One person was willing to imagine a fluid sharing of ideas if she could have "some drawbridges. Sometimes the mind needs to be somewhat separated."

New metaphors for mind came up: black holes sucking things in, gears turning other gears, liquid electricity "making things go in our minds and outside too," radio waves, moss, department stores receiving new shipments. Many people wanted to be sure I knew that minds could be private, and that people could "hide things in their mind." I figured that I had probably pushed the readability of people and minds a little too hard, too early. I did acknowledge this and asked only that students now and then notice how they interact with other people, in and out of school, in talking and in writing.

At other times during a semester I might talk a little more, either with individual students or in class, about the many images that have come up, and about my sense of a mind being drawn to attending things or focusing on them only if it feels swept into them, like a wave or current of water joining another. My mind needs to feel strong and full of energy in order to risk tangling with an other person's thinking or with some idea that feels foreign to it, I say; letting itself feel pulled into a whirlpool with another culture or another mind's thoughts needs my trust that on the other end of the funnel is new life and a worthwhile result. If students are struggling with ideas, I recommend that they trust the struggle as a stage in a process, try to talk aloud about it, and tell as many stories about the struggle and the ideas and the people involved as possible, even when it does not feel comfortable. Just as currents of water run into obstacles in their own journeys, yet come together with competing currents to create new figures and forms, so might people with opposing ideas who let their minds move together—even though tumultuously—find new ways to relate to each other and to foreign-feeling ideas.

I bring more images and ask for more back. Might they try thinking of their minds and figurings not as solidified into real brain-like structures, but able to shift shapes, feeling liquid when obstacles come, solid (but not dense) when ideas are being hammered into place, even expansive and fast-moving through the negligible resistance of air and its vaporized water? These are some of the figures of mind I ask students to consider, expand on, and argue with as the semester goes on, to begin to attend what it feels like to write and welcome complexity, to believe that equilibrium is more pleasurable when it follows a period of disequilibrium. To aid critical thinking, claims Susan Buck-Morss, we need to be finding ways to help young people abandon rather than seek a Piagetian perceptual equilibrium (112).

The word "figure" is meant to be a chameleon that will help them do that abandoning: it has always carried the idea of plasticity, or a molding or shaping of form (as Erich Auerbach discusses in his etymological essay "Figura"). This thought is in the back of my mind whenever I suggest that one way to understand how the mind *might* work is to think of it as humanizing the world, figuring it out with all those figures. Minds are so wonderfully diverse because they are more possibility than actuality, being able to decide where to go next and how to behave with the figures they meet there.

Greek scholar John Poulakos picks up sophistic ideas to claim that rhetoricians concern themselves "with the possible" when they refuse "to keep people in their actual situation" (43). From this sophistic point of view, Aristotle's association of the actual—*energeia*—with men, and the possible—*dynamis*—with women, can be thought not insulting to women: though of course Aristotle valued the actual more than the possible, we need not. Moreover, before *dynamis* ever meant "possibility" it was associated in ancient Greece with the idea of power, and also with the elements of earth, air, fire, and water. Coming together in all those shape-shifting images of a writing mind, then, are what feel like just the right historical and rhetorical connections to work what I always hope is magic. Weak magic, perhaps, but a little change in some minds' ideas about what they might be able to accomplish.

Figures of a physician

I intend the word "figure" to blend at its edges into other kinds of figures and I will usually say a little about these later in the semester if the timing seems right, either with a whole group or with single students. One such apt moment occurred in the summer of 1985 with a student named Roberto, in a required junior English writing course I was teaching at the University of Maryland. Our first official assignment asked students to write an autobiographical career goals statement, and Roberto had chosen to write his in the form of a letter to Johns Hopkins Medical School. He thought of this school as the one he would most like to attend, and because he was an honors student with a 3.5 GPA, this would seem a not unreasonable desire. But that surface desire seemed betrayed by some incoherent undercurrents in the letter he wrote, ones that led us one summer day after class into an interesting talk about double stories and allegories.

First the letter. Understanding that Johns Hopkins' medical school was one that encouraged a wide range of interests and backgrounds in its students, Roberto did not hesitate to tell the admissions people of his double major (English and zoology). But the way in which he chose to explain its effects on his life seemed at cross purposes with his stated goal. First, rather than giving English and zoology equal time, he chose to emphasize that "English education has allowed me to better understand the human mind and it has increased my level of maturity. As a result, I feel that I am better disciplined and better prepared to face the demands of medical school." No benefits from zoology were mentioned.

Next, there was a slight detour as Roberto told admissions about a well-rounded physician ("well-rounded" being a vague, undefined, catchall term for him), "liberally educated," having "a broader scope in his or her views of mankind than a physician who is strictly science-oriented." This is crucial, he said, in allowing "one to be tolerant of others. It can help one to be less judgmental and more accepting of peoples of differing races, creeds, or religions." A hidden agenda seems to be afoot here, but Roberto quickly brought his lecture to the admissions committee back to the work of physicians: "this can ultimately mean establishing sound relationships with their patients."

Then came a paragraph that moved the direction of the letter into an entirely different itinerary, away from Johns Hopkins to England:

> As I share the value that I understand you do on a liberal education, I would like to continue studying English literature beyond the undergraduate level. Fortunately, this is feasible as I understand that your medical school offers flexible options for obtaining a medical degree. I am especially interested in your delayed entry option. If granted a place in the program that allows this option, I would like to travel abroad and study at Oxford University as a Rhodes Scholar. This option is ideal because not only would it allow me to pursue advanced studies in English literature, it would alleviate many of the pressures involved with entering medical school directly after college.

By this time, the admissions committee may be wondering how strongly Roberto wants to be part of the Johns Hopkins Medical School. In a class discussion about the letter, he had claimed simply to want to be honest, believing that admissions would value that honesty. And he did, after all, add in his letter that "the decision to go to medical school has been one that has required a great deal of careful thought." Now, he claimed in the letter, "I am . . . eager and motivated to study medicine"; not so eager, the school might conclude, that he does not wish first to avoid its rigors by studying English at Oxford.

There were, to be sure, many angles from which we two could have approached the lack of confident force in the letter, its failure to communicate a coherent sense of vision and purpose. I agree with David Bartholomae's conviction that beginning writers (and I extend his discussion into thoughts about this junior writer—still novice) need to imagine their right to speak in a language that is not yet theirs, that the problems these writers face are as social and political as cognitive, a matter of "working against the inevitable presence of conventional language" (143). Roberto needed to imagine not only Hopkins conventions but those of my expectations and the university's as well. Double and triple trouble.

But interwoven with students learning to "extend themselves" (as Bartholomae puts it) into the networks and structures of university discourse, I think it important that they extend themselves into the cultural networks in their own minds that those new networks will need to embed themselves in. Bakhtin's idea that the psyche is a social entity penetrating "inside the organism of the individual person" (39) helps me envision the memories that might interrupt a student's discourse as sites of social and political conflict, ones to be negotiated with the memory-laden institutional discourses, themselves full of implicit histories, that students must learn to imitate.

The inadvertent detours in Roberto's letter and his willingness to explore the images in his mind that arose at the site of those detours, produced some rich and complex stories when we two sat down to talk. First came some confusion as to whether or not he actually wanted to go to Johns Hopkins (too hard, too much competition). Next was his real love as one of literature rather than zoology, and even his mixed feelings about his 3.5 GPA, since he was the only one in his family to go to college (the family had immigrated here from Cuba in the 1960s), and his mother sometimes accused him of trying to be smarter than the rest of them, even though she was also proud of his accomplishments. Roberto identified himself as a black, and freely spoke of his anger and resentment at whites for "suffocating" the life and self-respect out of blacks.

Then, related to the well-roundedness, came the idea that most doctors are not well rounded or humanitarians. Most of them, it turned out, and especially the kind of high achievers associated with having gone through Hopkins, were identified as the white, judgmental ones, little given to tolerance for and acceptance of "others." One part of Roberto wanted to be a doctor, but he did not want to be one of "them," and above all, he did not want to put himself—a highly competitive self—in a situation in which his intellect might be intimidated by more socially central figures. At least once before in his life he had been intellectually intimidated, that time at a high school for gifted students. His grades had dropped after entrance there, and the following semester he had returned to his old school.

Roberto was finding a double story in his letter, one that seemed—in a rough way—to express one desire, and the other, running along beneath it, to tell another that touched the first at breaks in thought. By focusing on those breaks as doors to important detours, by assuming that the first story would never be able to make sense unless the other stories reflected in it were brought into its midst, we both found a relief in the new, assuredly more complex level of coherence in the whole affair. The implicit detours became explicit ones, leading Roberto into memories, and those, into a realization that his letter did not "really" carry the meaning that he wished to enter Johns Hopkins. In a way, the letter could be seen as a question which his detours answered. We talked a little about allegory as a rhetorical figure *often* present in writing as an undercurrent of comment on a main line, but needing a real sense of ambidextrous, two-handed coordination (Quilligan 26) if it is to feel graceful to writer and reader. Allegory, says Craig Owens, is an uneasy marriage of story and figure (76). Walter Benjamin sees it as a kind of script or writing personifying the mind's movements, tracing a double track with that of an alien world (214–215). Allegory brings to a text the voice of *allos*, an "other."

Roberto's paper had elements of a postmodern, secularized allegory, in which one text comments on another and the meaning of neither ever quite dominates the other. It also bore semblances of a related figure called by Derrida "anasemia," a reversal of "meaning and the meaning of meaning" ("Fors" 92). Derrida takes the concept from psychoanalyst Nicolas Abraham, who used it to describe a mental process operating in everyone unconsciously, giving people a way to bury or seal off—"encrypt"—stories about important social relations, in a place that can only be known by analogy. The original event is already the memory's translation of other events, already a "radical semantic change" ("Fors" 93) from one string of events to another. In a writer's hands, it becomes a detour that sometimes pulls the main line of thought off its track, disguising meaning. The anasemic translation "swerves off at an angle in order to throw the reader off the track and make its itinerary unreadable" ("Fors" 108). Certainly Derrida must have been reading some of our student papers.

But an anasemic figure need not be thought a nuisance to be banished before getting on with the task at hand. Rather, the breaks in thought that signal its presence are more profitably considered an opportunity to take a side trip with students into some of those stories waiting to be retrieved. The braver among them will be willing to endure some of the turbulence involved in tangling with parts of their own lives and memories that feel incoherent with other parts.

Roberto was one of those who raised his own questions at points of disruption, with some prompting but not reluctantly. During the rest of that six weeks, he tried out different identities, though not necessarily explicitly. When I asked students to bring to class Xeroxed copies of one page of a favorite reading, he brought a page from a James Baldwin novel. And when I asked them to look at their pages for resemblances between themselves and any person they might find there, Roberto thought of himself as a figure of Baldwin himself, and experimented a little with a Baldwinian sentence structure he especially liked. When I asked the class to create figures of themselves as the writers they would like to be, Roberto neglected Baldwin's writing power and instead concentrated on some of Baldwin's worst fears: being chased through fields by an enemy. In this scenario, Roberto himself became a martyr in his writing; he lay down and "rolled my eyes toward the heavens," waiting for an ax to fall on him. During the ten minutes or so students were doing this writing, he moved himself into the hall so he could "concentrate better"; he wrote long after the others had finished, struggling with this image of not being able to escape, one that had recurred many times in his dreams.

At other times and in more formal papers, he experimented again with roles having to do with medicine; he wrote a superb paper on the concept of triage, then a so-so one on becoming a physician's assistant as a viable alternative to long, expensive, grueling years in medical school. In yet another he discussed shopping mall medical centers as examples of doctors' greed, then rewrote it when interviews with personnel at one of these centers convinced him that such centers were probably growing out of multiple and often more positive motivations. Roberto was moving in and out of "real" and "unreal" images and figures, testing his sense of himself against both antithetical and congenial lines of reasoning.

Stories at the edges of chasms

Whenever I see a gulf open up in the meaning of student writing, I suspect there is a powerful force somewhere in the mind swallowing presence and attention, an anasemic figure that signals conflict of interest between voices in an intrapsychic story, and therefore signals a context that can be negotiated. Students seem surprisingly open to hunting for images that might arise in their minds at the chasms readers have pointed out. In fact, some have told me that now they understand why they might have said X, connected as it was to Y image in their memories. They have liked thinking that their thinking grows out of images or stories that fuel whatever they write, even when the images might not have gotten into their writing or might not "make sense" of it in usual ways. No problem, I tell them; go after the competing stories that clash with each other. In the long run, what seems to make writing more complex now will simplify it later, when the parts come together more coherently.

"Figures," says philosopher Amelie Rorty (referring to figures of persons), have traditionally been "defined by their place in an unfolding drama" (307); they carry their cultural history with them because they are signs of the typified others we link them to in similar narrative situations, others we sense we can resemble, imitate, be like in certain situations, "characters writ large," as Rorty calls them. Figures that have acted as external models become internalized, she says, naming such archetypal figures as Adam and Christ, or ancient types such as pilgrims, tempters, innocents. Differently from persons as selves, persons as figures are social: those who act amongst others who themselves act. Their early connection to plastic form connects them to the arts—visual and literary—and to an interpretive act that covers the painting of a model as well as the writing of drama or even of one's life's texts in the memory. Figures function. There is a story that goes with them.

We can turn, then, to the way writers make figures of themselves and their readers: to write is to figure out the very palpable way in which the mind reads the world and then writes it in the memory so that it can read it again someday.

7

Time Passed from Reading to Writing to Reading

Sources of interest in reader-writer interaction

Even though composition teachers may have long known that reading and writing are closely related activities, only recently have studies of the relationship begun to mushroom. Now it is almost a commonplace among us that writers cannot write nor readers read unless they collaborate and negotiate with each other, and that though they may be separated from each other in time and space, readers and writers need some way of understanding their expectations about each other and the material at hand if the communication is to work.

Interest in the relationship has come from several quarters. First, studies in literacy have moved in recent years beyond what used to be an emphasis on reading into its pairing with writing, picking up not only on comparisons between oral and written forms of language, but on political overtones. "Writing ability is unevenly distributed in our society along class lines" (Kintgen, Kroll, and Rose xvii). Second, researchers in the fields of education and cognitive psychology have begun to study similarities and mutual influences in the two processes, noticing, for instance, that composing and comprehending are functions of *both* reading and writing (Flood and Lapp 10). A third source of interest in the relationship has grown out of literary studies and their move away from New Critical thinking in recent years toward an involvement in both reader-response criticism and poststructuralist criticism. As Edward White points out, the New Critical idea "that meaning resided in the text" led us to analyze student writing as *only* a product, and we edited every composition as if it were "a failed Shakespeare sonnet" (87). As teachers of literature began losing interest in formalistic focuses on texts, so did we in composition start finding common ground between literature's "examination of the reader's movement through the text" and our own research in writing as process (White 92). The text had lost its "privileged status," and as we turned toward how it is created by readers and writers, we began noticing, with poststructuralists, the many ways meaning slips through the cracks between any reader and writer (94–96), be they novice or expert, student or professional.

Though strands of each of these interest groups have found their way into studies of the social and cultural contexts of the reading and writing pair, these studies are especially alert to issues of hierarchy embedded in acts of reading and writing. Richard Ohmann, for instance, points out that the privileging of reading in literature departments has not been free of an ideological duality and tension between the supposed mental or spiritual work of reading for a "refined leisure" and the supposed physical work of writing with the hands in the marketplace (21). George Dillon describes how writers recreate cultural codes that establish their authority with readers (*Rhetoric* 7–11); David Bleich undoes the hierarchical opposition between written and oral language to situate their use in "the palpable social and bodily presence of the individual among members" ("Reconceiving Literacy" 33).

Expanding the meanings of reading and writing

Innocent or neutral interactions between readers and writers cannot be presumed, then, no simple passing between individuals of information that is not already tacitly marked with histories and instructions about what can be said and how it can be said. And if meaning is made on both the reading and the writing sides of the interaction, it can be seen that any notions we have of "reading" and "writing" are inevitably set into larger semiotic webs, or as David Kaufer and Gary Waller put it, "we read each other, the signs of the world, the nuances or blatant assaults of political, commercial, cultural signs; and to read is to find ourselves within "writing" (83). As Ann Berthoff quotes from Paulo Freire's talk in Boston, "For me . . . the fundamental task of human beings should be reading the world, writing the world; reading the words, writing the words" ("Reading" 129). That task is a very large order for all of us to become better readers and writers of everything by learning to think in terms of the world and our experience in it as signs of each other.

Students do not have an easy time hooking themselves into this concept, but beginning early in the semester with the idea that their minds are already good at figuring things out (if they will only notice, I say), I elicit more and more of their figurings, and stress that experience is itself a figuring or reading of signs. (And I begin, gradually, to interchange these two verbs, "figuring" and "reading," in order to broaden the scope of each.)

Double readings

In fact, what I am trying to do from the beginning of any semester is help them develop a repertoire of ways to double their own readings with those of others in the classroom and those about other people at the edges of their own minds. The hope is that mental flexibility will begin to alert them to the ways they read and write with the cultural patterns written in their memories. These patterns I take to be inscribed in voices that are real forces interacting with other forces in the memory and others in "reality," voices that tend, one way or another, to work themselves into whatever writers write about. The patterns of voices—the stories—often become hidden agendas, as they did with Roberto. Finding ways to double these movements of mind with as many perspectives on a matter as possible—ones read through observations, through memories, or through live interactions—sharpens the edges between the perspectives. New life is born there, new angles of vision that disrupt sterile or single-parented reproduction of sameness. The process is not unlike George Dillon's "stereoscoping" (*Constructing* 98), or the "cognitive stereoscopy" described by David Bleich ("Cognitive" 99), a seeing through at least two perspectives at once. It resembles, too, the logic of mutual causality that Magoroh Maruyama calls "polyocular vision" (209) and believes to be more prevalent in non-Western cultures, those in which growing children are exposed to the many adult viewpoints of extended families (208).

Reading for ensemble

The idea that signs are always signs *for* somebody brings people and their multiple readings to the center of writing classrooms and gives a basis for questioning authoritative meanings that might stop dialogue. The goal is not relativism, but ensemble, attentiveness to patterns of interaction. (The very idea of relativism is an individualistic one, assuming multiple units *not* internally related). Twenty minds alerted to how they can *pattern* differences, neither minimizing nor accentuating them, can be a good start toward learning how reading (in its broad sense) grounds writing. I use three initial strategies, each intended to make more familiar a multicultural world whose forces and viewpoints need to be understood before they can be negotiated or argued with.

First, I urge students to share as many of their readings about their worlds and about each other and the class—whatever is drawing their interest—as they can manage and we can manage in our limited time together, either in small groups or the larger class. But I ask them always, as Chris Argyris suggests in his ideas about double-loop learning (*Reasoning* 103), to test their readings of situations with others by giving the concrete "data" that led to the reading, and then asking if their inferences are shared. Because the testing creates a structure and a measure of safety, people will often feel more courageous about venturing negative readings, which need to include the *continuum* between "data" and reading. For instance, "I don't find these groups at all helpful" would be followed by either a volunteering of or questioning about what goes on that makes them unhelpful, and what they are not helpful for. Then others share their own readings.

I put the word "data" in quotation marks to emphasize the need to understand even data itself as already read and therefore as a slightly different phenomenon from what is ordinarily meant. The difference between data and inferences, I emphasize to classes, is one of degree: Social agreement, cultural habit, and the material life of sensory experience lend themselves to our sense of what counts as "fact." The usefulness, then, of this intermittent activity of testing readings is twofold: there is a certain tone of empiricism in our class's practice of separating facts from inferences and these from "opinions," but more than simply empirical testing, I mean the activity to encourage a way of understanding observation itself as a sign of the observer's habits of reading or figuring out a situation. Closer to what Charles Peirce calls "abduction" than "induction" (413–414), it is a tentative inferring, a guessing about how a given experience might be interpreted, a guess that is drawn toward other guesses for stronger grounding. Abduction encourages a doubling frame of mind, multiple readings superimposed on each other and undercutting the idea of single, correct views of matters. As educational psychologist Gary Shank puts it, abduction is a way to read signs that leaves open a rereading of circumstances "in order to come up with an alternate reading" (288). "Too often," he says, "we are willing to accept observations as facts, without seeing the underlying structures of assumptions that are built into the observations" (289). Encouraging students to think of their observations as readings to be tested against those of others will help them learn to revise their initial readings.

Second, I ask students to watch for as many ways as possible that they let parts of themselves be dominated by other parts, squeezing the life out of the subordinated parts. Usually, for instance, the head is the only sign-reader or figurer any of us considers useful, but as Sondra Perl and Arthur Egendorf argue (using the work of psychologist Eugene Gendlin), one of the best ways for writers to begin knowing what they know is to pay attention to messages from the body, which they (and Gendlin) call the preconceptual "felt sense" of experience (122–123). The meaning any of us gives to our experience, they say, begins in the way our bodies "organize the situations we live" (125); paying attention to and describing the way it feels lets us discover attitudes, structures, direction.

Julia Kristeva's idea of a presymbolic, prelinguistic sense of rhythmic ordering of energy (*Revolution* 25–30), Derrida's positing of "a fundamental synesthesia" related to nonphonetic writing (*Of Grammatology* 88–89), and anthropological studies such as those of Ron Scollon about crossovers between biological, mental, and social rhythms (335–349) all attest to the need for an expanded conception of mind and thinking that will remove them from the tyranny of the brain.

If attention can become attuned to multiple messages needing to be read (almost) simultaneously, a sense of rhythmic resonance is called on in order that many body-mind sensors or channels move together, opening dimensions of awareness to each other. When I tell my students that my way of getting ideas together for writing is to jump for ten or fifteen minutes on my mini-trampoline, they laugh, but I hope they laugh believingly (I have never asked). Nothing can come to consciousness unless it can be sensed in "a relationship of bones, muscles, and breath," claims one dance teacher (Wiener 27), and though the idea might sound extreme to a teacher of writing, we should remember how culturally dictatorial have been attempts to convince women, for centuries, that heads (of bodies, states, or households, for instance) are smarter than non-heads. We might begin to reconsider the assumptions and the rationales for this belief. Many teachers of writing have regretted that we need to overcome in our classes a TV generation's worth of changed perceptual structuring, with loss of the image-making capacities and auditory sensibilities needed for the reading/writing cycle. But neither visual nor auditory images are only themselves; they can be awakened to each other and to other kinds of perceptions. The more we encourage multiple channels of readings—social ones, kinesthetic ones, emotional ones, for instance—the less single-minded will our students be about their writing.

The word "expert" is etymologically related to "experience" and "experiment"; the connection is not an unfruitful one to make to students who might like thinking that expertise grows as much out of the number of experiential "channels" they experiment with as it does out of the number of hours they spend at their desks. Letting other people serve as the experts over one's own reading and writing is tantamount to giving up an engagement with these tasks. Noticing the many ways bodies and minds work together can bring it back.

Reading and writing into ensemble

Finally, because time scales involved in reading and writing vary so drastically and often so disablingly, I try to sensitize my students to the way the felt discordance can be brought into awareness and negotiated into a sense of ensemble. This matter of differing time scales is beginning to be noticed more now that interest is growing in social contexts. Let me explain.

When teachers move out of a psycholinguistic perspective on the reading/writing relationship into a more socially and culturally interactive one, they are apt not to concentrate so much on the one-way action from speaker or writer to audience as on what Martin Nystrand calls "transforming a shared knowledge base" (41). Instead of uncritically accepting Grice's advice that we get our messages accepted by assuming a Cooperative Principle (only passive, cooperative accepters out there), we would expect to hear too of a second—receiving—voice with its own agendas, not always in accord with our own. And Nystrand does indeed discuss that second: claiming, first, that "discourse is not so much the encoding and transmission of what the speaker knows as it is [a matter of resolving] discrepancies between what the producer has to say and what the receiver needs to understand" (44).

Nystrand next claims that both speakers and writers are able to do this resolving because both operate in the two contexts that support it, one of production and one of use. The major difference between the two is that writers must operate in a "context of eventual use," rather than the one of immediate use belonging to speakers. And even though their interactive resources are different, writers have no fewer of these resources than speakers do. (Genre conventions and punctuation, for instance, replace intonation and gesture as ways to suggest "tone and attitudinal coloring" [46].) The delayed context of use simply means that writers must find ways to build the future into the present and cope with the impingement, trying out the text themselves, bringing readers' feedback into their own minds and alternating it with their writing, moving back and forth.

Nystrand's social perspective on writing and reading is an important and enabling affirmation that writers' work is every bit as reciprocal with readers as speakers' work is with listeners. Using work of the Norwegian psychologist Ragnar Rommetveit, Nystrand makes a subtle but significant turn within cognitive studies for writers. Rommetveit has described the difference between a Cartesian cognitivist who studies individual "mental states and processes" and a more social-minded cognitivist for whom "meaning and understanding" are important, and who studies interaction as an essential component of mind rather than an added-on auxiliary idea about context (Rommetveit 93–94). Nystrand takes the social-minded stance and assumes that writers and readers must necessarily collaborate with each other (40). Cognition, then, becomes embedded in social situations, divorced from computer-inspired models, and forced to include what we in composition have for so long called matters of *content*. From this point of view, neither the old formalistic models nor the newer content-inspired ones (often associated with writing-across-the-curriculum) are as useful in the writing classroom as models that acknowledge both content *and* structure in *action*. Attention shifts to the time- and history-ridden importance of subject matter as it interacts with time- and history-ridden readers and writers. The "form" of human time is rhythm, and its context is rhetorical interaction. Writers are thus called on to sense the special qualities of their medium as embodied rhythms of rhetorical contexts.

The "eventuality" of the writing context alludes to writers' need to imagine, without immediate sensory cues, times not their own, embodied futurities. Moreover, they need to be able to keep their sense of rhythmic voice attuned to reading speeds when what writing is doing to their minds is slowing their time sense to a snail's pace. Mentioning Richard Lanham's thought that readers assume no difference between their reading time and the time it takes to write, George Dillion comments:

> This observation comes as close as anything I have read to explaining the fascination writing has for me: to read what I have written is to think faster, more sustainedly, coherently, and effortlessly than I do in composing. This effect explains why authors may be caught at odd moments reading bits of their own writing with a satisfied smile. It may also explain why some very good student writers find revision almost impossible. (*Constructing* 32)

When all the other good reasons for practicing a multivoiced rhythmic resonance are thought not good enough, the need to create and maintain a sense of coherent timing between reader and writer creates a necessity for that practice. Writers must be able to change their speeds of thinking and do it often in order to gather many webs of mental rhythms into their texts (so that, as linguist Wallace Chafe puts it, "the abnormal quickness of reading fits with the abnormal slowness of writing" [37]). They need, too, to sense how matters of time pervade the sequence of writing events: their work becomes written into their memories, part of already-read material gathered into a background hum where discordant rhythms have been already made concordant. The thought of revision must surely seem like arrhythmia.

Rhythms "actively sought out" can "ward off tension and anxiety," claims Joost Meerloo (95), a useful function for any of our students, especially when writing is slowed to a halt, as it inevitably and often is. At such times and at times of revision, writers need to find ways to read the many layers of discord as irregular rhythms, tolerable if not comfortable.

That kind of reading is part of the path toward home, toward a gathering of materials into an ending in ensemble. It is a moment of challenge during the experience of flow for a writer, leading into an experience of flow for a reader. Texts are embodied records of dissonant contexts turned consonant, integrations of process with product. Louise Wetherbee Phelps calls such an intersubjective coherence the "Dialectics of Coherence," an "ability to negotiate thought objects of great complexity, depth, and scope in discourse" (23).

Pia's gathering

I would like to describe now the way one of Roberto's classmates was almost able to achieve that coherence. The way it was done yet not done held a lesson for me in how reading and writing and the larger rhythms that embed them can so easily slip tacitly into issues of gender.

Four of the twenty students in that summer class were Hispanics, and there was a sense among them that forces were afoot drawing them all together. Pia, a young Mexican mother of two small boys, was sure those forces were complex and her mission in that class even more so. Pia was an art major who had returned to school after the birth of her children, and who had read eclectically in the intervening years. One love affair at the moment was with Jungian works. From the beginning, she had caused a sensation of sorts in the class, partly because of all the antitheses she seemed to embody.

The first day's image was that of a caring mother (one son came to class with her), but on other days her scanty dress and flashing eyes created in some male students confusion about her "role." Her perceptive and bright comments in class would alternate with questions that were surely, I would think, those of someone not listening in. Shy at one moment, outgoing the next, Pia exploded into anger in my office one day late in the second week. The anger was toward William, an evangelical Christian, who had the day before returned her journal (students were exchanging and commenting on each other's entries), not only having written patronizingly about her writing, but having observed (in writing) that she was obviously "madly in love" with him and he was sorry he could not respond, but he had made other decisions about life.

Pia felt misunderstood and a little frightened (her husband met her after class every day from then on; William himself asked me the next day if I would ask Pia to dress more fully and behave less provocatively). But even more than feeling misunderstood, Pia seemed suddenly catalyzed into the role she would now assume in that class—that of the compassionate mother who would save not only William from his delusions but the rest of the class from their ignorance of a new kind of consciousness struggling to be born in the world and in our own class. It was a consciousness, she felt, that would allow sensuality to live comfortably with spirituality, and art with science.

To be sure, this was an agenda I did not feel unfriendly toward, but at this point in the summer session, Pia's agenda seemed at cross purposes with my own, which was to urge her to tackle something less global to define than planetary consciousness, and to help members of the class ground some of their own airborne ideas in earthly images.

But she sensed we had reached a point of struggle in this class in which many people were feeling discouraged about their work and unable to fit their own ideas into the required junior English formats of the papers. She believed that the nascent cohesiveness of the group was in danger of being destroyed by the low ebb of energy. Therefore, when I asked her to bring her own airy paper to class for help in grounding it, she took my request as an invitation not only to make connections with readers, but to do so in a way that would gather that class together in a surge of inspiration. The way she chose to do it taught me something about creating ensemble in a classroom, even though I was left with a question about how Pia might have achieved her purpose with the class (which she did) as well as my purpose (and, I wished at the time, hers) with her paper (which she did not).

Here is the beginning of her "gift" (her name for her paper) to the class:

> Right before a child is born, his or her head turns to the side so that it can fit lengthwise through the birth canal. As it comes through, it turns back around to line up with the shoulders. The movement is called restitution. The synergy between physics (the head is elongated at birth and the canal is longer vertically) and instinct (the baby turns his head by himself) make it possible for birth to take place. In the same way, we are now turning our heads in order to be born to a new era. We are undergoing a transition in consciousness from a dichotomy to synergy between intuition and intellect. We are learning . . . that there are many colors in the rainbow. . . . We are learning to see patterns in order to restitute unity in the planet. Although it sounds complicated, it is very simple.

At this point Pia began to prove its simplicity by translating it for every member of the class she could manage to include in her paper. To all of us she gave a visual image: "the old image or archetype of ouroboros, a serpent with its tail in its mouth." To Marlon the scientist she gave:

> When the nineteenth-century chemist Kekule was researching the molecular structure of benzene, he dreamed this image. He interpreted it to mean it was a closed-carbon ring. He restituted this message from his unconscious with his empirical knowledge of chemistry. This gave birth to his "Textbook of Organic Chemistry" (1861). His intuition and intellect enhanced each other's effect by working together. This simultaneous enhancement is called synergy.

For Scott's interest in TV and Cassidy's in the arts, she brought: "The surrealist artists tried to bring forth their archetypes. They painted dreamlike images like some seen on MTV today." For Wendy the feminist she said, "The women surrealists however made highly personal images which they all claimed were not related to anyone else's. Though these women had not seen each other's works, their images were remarkably similar." For those like John who were tired of this rigorous university life: "These things happen to everyone. They are called synchronicities. When one is away at school thinking about an old high school friend and we run into them at Georgetown on the weekend at home. Or thinking about calling someone we haven't talked to in years and they call us." For Alison who wrote often about motherhood: "Mothers seem to have extraordinary powers sometimes because they can feel things from far away." For the many skeptics: "Some people are afraid of psi because it is the unknown." And above all (she later told me), a long section for William, beginning with "Religions have scores of events where prophets and leaders perform miracles of mind over matter. . . . since God created man in his image those abilities are there to be put to a useful purpose."

To gather up all the discouragement about the difficult intellectual task afoot in this class, here was a message both for me and the discouraged ones: "The English department could be the place where intuition-art and intellect-science can find meaning to a new way of saying things. Instead we are separated into three-ninety-ones and three-ninety-threes. . . . it was Marlon, the engineer, who made the intuitive connection in class. . . . scientific knowledge serves no useful purpose without [intuition]."

Class members seemed haunted by Pia's paper. They talked about it with her and with me; she had gathered them into her synergistic project, arranging the paper as if she were handing food to each person around a large table, designing for everyone the figure of new life that raised the spirits of the class, it seemed to me. I was at the time caught up in the role of rule-giver for paper formats, and as I look back on the day Pia read her paper, I think I was glad to have her take over that role, to hold my authority in tension with her bringing back onto center stage minds that were feeling marginal to rules.

I was puzzled by the paper, though. I wanted her to treat it as a draft, to bring it to a point that would pull its circular structure together for a reader, make it go someplace in a line of thought. As it was written, I—as a reader—looked from one story to another, feeling I was sinking into each with no life line to draw me out of the water. But Pia and I absolutely missed each other's signals about the purpose of this "draft." I began showing her ways she could revise; she seemed surprised and hurt that I would even imagine this gift to us all might be changed.

Long after the course was finished the whole scene cleared up for me and I wanted to call her back to add my own voice of appreciation to those of her classmates for what she had accomplished.

Here is what I finally figured out. Pia was not trying to write a paper; she was writing, creating, and designing a class mood or tone, using the paper only as a prompt for her gathering. She was an artist, and it was as a piece of art that she wanted to structure that class. (I think now of Judy Chicago's *Dinner Party*, with plates of china set around a table, each representing one memorable woman in history.) What I wanted was sharpening, a point. What Pia wanted was a gathering. I would have liked a spiral gathering, reaching up. She gave us a ouroboros, a snake eating its own tail, all on one level, beginning where it ended (after many digressions), going nowhere.

She had meant to design the paper/class that way, for her whole point was restitution—a return to beginnings. It is a spatialized kind of writing, a painterly one, and if it is to communicate to the reader any kind of movement, it is apt to do that not through the controlling ideas of predicates or verbs that move things along briskly by building on what has gone before, but through the superimposing of one scene on another, slightly phased, almost like the cubistic experiments with changing perspectives on a flat surface: here it was chemists beside artists besides feminists, all vaguely, or perhaps it might be said, paratactically, connected to each other in being illustrative of a new/old consciousness. Pia had come into this class, she once wrote, with the hopes that she might "focus on the images so that I can see them in words." In a sense it was a move out of silence into a voice, and her paper was a record of that transition.

That transition spoke, I think now, not only of the artist's culture she was a part of, but a culture of mothers too. Though the single-minded might have trouble knowing how to read Pia (William seemed to be able to handle only one role at a time when faced with this multiform goddess), she grounded herself and much of her summer writing in thoughts about childbirth and creation myths: pregnancy, labor ("like waves in a seastorm"), birth ("order re-established"), Mexican goddesses and feathered serpents, DNA and—in the next breath—woman in transition, "giving birth to herself" by synthesizing "ancient civilization and the future." Heady. Not what the University of Maryland had in mind for this course. But certainly situating itself in an identity related to what Julia Kristeva calls "women's time": a feminist identity "exploded, plural, fluid," spatialized, outside linear time but rejoining "the archaic (mythical) memory and . . . the cyclical or monumental temporality of marginal movements" ("Women's Time" 19–20). These were Pia's times, with which she was beginning to break her silence.

There were marks too, in the restitution paper, of a centuries-old Spanish culture that values digression (Kaplan 12) and a less businesslike pace than the pragmatic North American let's-get-on-with-it. But the way that paper played out its spatialized, cyclical time seems most interesting: its wholehearted embrace of, and moving into, little whirlpools of thoughts with the interests of all those students in the class. Theodor Schwenk writes of how much thinking is like the flow of air and water currents: "The activity of thinking is essentially an expression of flowing movement"; but then he warns that the ability to coordinate streams of thought and the forms congealing in them can sometimes be interrupted by digression—the creating of "'whirlpools'" (96). I have been recommending that writers urge themselves to move into the whirlpools so that they can tangle with other minds and then bring the minds into their papers with them. Pia went gladly into the whirlpools, but never gathered them sharply into *her* line of thought. She gave herself over to each one, fluently, fluidly, bringing each one her dream. But when she came up for air she skipped right by any solid or earth-like resistance (no struggling with the words in the text, how their meanings relate to each other) and went straight for the airy regions where thought moves far and fast in the big sweeps of monumental time, "space-time," Kristeva calls it, "in infinite expansion" ("Women's Time" 17). For Pia it was an explosion everywhere into a new age.

She was superimposing many scenes on each other in this paper and in those of the whole summer's writing, looking through them, as if they were translucent, and this was her strength. It was a kind of dream time that let what "solid" logic would call "incongruities" live together. Solid (Aristotelian) logic says something cannot be itself and something else; Pia's logic that looked right through one thing to another (DNA to ancient myths, for instance) said it could.

But we writing teachers will want to acknowledge that most readers in the larger culture our students will be writing in will expect lines of thoughts to be clear; readers need these cues and have a hard time reading without them. Realizing this, I began digging even further into lines. The way Pia bypassed them made me think that the differences between reading rhythms and writing ones bear marks of the way gender roles are often traditionally conceived: men live in the world of public struggle, so the story goes, where they need to make their mark against resistances that are often material (and material resistance can slow minds down, we might add, the daily conflicts destroy any sense of synchronized rhythms). Theirs is the blade culture, the one we see through big phallic styluses like the Washington Monument, set firmly on the ground, reaching upward to the sun that has always been a male god, a symbol of the daylight, public world in which men make their mark. It is a very writer-like culture, inscribing its rules and laws against resistance.

Women's lives, so the other half of the story might go, are more hidden from public view, more reflective of the public life of men. (Think of political wives, the Nancy Reagans with strong voices; those who do not stay in their off-center spots, reflecting ideas of their husbands, sometimes draw down the wrath of Zeus on themselves.) Women's lives are more like the moon that has often been associated with goddesses, a reflected light that can at least, so it has been said, give them a little illumination for their worlds hidden from public view. Their roles are more reader-like than those of men: They need to read or see their own needs through the eyes of what others have written or decreed. And although we might claim nowadays that readers are after all active participants in making meaning, there is still a sense in which they take in as opposed to a writer's sending out; they open their mental borders to writers, drawing in before they move back out to negotiate meaning. Their mental movements need to be quick ones, gatherings of many strands of thought, many scenes, into a contrapuntal response that can follow a writer's line of thought. Women are intuitive, we hear, able to put themselves in the minds of others ("yes," we might answer, though intuition is simply very speedy thought). Women, it might be said then, have a more reader-like culture than men do.

This dualistic picture, though not without value as a starting point for discussion, of course has flaws. Its usefulness is that it captures an important part of a big picture without considering subtleties, and that looking at a few more subtleties of an individual case—Pia's—might show us just where the picture could be changed.

Pia wrote her paper the way a woman-mother might, like a reader gathering up the strands of thought without ever drawing them into a sharp, inscribing kind of linear time, no single line of thought hooked to another. (She had not the male, linear kind of birth consciousness in which Adam begets Cain begets Enoch, and so forth.) She had the beginning and the end, the mouth eating the tail, but no middle progressing up the mountain through rough earth-like terrain. This seemed almost like a woman's version of single parenting—large, expansively generous, supporting, but not caught up in the world's business. There was no line drawing the two-dimensional circle up into a three-dimensional spiral, no father interrupting the mother-child unity. She should have been able to incorporate enough patriarchal conventions, I might have concluded, to fit in the big culture she would have to write in some day.

But when I realized that Pia was designing the class mood with her new voice as much as she was writing or designing words on that piece of paper, I decided I had been looking in the wrong place for all these coherences and lines of thought. Her object was to "restitute" the enthusiasm with which her classmates had begun the summer session. Once I saw the way she was trying to do that, the paper and even some of the interactions in class looked different to me. One story she had told me and one comment she wrote about twilight gave the clues that helped me rethink what she was about.

Pia had given birth to one of her children alone, in her home, and after feeling frightened initially when neither her midwife nor husband could be found quickly enough for this unexpectedly quick labor, she had found a deep satisfaction in the delivery she was able to handle successfully alone. And there it was, I thought when she told me about her experience, this unusual, fascinating, many-sided woman doing things independently, able even to give birth self-sufficiently.

But she had *not* conceived the child self-sufficiently, nor could it be said that she withdrew by choice from relationships, so I had to give up at least a good deal of my picture of her self-sufficiency. Rather she had had in that self-tended delivery what many women nowadays do not have, an absolutely essential need to put herself in partnership with the life rhythms of her body and those of her child—invisible ones, out of her control, but ones she became so attuned to that long afterward she was still full of wonder at the process. There were no other partners around for her to depend on. I realized finally, in thinking about women and receptivity in this context, that a birth "arranged" with such a partner is a powerful model for the side of the reading-writing partnership often missing from academic discussions: Writers need to gather the discordant rhythms of readers into a figuring or reading of the whole, superimposing them on their own struggles with words, for the purpose of creating coherence or ensemble in the writing. Both unity with reading rhythms *and* separation from them (during self-absorbed struggle) can then take place, each in its proper human time.

There is, of course, a missing time line that moves the whole affair *through* struggles into new histories and contents, new discordances to be grappled with. Pia knew how to grapple with material forces but not how to bring those struggles through irreversible time toward a point. Her time was human, but only repetitively human, birth over and over without an allowance for discordant differences that cannot so fluidly be banished. She was a reading kind of writer, reading fast, pulling things together with intuitive ease because nothing ever went so far that it could not be restituted, brought back to new beginnings where rhythms from other worlds already written can guide action when superimposed on one's own. Though incomplete, the vision allows an important kind of light into the reading-writing circuit.

Though the rhythms are of course strongly sensed in childbirth, there are rhythms everywhere to be sensed, large ones, small, biological, linguistic, musical, seasonal, diurnal: Once attuned to, life rhythms are one of the best resources for writers, because they can be sensed in their overlappings and orchestrated into breathing, thinking, writing, reading, talking, moving. Scollon claims that learning to learn (what I am calling double-loop learning) is not only embedded in interactional dilemmas born of contradictory needs (needs of participants both for bonding with the other's concerns and for remaining free of them), but grounded too in tempo, in an ensemble that "holds participants together in mutual attention to the ongoing situation" (344). Tempo is the means speakers use to negotiate, he says (340). Writers, I would add, create ensemble with readers by drawing reading tempos into their writing ones, creating a rhythmic environment that lets readers stay with the messages and concerns of writers. The more ensemble is created, the more chances both writers and readers have for double-loop learning. Learning to sense the rhythms inherent in everyday activities can help.

Pia wrote about sensing a child's separation from its mother as like twilight "when both the moon and the sun are still in the sky." It does not matter, I think, whether this image of changing half-light and betweenness came to her during the event or in reflection. She herself seemed comfortable in a kind of thinking world that values metamorphoses at such points of betweenness: flexible identity, changing boundaries, dream time mixed with conscious time, and especially a kind of living in what Rothenberg calls "homospatial thinking," superimposing many images over each other in a single creative space (69). Pia took a hand in writing a class vision out of many kinds of people—making a mark on the behavior of the whole. To do that she needed to read those others well, to make figures of each one and superimpose them in her vision.

Though I cannot go so far as to say the class was finally a work of art, there was an energy in it that she helped create and felt responsible to keep an eye on. Especially did she tune into the way discussions moved when any of the other Hispanics were involved. She echoed them in class as she had in her paper, giving a kind of dream-like or dream-time support, a little hazy, not always "there." I think she *was* there, though, but there to help some others to shine, like a reflecting mother, and the scene she sensed was always plural. I scarcely noticed the subtle support she gave Gustavo, for instance, until much later. *He* was the one in the public eye; *she* saw to it that people understood him, then after her work was done, let others take over in supporting him. To this day I believe she sensed that he could provide the missing half of her vision.

Gustavo's lines of thought

Here is the sequence of events. In the first week of class, I asked people to write for five minutes in answer to the question "Who Am I?" Gustavo did not need five minutes: "I am a foreigner," he wrote. "That is the only English word that fits me."

He was an Argentinian, tall, studious, proud, polemical with me, shy in a large classroom. The day after the five-minute writing he came to see me after class, concerned with our in-class discussion about the differences between writing for readers and writing for oneself. He complained that he would lose what he wanted to say if he could not either choose his own reader or just imagine himself as reading his own writing. "They" (presumably teachers) always want "clear writing," he said. This demand felt to him like a restraint on any pleasure he could feel in writing. I was not unsympathetic; certainly it seemed reasonable that one could feel pulled off-course by turning attention away from one's subject matter. But Gustavo's complaint seemed stronger than most others I had heard. He was adamant about not wanting to be burdened with imagining himself being heard or read by those who might not understand him.

Gustavo might well have agreed with my silent thought that his reticence was related to his unwillingness to negotiate with the cultural values of his classmates and me. But I doubt that he would have agreed with my sense that fear of losing his own identity and culture in those middle-class values was also a motivating factor: he thought of himself as a revolutionary thinker but lived a comfortable life with his family in Maryland, a hard enough combination to juggle without adding any comfort that might develop with American classmates. He set himself up on another day to simply ignore their ideas: "I don't mind the class reading [my] papers," he said. "I think they would make a lot of comments but I most probably would disregard the vast majority of them. . . . I do not accept their style so I would not accept changes that would assimilate my writing to their style." How different a kind of thinking from Pia's. She read people, spread her mind out to enter their thoughts; he skipped the stage of reading others, wishing only to write his single-minded line of thought.

Gustavo readily recognized himself as an isolate among his classmates. The Xeroxed page he brought in was from "Thus Spake Zarathustra" in *The Portable Nietzsche*, and he had underlined "Whoever does not believe himself always lies." So unsteady on his cultural and psychological feet, I thought, that he can only chance self-readings, and even those are not to be trusted very much. He did indeed see himself as a Zarathustra "despising man. . . . I hate the world because I cannot change it." I was not sure, at that point, how to read him, how seriously to take his separatist stance. I was sure, though, that he was uncomfortable with most of his classmates.

Nevertheless he came into my office for long debates about anything I was willing to talk about: politics, writing, society, people. I found his ideas sharp and stimulating, but his writing obscure, with gaps between sweeping generalities that raised questions he never answered. Often those questions were simply about when and where these abstract ideas were to be implanted; only under pressure would he orient his topic of subversion, for instance in names of real nations. The reticence was extreme, and had to be that of a person, I figured, who plainly did not want to communicate with people he was sure would not understand. Us.

But class trust was increasing among most people in the early weeks, and though he certainly did not hint at greater comfort, I suspected Gustavo was learning to trust readers a little. Journals were being exchanged and the three other Latins were openly supportive of Gustavo's challenging entries, and Pia talked often with him during breaks. Others seemed also to say "I understand" to such statements as "Just because Time magazine says it is so it isn't true." Our talks in my office, though still full of his protest against things I would say, began concentrating on my thoughts about what would make the papers understandable to American readers. "In Argentina they would understand these political matters; here they are so ignorant of them."

The topic afoot on one particular day was the U.S. presence in Latin America. The draft of his evaluation paper that I was looking at in my office was nearly unintelligible to me, but I urged him to let the class work with it, because I knew he had supposed this one to be prepared for readers. My problem was that I could not understand how it fit not only with readers, but with his mumbling something about having listened to an evangelical sermon the Sunday morning he wrote it. I hoped the class could help. I had spent some time urging everyone to see that no writing could be powerful that did not allow its own gaps and inconsistencies to surface in questions readers might ask about it. Only when a writer hears or imagines those questions, I had claimed, will she be able to pause at problem spots, back off, go jog a little, and see if conflicts *or* connections come to mind. Questions are wonderful because once asked, answers are nearly always just behind.

Gustavo's paper did not show any signs that he had imagined readers' questions. At least I could not find those signs. Instead it split into two seemingly unrelated (or only slightly related) parts, the introduction about capital punishment, the rest about the U.S. presence in Latin America. Between the two parts was a semantic chasm. The class tried to stumble through the beginning.

> What is the purpose of capital punishment? More than just a punishment for a murder or other heinous crime, it is a preventive measure. Probable criminals are not only deterred but also punished criminals will never act again. This argument would become inexorable if, by a historical peculiarity, prisons did not exist. It would only serve justice to execute a murderer so as to prevent more atrocities, especially if the villain has a history of reprehensible crimes. Furthermore, if by another historical quirk, these criminals could not be brought to justice, would not the people have the right and obligation to protect themselves and their society from such a perpetrator? Would John Wayne not right this wrong?

I knew Gustavo did not believe any of this, nor could I understand before this day what it had to do with his having listened to that evangelical sermon.

Suddenly during the increasingly heated discussion in class I realized what he was trying to do. The second paragraph began with "Such an injustice occurs in Latin America. For almost one hundred years an organized band of criminals unprovokedly has murdered thousands of innocent people: The United States Armed forces and it covert partner, the CIA." What Gustavo had done was create an introduction for the most difficult reader he could imagine: an American, right-wing, evangelical believer in capital punishment, whom he assumed would become warmed up by what I now realized was supposed to be an imitation of sermonic style, including pointed questioning by the minister. The fact that William was an evangelical Christian as well as one of our most vocal students probably influenced him, but unfortunately, William read Gustavo's paper as "a piece of propaganda," himself not capitulating to what we were all beginning to realize was the "real" argument against the U.S. that concluded, "But just as John Wayne, the people [in Latin America] have begun to take action against these murderers. More and more they are being brought to justice."

Gustavo was making his case to those he supposed not able to understand or read him well, and therefore the case resembled the revolutionary attack he believed necessary to create change. I was convinced, too, that he was ironically feeding us John Wayne to appeal to our love of actors or entertainers in high positions.

The surprise, to me anyway, was not the shock but the seriousness with which the class took in his argument (two sources for statistics were even given in the paper), and the passion and concern with which the electric exchange took place. No one attacked Gustavo; even the comment about "propaganda" was couched in careful terms. Most students tried to help him find a more effective way to say what he needed to say; someone suggested, for instance, "Substitute a name—Roosevelt—for 'Americans' in that paragraph about the Marines in 1936, so you're not including all of us. Then we can listen better." One student, disbelieving (it was 1985), said his country would not do those things; other convinced him it might.

Pia gave an impassioned plea for better understanding of Latin American problems and seemed to speak for Gustavo, who said almost nothing during the debate. It was long and earnest. People did not want to stop talking about the paper. Gustavo's penchant for titles was lost on no one: "The Name for our Profits is Democracy," he had written, and Pia wanted the class to know that "profits" could be played with as "prophets." Then a new debate started about American prophets "teaching" other nations political right from wrong.

She was there, understanding him and pleading his case articulately. I cannot tell if he might have begun to trust their interest without her, but I believe the debate she fueled played some part in his throwing out this draft for his evaluation paper and writing another, called "Ignorance is a Thin Veil for Apathy." Its arguments were now nearly *all* documented or personally supported, and it even contained a quotation from one of his old professors in Baltimore. It is the answer he was too shy or perhaps too unprepared to give on the day of the debate, but others had in some ways given the gist of it to him by raising the questions he answered. I quote here over a page of it in order to show the control he was able to develop after that contact had been made and he had heard questions he knew these people really wanted answers to.

> There is a saying in Latin America that every person in the world should vote in American elections, everyone except Americans. Most Latin Americans believe that Americans, as proud as they are of the power of their nation, are ignorant or misinformed about Latin America and the actions of the American government in the region. My personal experience in the United States has, unfortunately, not disproved this belief.
>
> As a college student in America, I have, on several occasions, brought to the attention of American students shocking and terrible acts committed by the American government. The few that pay any attention argue that they did not know about this and that their ignorance acquits them from responsibility of their government's actions. They are wrong. Ignorance does not absolve them.
>
> In America, people have the right to be informed. The First Amendment guarantees this right. Furthermore, the Freedom of Information Act and similar legislation have restated the right of the American people to know the activities of their government. In addition, hundreds of groups and organizations constantly monitor and publicize the activities of the government. Specifically, college students have vast and accessible sources of information. The libraries, courses and professors in American universities can provide anyone who is interested with information on any subject. Yet, American students choose not to know.
>
> As studies have shown, American college students are significantly less aware of the rest of the world than their European counterparts. Most, one study showed, do not have a reasonable knowledge of world geography. This lack of interest towards the rest of the world is also evidenced in the decline in the enrollment in social and political science courses. This decline has led many universities to require students to take courses in these areas. Doctor Augustus, Professor of History at the University of Mary-

land, noted "students today are only interested in what affects them directly. They are not interested in learning about other countries or other times."

As in most countries, ignorance is not an excuse in the eyes of the law. If a person unknowingly commits or aids a crime, he is at least partly responsible for that crime. For example, if a person carries alcoholic beverages over the state line, he can be arrested and prosecuted, even if he did not know that this is a crime. Every year, many people unknowingly commit this crime. Even though the few that are caught seldom are punished, most are found guilty. Similarly, if the American government commits a crime, the American people are responsible. It is their duty as human beings and citizens to be informed. . . .

In a democratic society, the people choose the leaders that will represent them. If these leaders act unethically or immorally, it is a reflection upon all citizens . . . If Americans allow their leaders to act wrongly, they cannot consider themselves moral and just persons.

Gustavo's response is by no means a sudden friendly merging with the class's ethos, but it is no longer a withdrawal. Rather he is moving forcefully toward classmates, negotiating with them and their beliefs with a pattern of answers to their questions. The draft the class had first worked on had failed to make a coherent turn from American sermon to Latin plea, and had failed, even, to reflect an accurate reading of most of these students. But when no one in the class retreated from hearing this foreign voice in its midst, when they all searched for ways to make sense of it, and when Gustavo could watch Pia imitate his voice with added passion, he was able, I think, to turn toward them full face. She would have called it restitution, a return to an original order of understanding.

He left at the end of summer believing he had not really negotiated with classmates because they represented the colonizers and negotiation could only take place between equals. I tried convincing him that formal networks of negotiation are often not nearly so effective as informal ones—even in large institutions—and that he had been, after all, practicing well the art of making interactional moves. He was still practicing those moves in a letter I recently received from him, asking me if I would write him a letter of recommendation, telling me about an Argentine novelist he liked, about his travels back home, and about feeling "the need to support this last statement with several concrete examples." I still did not know exactly how to read him: a little joke here, a little seriousness there, and then his still-present cultural split that created, he said, "a schizophrenic fog that pervades my whole existence." It did not yet seem possible to know whether he was serious about things or putting me on. Then he ended with a postscript: "Forgive me, but I did not know which was the correct tone for this type of letter so I used them all." Indeed he had used them all, practicing the kind of superimposition of identities that Pia would probably have appreciated.

Silent partners

Pia I would like to have lunch with once a week for a year to talk about ways women and people who feel silent might use their heightened sense of rhythmic interactions to negotiate readings fearlessly and write with lines of thought that incarnate strength of vision. Women have often seen themselves (or been seen) on the sidelines, cheering on the texts at the center, looking good and sounding good as echoes for those centers. Mary. Pia. Deborah Cameron writes in *Feminism and Linguistic Theory* that "women communicate adequately with each other but are institutionally constrained/negatively judged in the public (male) arena" (108). Instead of trying to insert themselves in a preexisting linguistic order of fixed meanings (as French psychoanalyst Jacques Lacan, for instance, assumes necessary for language acquisition [Cameron, 124]), they might better use those resources they have already developed *away* from public discourse to enter it, she believes. Then they will learn to create "meaning in specific contexts, negotiating where necessary in order to achieve as fully as possible their communicational aims" (140).

But the split is not so neatly genderized as this very often, any more than readers can be so neatly separated from writers. Some of my most chilling conversational encounters have come with women executives who guard their linguistic categories fiercely (thoroughly converted to patriarchal habits, some would say), while some of the most enabling have been with men who understand feminist thought patterns as well as or better than I. Better than thinking in terms of sides is thinking in terms of the questions that are apt to arise at the margins between those sides, there where meaning often feels muddled and a faint stir in the solar plexus says do not cross these borders. Authority probably lurks there in an "of-course" attitude, and it is not only women who benefit from challenging that authority and speaking up from old positions of silent partner-hood. As Hélène Cixous says,

> There is not a soul who dares to make an advance in thought, into the as-yet-unthought, without shuddering at the idea that he is under the surveillance of the ancestors, the grandfathers, the ty-rants of the concept, without thinking that there behind your back is always the famous Name-of-the-Father, who knows whether or not you're writing whatever it is you have to write without any spelling mistakes. ("Castration" 51)

To the bodies of rules we all feel behind our backs I turn now, and to ways we might turn *them* from tyrants into silent partners.

8

Grammar, Style, and Politics

Teaching "formal grammar": the controversy

Students of composition who find grammar a less-than-stimulating body of rules might be puzzled if they could hear the passionate tones with which its place in their classrooms is sometimes argued; we teachers so seldom seem neutral about whether or not we should teach them rules of grammar. After Patrick Hartwell argued against such teaching in the pages of *College English*, for instance, the "Comment and Response" sections of later issues brought readers a lively debate, one that had actually begun with the publication in 1963 of the famous Braddock, Lloyd-Jones, and Schoer report and its famous conclusion: "the teaching of formal grammar has a negligible or, because it usually displaces some instruction and practice in composition, even a harmful effect on improvement in writing" (37–38).

Hartwell himself claims in his article that the grammar issue had been settled for him by that conclusion. Having followed arguments over the years both for and against, he decides that those against the teaching of grammar have a model of literacy that "predicts a rich and complex interaction of learner and environment," one that he implies is more interesting than the one used by the defenders of grammar teaching. Those defenders "tend to have a model of composition instruction that is rigidly skills-centered and rigidly sequential: the formal teaching of grammar, as the first step in that sequence, is the cornerstone or linchpin" ("Grammar" 108). Given these loaded terms, the either/or choices, and the rather patronizing tone with which he dismisses both dependence on experimental research (positivistic) and the "worship of formal grammar study," it is not surprising that his article drew forth protests. I for one would not want my interest in the study of language and its forms to be caught in his dichotomies.

Hartwell's major strategy is to divide grammar into five categories: (1) unconscious patterns familiar to all native speakers, (2) linguistic description of those patterns, (3) linguistic etiquette, (4) school grammar, and (5) style, and to claim that the second, third, and fourth—as bottom-up strategies—will not help native-speaker writers access the unconscious knowledge of the first category or master the complex codes of print. The solution then? With some guidance in rhetorical matters (contexts, purposes, discourse procedures) and metalinguistic ones (the stylistic concerns—"surface form"—of the fifth category), writers can access unconscious codes, practice written ones, and, therefore, have power kept properly in their own hands instead of in the hands of those who dispense rules of grammar.

Objections to Hartwell's categorical dismissal of "formal rules" ranged from mild to intense: Joe Williams urges development of a different kind of grammar *"dedicated to teaching style"* (642–643); Richard Cureton claims that students do after all need a way to talk about structure, form, and function (643); Carole Moses pleads for more "imaginative ways to approach grammatical instruction" (647). By the time Martha Kolln registers regret that since 1963, writing teachers have mistakenly thought teaching grammar to be "harmful," the controversy heats up: she complains that Hartwell has misrepresented her published position toward grammar (she wants it used rhetorically; he has claimed she wants formal grammar centralized in the classroom); he bypasses some of her direct confrontations to claim she is "flat out wrong" to believe we have "a generation (or more) of students who have no language for discussing their language" ("Response" 876).

A close look at the way Hartwell uses some of his other sources produces the suspicion that he may be setting up some straw men (and women) to fit his dichotomy: Metalinguistic awareness is acceptable and congruent with a nonrigid classroom; "formal grammar" (a monolithic, untransformable pairing of terms in his hands) is not, and seems to be equivalent to "learning about language in isolation" ("Grammar" 125). The first group, he thinks, leaves power in student hands; the second takes it away and sets up

an authoritarian mix of structural and usage-oriented "incanta-
tions" to rule classes in old and unenlightened ways. The similarity
between ruling students' minds with grammatical categories and
ruling other scholars' subtle positions with one's own stereotypes of
those positions seems to escape his notice.

For instance, Hartwell uses material from an article by Robert J.
Bracewell to support his own claim that "we need to redefine error
. . . as a problem of metacognition and metalinguistic awareness, a
matter of accessing knowledges that, to be of any use, learners must
have already internalized by means of exposure to the code"
("Grammar" 121). No problem here, at least on the surface. Bracewell does certainly see a difficulty in transferring internalized codes
to written products, and although he does not use the word "metalinguistic" (as Hartwell does in intimating that he is following
Bracewell's "insight"), it is probably fair to connect Bracewell's talk
of "conscious awareness of language form" (Bracewell 418) with
metalanguage. He does, after all, use "metacognitive" to refer to a
conscious employment of particular cognitive skills (as opposed to
simply using them without conscious intent), and claims that metacognitive activity is an "executive processing that is guided by
executive schemes" (401). In an effort to support Hartwell's implicit
attribution of the word "metalinguistic" to Bracewell, then, one
could understand Bracewell to be implying that consciousness
about one's cognition and one's language could be understood as
"meta" matters, though certainly separate from each other.

Hartwell, however, not only blurs any distinction between "metacognition" and "metalinguistic awareness" that Bracewell may have
in mind (no definitions in Hartwell's article), but ignores a crucial,
subtle difference Bracewell finds between experiences of reading
and writing, a difference that surely raises questions about Hartwell's own favoring of print codes being mastered "top down, from
pragmatic questions of voice, tone, audience register, and rhetorical
strategy, not from the bottom up, from grammar to usage to fixed
forms of organization" ("Grammar" 123). Bracewell stresses that
preteen readers are quite able to master print codes through their
reading, but that this mastery is itself a roadblock to their writing,
once they realize that a gap exists between their own writing technique and that of more skilled writers. Any metacognitive skills
they may develop for purposes of writing, he claims, have been

shown *not* to be strong enough to bring the syntactic ones along with them. Reading ability seems to hinder production: young writers have trouble bridging that gap between their developed processes of reading and undeveloped ones of writing. Bracewell hopes that students might learn to "gain deliberate [metacognitive] control" over language form skills (419), but "it remains to be seen whether . . . language form at the sentence level" can be thus controlled.

In other words, though students need to gain conscious access to their tacit knowledge of syntactic form (and surely Hartwell cannot deny that such matters are "metalinguistic," a term associated by others with use of both grammatical terms [Frank Smith 55] and linguistic codes or glosses [Jakobson 356]), that access is not easily gained simply through metacognitive skills. The reader is left wondering, at the very least, about how Hartwell believes students can gain "mastery of written language" ("Grammar" 123). Top-down metalinguistics can surely just as easily be bottom-up grammar, but the one will do and the other won't.

Why does it matter? Hartwell's 1985 article is still talked about among composition teachers, and Bracewell's differently and more clearly reasoned one is less well known. (I am not claiming agreement with Bracewell's tenets, only interest in and concern with the results of the studies he discusses.) Moreover the associations Hartwell creates between teachers who bring talk of grammar to their classes and teachers who dispense rules in authoritarian ways are pernicious, creating the impression that his grammars 1 through 5 are neatly separated from each other, and that those who do not restrain their grammatical doings to something in the area of grammar 5 (perhaps psycholinguistically tinged, it is hinted) have not done their homework in either metacognitive affairs or the humane treatment of students.

The Braddock report did create powerful negative waves against grammar in the profession, but as Kolln points out in an earlier article, those waves may have caused a premature shutdown of interest in ways students might access matters of structure in their language ("Closing the Books" 139–148). Many repercussions have been felt nationwide as a result of the report; I know of at least one large school district that has until recently at least implicitly discouraged its teachers from dealing with the subject of grammar in

English classes. (Its stance, I admit, has multiple causes.) I am sorry that more of my students cannot at least find the subjects and verbs in their sentences (especially when so many of those sentences cry out for a reader-writer dialogue needing a common vocabulary), and I can only wonder that Hartwell's students do not have any of the problems mine do in lacking a language to discuss their language.

Hartwell's belief that mastery of language use needs to be embedded in pragmatic questions of context is my belief too. His desire that teachers not monopolize center stage in classrooms is also mine. But his confusing and allergic handling of "grammar" cordons it off from teachers' attention in an either/or, value-ridden way, preventing the possibility that doubling and superimposing talk of forms and syntactic images and rhythms on each other and on student writing might help students know and feel the language of their work in their bones. Banishing talk of grammar is not the way to defuse its position of authority in minds that rebel against it; Sennett shows us that rebels are still in thrall to and fearful of who or what they rebel against. Giving grammar a voice now and then in our classes as an interactive force rather than an authoritative one lets it be understood always to be dwelling *anyway* as a silent partner in everything we say or write.

Metacognition, context, and cultures

Although Bracewell's orientation, too, seems to me restrictive in its cognitive assumptions, his point, divergent from Hartwell's, is an interesting gateway into issues of language and form. First, a clarification: Issues of metacognition are contextual ones, requiring learners to access whatever they are learning to deal with (a text, for instance) from its context: questions about what, when, why, or how it is important (Smith-Burke 230). Most psycholinguists see context as internalized within individuals, writing as solitary, and its language as noninteractive (as an educational psychologist, Bracewell shares this view). Many anthropologists, on the other hand (and those influenced by them), describe contexts of language use as highly interactive, whether involving internal voices or those in actual social situations. Bateson sees minds' shifts from text to context as throwing "unexamined premises open to question and change" (*Steps* 303), Argyris and Schön, as creating double-loop learning.

We can look again, then, at the writing problems Bracewell discusses, with hopes that if writers might understand rhetorical context in a more interactive and dynamic way than do those who imagine it as metacognition inside a head, they might find it a useful start after all in bridging the gap between reading and writing skills. The study from which Bracewell drew some of his conclusions involved a group of eleven-year-olds, who, as they began to notice their own writing in the context of their improved ability to read, became increasingly aware "of the significance of technique" (419). Better reading caused them to sense their own discursive and syntactic shortcomings, begin to notice their inability to produce readable writing. Their confidence in themselves as writers dropped, they could not see the *relationship* between themselves as agents and the context in which they wrote, and they could not see through the reading to the writing. We can conclude that these activities were opaque to each other, and that rather than an interacting system, they sensed a mutually exclusive, either/or pair, one side (reading) ruling the other (writing) and weakening it. Their ability to contextualize their writing in terms of their reading (in an unequal, irreversible way, though) was throwing them off, and thus began their own desire to minimize writing activities during their school years.

If we put this problem in a less cognitive and individual context and extend it beyond the eleven-year-old age group, we can take the individual writer out of a problem created between cognitive and metacognitive levels of her mind and put her in one that might be addressed culturally and interactionally. Because (as Bracewell notes and I myself have experienced) the same problem of alienation from their own work occurs when ten-year-olds work in the visual arts, the problem seems apt to have relational and political overtones, to say the least (as has been noticed by at least one art educator [Lewin xiv]). Might students not sense cultural values being placed on mistake-free reproduction of sameness, of a valued "original," rather than on partnered reproduction of sameness with differences? Schools do, after all, as a whole usually value correctness rather than agency, and classmates under such conditions become highly competitive and critical of deviation from norms.

Rather than being mostly a matter of translating tacit language codes to metacognitive control, as Bracewell suggests, the difficulty in coordinating reading skills with writing ones might then be understood in wider terms as one that begins in social and cultural contextualizing, in students accessing themselves as agents into the larger cultural systems of which they are a part. This suggestion has been made by Linda Shaw Finlay and Valerie Faith in an article describing their classroom experience with a group of twenty-seven upper-middle-class college students, most having what other teachers had called "linguistic inadequacies" (64).

Makers of culture

Finlay and Faith found that these students not only deeply distrusted the way language is used in schools ("they both acknowledged and denied its power" [71]), but resented the need to attend school in order to achieve success in a society they also distrusted. They valued "body language" (hitting, touching) and their private lives, and believed they had some control over these as contrasted to their school lives. They reacted in anger to any suggestion from their teachers that knowledge about the public, distrusted world of institutions is created not on the basis of an objective reading of truth, but by people on the basis of their interests and values. Yet these students did not believe themselves connected to the "objective" language of that knowledge, and "were often literally unable to understand each other or [the teachers] because they responded to words not in terms of their common meanings, but as stimuli that triggered a chain of emotional associations" (73).

A breakthrough in their control over their own language came, say the authors, when students began to realize their own part in sustaining the system they distrusted and to understand their attitudes as making them "complicit in what they perceived as their personal destruction" (75). As they began to talk about their alienation, their attitude toward language and writing shifted to a less alienated one. But at the same time Finlay and Faith noticed that

> students habitually discussed their ideas in the passive voice, bring-
> ing themselves into the grammatical position of the object ("It has

been demonstrated to me," rather than "I learned"; "It has been noted to me," instead of "I saw.") They did not fully perceive themselves as subjects, either in the grammatical way or in the way that Freire uses the term, as free human beings who are capable of taking action on their world, and their writing reflected this subconscious judgment. (79)

Further evidence of structure being a silent partner to students' judgments about themselves came in their frequent use of sentence fragments and run-ons, in both cases presenting a confusing relationship between subjects and predicates. Students "lacked the confidence," say the authors,

> that they were qualified, or allowed to make the judgments that active, declarative sentences required. So they didn't write them. Their *psychological grammar* was quite accurate. They did not believe it to be within their power to make judgments, statements, decisions, and to act on them. Before they could begin to find their own natural voices, they needed to see themselves as subjects, as knowers, as persons responsible for taking action in creating their world. (80)

Finlay and Faith believe that the problem is "attitudinal and cultural rather than mechanical and individual" (83). These students accurately perceived "the gulf between the use to which language is commonly put in our society and the ideal of language as a means of analysis, illumination, self-expression, and communication" (81).

I would want, like Finlay and Faith, to raise questions of attitude and culture with students whose words and ideas seemed divided from each other. I would want, too, to begin doubling talk of culture with its structural counterpart when papers are being looked at in a class. I would want to remember how difficult it can be to try to learn a new language as an adult without also learning something of its structure. Writing must surely seem a foreign or second language to our students (granted, the parallels cannot be infinitely extended); there is no need to deprive them of the possibility of more conscious and pleasurable control over its workings. We want to defuse some of the cultural intimidation of structural matters, then, rather than give structure (and not simply "surface" structure) up altogether simply because it has been used politically so badly in the past. We want students to understand that *people* make culture and knowledge, structure and usage "rules." As potential makers, students are at a distinct advantage with the language that participates in that making if they can become sensitive to the multiple ways it works.

Coming at sentence problems from many angles can boost confidence all around, but we need to keep in mind that (1) when eyes glass over at the mention of grammar (*rules* feared afoot), stories from students or teachers at the site of forbidden borders can make the borders feel more fluid, and energy and language flow more freely; and (2) the more conceptual and perceptual channels used, the more memorable and usable the material; and (3) the fewer basic concepts used, the more likely students *and* teachers will create and understand clear structural paths; and (4) the more structure talk becomes structure-in-motion or rhythm talk, the more likely the impression will be felt in the bones and translated into linguistic action; and finally (5) rhythm talk can be attuned to culture talk and to felt dissonances between reading and writing. Dissonances can be acknowledged and even dealt with as challenge and obstacle on the way to an experience of flow for both reader and writer.

Analog and digital communication

All five of these needs relate to the two larger ones alluded to in the last chapter: a reading of background material that gathers it into a wide focus and a writing with it in a narrow focus, incisively drawing it into lines of thought. This simultaneous broadening into fluid boundaries between lines of thought and narrowing into discrete points is an important ground on which to lay the teaching of structure in any writing class. Anthony Wilden calls such widening and narrowing "analog" and "digital" communication, claiming they act as context and text for each other. Simply put, digital communication is denotative language: it is the discrete, either/or, on/off, and yes/no, syntactic patterning that punctuates the connotative qualities of analog communication. The analog is the fuzzy, unnameable, both-and continuum of everyday experience, says Wilden, the source of meanings that can be known only through analogy because there are no clear-cut boundaries, only areas of more and less: emotions, relationships, "'gesture-language', posture, facial expression, inflection, sequence, rhythm, cadence, and indeed the CONTEXT within which human communication takes place, is a type of analog or iconic communication" (*System* 163).

Behind the digital codes of both oral and written language lie the analogic relations in which they are embedded, as syntax is in semantics, both parts of a single system. The mistake people make, thinks Wilden, is to believe that the either/or codes of digital communication which pervade educational systems are more basic than the analog meanings from which they are drawn. But though they require a different kind of reading from digital cues (analogs are imitative, iconic, and often multiply referenced rather than single and definite), analogic ones are just as communicative, alone or with digital cues, in the drawing of attention into figure from ground, for instance, or in dealing with "phenomena at the fringe of consciousness . . . in pattern recognition, in the context-interdependence involved in language translation" (*System* 157). To decide on how the widely focused analog meaning is to be narrowed into digital categories is a function of "those who have the power to punctuate" he claims, and "the punctuators tend both individually and collectively to be white, male, industrialized, affluent, and usually Protestant" (*System* 116).

Wilden's thinking is useful in the present context in that it opens the governed study of language onto other less rigidly coded life experiences, and especially to those often thought less worthy of scholarly study (more given to "women's interests"?) or else separable from the study of linguistic codings. In Wilden's explanation, the analogic, doubling, relational, imitative and iconic experiences of everyday life can be read and trusted, and *need* to be if we are ever to change cultural codes. Moreover, frequent reminders in writing classes that language is embedded in life experience can undercut the temptation to extend language's digital, yes/no, right/ wrong qualities into contexts of use, where they can so easily intimidate students' thinking. Everybody reads more than linguistic signs every day—pictures, eyes, gestures, movements, even building designs or classroom arrangements—and we read them through each other, unless that ability is squeezed out of us by years of hearing that we can only know what can be said. How many times have we said to students that they do not *really* know something if they cannot put it in words? Once I realized the implications of that statement, I stopped saying it. Any time all data are collected into airtight categories with nothing left over, either/or digitalization has taken over. Even some of the most worthy-sounding programs being instituted in English departments are guilty of this thirst for the finality of language's governance (and perhaps their own authority as its representative) that leaves no room to breathe. One description claims a curriculum that

> will involve showing how the fundamental language systems and codes of our culture *govern* [my italics] our structures of perception, values, exchanges, and practices, establishing for every man and woman the empirical order in which we live and interact. We hope, as well, that it will be fun for students. (Waller 9)

I hope so.

Reading and writing life worlds through structures and styles

Those writers—eleven years old or twenty—who have found that their writing does not measure up to their reading standards need to learn to read their own and others' texts from and through peopled contexts that overlap each other, analogically, imitatively, multiperspectively. Feeling tones, emotional nuances, the rhythms of language, breathing, interactions, imagery, body responses—writers can begin to trust their readings of a wide range of signs, the network of forces that embed and are embedded in their language and others' language. This way they get some control over and become part of the context, whether syntactic or cultural, because it can be "rightfully" experienced in a relational, both-and way, open to more ways to differ from it the better it is known and understood.

Because digital language forms grow out of the felt forces of syntax in motion, bringing those forms into a class cannot feel like a political clobbering if they are embedded in this both-and setting. The more analogies, the more rhythms and icons that can be integrated, the more memorable the structures-in-motion. The important task is to get the writer on the margin between the language and the context, reading the signs there of the meeting—the rhythms, the dissonances, the fears, the frustrations. If we encourage a kind of open focus that will take in as much as possible from both analog and digital sides, attention can learn to narrow in the context of widening.

The distancing of Vivian's world

These two kinds of focus or attention are exactly what one art educator has worked into a highly successful method of teaching both children and adults to draw, and the problems of alienation from the medium and lack of confidence she deals with are the very ones that Bracewell mentions showing up in preteen students in both artistic production and writing, and Finlay and Faith describe in their "linguistically inadequate" students. What Mona Brookes has been able to accomplish gives writing teachers a useful allegory for their own thinking about form and structure, an allegory that gives our heads just a little turn into a double of our own work.

But first we need to look at the problem that will lead into her work as a solution. When I was teaching art to preadolescents, hands were often thrown up in despair over inability to shape what those young artists knew they wanted to shape on paper. They had begun to read their own work in the context of those more professional than they: the illustrators of their books, for instance. Fifth grade was an especially difficult time, when those who had loved to paint the year before were giving it up for the challenges of social life in the art room—paint brushes, paste, papier mâché—all were finding their way across the room between boys and girls who were not yet sure whether to hit each other or smile invitingly.

Vivian stands out in my memory: restless, unhappy, often at odds with her two girlfriends, not yet rid of enough fourth-grade chubbiness to be sending challenging looks to boys, and above all (above all to me her art teacher) unable to make the grass look right under her flowers. She was a flower lover in her drawing, had been through the years I had known her, but her fourth-grade line of grass across the bottom of the paper was no longer satisfying her as a setting for the flowers, so she mostly sat at her round table and pouted or teased her friends, unwilling to explore new artistic avenues.

Vivian, like Finlay and Faith's students, had split one of her worlds off from another. She had grown out of her early childhood reliance on what Angiola Churchill calls "body feelings, tactile sensations, and a subjective relationship to space" (68) where flowers and self are all of a piece, together on a symbolic base line. Vivian was now looking at her flowers from the outside in, not willing to part with them, but no longer able to believe herself in the midst of them, part of their world. Distancing herself, she looked back in at those flowers and saw herself alienated from what seemed now, from the outside, a longed-for, yet separate (three-dimensionalized), and therefore uninteresting world she could no longer imagine cocreating.

Needing techniques to depict a world become foreign and assumed "objective," fifth-grade artists as well as college writers lack a bodily, rhythmic, participatory sense of their media and subject matter, so the media become stiff and ungraceful in their hands. As Churchill comments, "objectivity is controlling, often suppressing, the emotional response" (69).

For fifth graders, all this is occurring along with a need to suppress as well as acknowledge dangerous-feeling bodily changes that are associated with their social lives. For college students, there has often been a successful separation of those body feelings and social lives from the more public institutional lives they sense connected to linguistic media, from which they had learned to distance themselves ten years earlier.

The problem then is, as Finlay and Faith realize, that because habits of writing (or drawing) reveal habits of reading the self in the world, students who distance themselves from the guts of a written language perceived foreign to them will write as Vivian painted: with dissatisfaction and conviction that the finished product does not look right (or sound right to eyes and ears that can only see or hear in an uninvolved way). The surface problem *could* be seen as the cognitive one Bracewell mentions (students' inability to access codes learned in reading), but that problem needs to be set into a much wider and more political focus. Its roots, I think, can be found in an educational world that values a narrow, digitalized kind of reading and writing, reading as a correspondence between the reader's mind and the printed content, writing that is valued in a good/bad, right/wrong way as according with rules laid down by societal standards. What is missing is the wider focus of analogic context that would let "right" and "wrong" be understood in a reading of social and cultural connections. Whether it is a scientist's social context, a politician's image-creating one, or a student's psychological and cultural moorings, the world of analogic relations is not often considered a legitimate subject of inquiry in schools that value "reading" the printed page in isolation from its political, social and cultural matrix. And a writer or speaker's "style" is imagined to be simply the surface of his words, unconnected to his habits of thinking and behaving in the world.

Separating digital from analogic reading and writing has historical roots in matters of gender. Almost four hundred years ago, as Timothy Reiss points out (drawing on the work of Foucault), the telescope was adopted as a metaphor for the proper kind of distancing perception needed if man were to discover truth, a distancing that would replace thinking about the world through resemblance with thinking that analyzes the world. Francis Bacon wrote in *The Masculine Birth of Time* that legitimate scientific discourse is the son born in this new age from a marriage of nature (the woman) with a legitimizing father of discourse, who watches for errors of thinking and furnishes (in Reiss's words) "a suitable analytical method . . . that can 'dissect' nature and reveal the lawful order of the composition of things" (220).

The world of education, along with the Western scholarly world, has used that dissecting method ever since. Mona Brookes' grounding in the icons of the art world gives teachers of composition a different kind of method, a needed allegorical current that can run alongside the "analytical method." It has less interest in dissecting women and nature than does the one we are so used to. To Bacon's idea that the world is made of "alphabetical elements . . . 'filling out'. . . a kind of natural grammar" that teaches "right reading and a true writing of the (alphabetical) order of the world" (Reiss 210), Brookes brings a matrix that embeds the world of "elements" in a more enabling, less right/wrong environment.

Mona Brookes' solution

Here is the way Brookes solves the problem of loss of interest stemming from loss of partnership with the world, itself extending into inability to focus on techniques of media (the structures of writing or the shapes and patterns of visual art) because they are on the other, socially valued side of the border between the self and the authorities who use them.

First, granting that most children and adults have learned to listen to a silent critic within themselves about their being unable to draw, Brookes encourages descriptive talk about technique rather than judgmental, and values noticing of differences between one work and another instead of goods and bads. We teachers of composition have certainly learned this way of thinking, but have found it hard to practice when we must assign grades, and even when we try to embed writing problems in problems a *reader* might have with them rather than in old categories of right and wrong. Still, if we embed the talk in a consciously created relaxed atmosphere (as does Brookes, even using relaxing techniques), and find time to *value* reading problems as masking hidden stories, we encourage a wide and interactive focus to discussion of technique.

Second, Brookes uses as many experiential, sensory-oriented words as possible for her technical talk: profiles are "side views"; vertical lines, lines "standing up, for instance" (33). (We could find counterparts in several ways, as I will discuss in the next section, even including a little talk about ancient Greek verbs moving from the upright standing of present tense, to the leaning away from that position of past tenses.)

Third, Brookes does not believe that if students practice enough they will build technique; she gives them guidance in shaping their media. When I first taught art, coloring books were thought to be the devil's creation for little children because children should find their *own* lines. Though I have never been able to embrace the idea of coloring books, I think more and more that we can find nonoppressive and workable links between negotiable parts of either painting or drawing and less negotiable matters of structure. Brookes bases her work on students' "ability to recognize and draw . . . five elements of shape" (37): she *assumes*, in other words, that her students will make the transition between reading the shapes and "writing" them, and to that end, she makes what I see as analogs of their sensory worlds which they learn to use with increasingly subtle manipulations. They learn to find in those worlds dots, circles, straight lines, curved lines, and angle lines (37), and

Brookes claims (and illustrates) that as they bring these "elements of contour shape" into their seeing, their drawing becomes more perceptive, more skilled. "Students report that seeing the edges of everything in terms of these five elements of shape is the main thing that got them to relax and feel confident" (53).

I think we can make more concrete, more visual, more analogical, more elemental, and more easily remembered and usable, our talk about grammar. I think we can think a little along the lines Brookes does when she tells her students, "It is the artist's connection with energy, life, light, feeling, and mood that captures our attention"; "keep the flow," she says, "and follow your feelings" (76). We can embed talk of narrowly focused, structural matters, in other words, in as wide an analogical focus as we can. One way to start is to lay a groundwork in rhetorical or interactional contexts.

From rhetorical contexts to rhythm and style

In writing classes at any level, I like to assign one or two early writings that ask for some outside, preferably live interactional research (in other words, not book-bound research) and some explanation about that interaction to me as a reader who wants to know as much as possible about it. I never grade these assignments, but rather use them to model for students a wide range of ways to read them, as wide as students and I together can go, ending in matters of syntax and structure. The seven I will look at here, for instance, were early memos to me in an upper-level informational writing class, part of a sequence of assignments that would move through a proposal and finally into a ten-to-fifteen-page report.

The term project itself is a variation of one many teachers use in the junior English technical writing course at the University of Maryland, one I have transported into a Towson context. My version asks students to (1) think of a dissonant state of affairs in some organizational setting of which they are a part, and (2) find someone in that setting—a supervisor, perhaps—who can think of a problem of some sort, one that could use the student's help this semester in researching and reporting on it, perhaps recommending some solutions. The hope is that the two activities might mesh, or that negotiation will bring the two problems together. I ask that students also be thinking about how they might apply some work related to their majors to this project, so that besides researching through interviews, personal observations, and questionnaires, they will spend some time in the library reading pertinent material. Because all but two or three students in most sections of this course I have taught have had part-time jobs where they spend many hours a week, problems are nearly always pretty well identified within a week or so after the assignment is given. I encourage wide latitude in interpretation of the assignment for those who feel stymied, and have a stock of over a hundred old reports to give people ideas. Audiences vary throughout the sequence, ranging from me in the beginning to four classmates for the proposal and progress report, and the outside reader plus other interested people for the final report.

By the time students begin working on their first two "in-house" memos to me for this project, I have established nonnegotiable policies on the syllabus and three nonnegotiable convictions about writing (in other words, beliefs I carry that influence the way I read, and that I feel too settled into to stay very open about). The convictions—which students need to know I believe and act on— are first, that no matter what its purpose is purported to be, all writing is socially grounded, communicational, rhetorical, dialogic, embedding answers to questions the writer has taken in from his reading of his life world on whatever level, and embedding questions implicit in those answers. Even sentences themselves can be seen as answers to questions raised by preceding sentences (Coleman 35) or even to questions within themselves (Bruffee 107–108). Students will believe they are writing about ideas or giving information, and they are, but they are also, I tell them, writing about their sense of how they relate to both readers and the people they are writing about, both groups of whom either engage them in dialog or are imagined to do so. When a piece of writing seems *not* to communicate, it is simply communicating some other agenda from the one it seems to be at first glance, and we can probably unearth it through yet more questions, coming from the writer and anyone he trusts to engage with.

The second conviction is that what holds readers and writers together are the rhythms of the writing that entrain or carry along the attention of a reader, subliminally, letting her mind sense the direction and flow of the writing because she is able somehow to imitate those rhythms on a mental and even physiological level. I keep Susanne Langer's description in mind: "The essence of rhythm is the alteration of tension building up to a crisis, and ebbing away" (324) and tie it in during the semester to the writer's and the reader's experience of flow. Students usually think of rhythm as somehow a surface quality of writing (if they think of rhythm at all), a nice little touch of style added to a piece of writing that needs to be judged more on its "merits" than its style. I hope to convince them that rhythm has to do with the way ideas, meanings, time, and events move together in both large and small units of a piece of writing (Baum 22–36), and that they can begin to sense how their own sense of rhythm in what they are experiencing gets into their writing and into the mental movements of readers. They can attune themselves to listening for it or feeling it in their muscles and looking at it on their pages. Punctuation is part of it, guiding reader's movements through what they see, what they feel bodily, and what they sense as places of silence (Poyatos 91–103).

And finally, those first two convictions are part of the third, that the rhythms have a lot to do with who is talking in a piece of writing (a Bakhtinian idea [Holquist 312]), whose voice is answering whose and punctuating (in the wide sense) the meanings. The voice of the writer is a reader's evidence of his style, I tell students, and although some discourse analysts claim that words on a page are not a reliable indicator of what is going on in a writer's head (Potter and Wetherell 12–14), I am looking less for signs of activity under a skull than I am for patterns and tendencies in the ways writers read themselves and others in action. Style, says Berel Lang, "is both a person and the field of agency or vision of that person which acts on the viewer [or reader] as he discerns the style" (730). Cultures have collective styles (Kochman 130–152, Hebdige 117–127), and people have styles. Styles echo the way people think about themselves in relation to others and they echo motives (Lang 738). I will not tell a writer that his style tells me something about him, but I will tell him how I read it in this particular context, what kind of figure it presents to me, and ask whether his own reading agrees with mine. If not, we negotiate readings. Readers do create figures of people based on how they read their writings, I think, doubles that they can check out with those writers in order to learn something new about how both parties experience social boundaries and the powers of language.

With a one-page form of those three convictions given to a class, and with a class having been spent on the importance of the relation between purpose, reader, writer, and subject, I pass out writings from past classes to look at: My informational writing course gets two sets, one for each of the first two assignments for "in-house" memos to me.

Here is the core of the assignment for the first memo:

> Find someone who can help you formulate a problem area for your term project. Talk to that person; ask questions and/or try out ideas. The ideal person is one (1) whose job could run more smoothly if certain bumpy areas were removed from its functioning, and (2) who therefore has an interest in your researching ways to remove those bumpy areas, and (3) who may serve as primary reader of your final report.
>
> After your talk, write a memo to me about the exchange between you two; tell me in what way the talk helped you (even if the ways might seem negative at first) and on what path you must now travel.
>
> Consider this an informal memo with a conversational tone.

Because the memo is an easy one to write, helping students to become attuned to interactive ways of thinking, I rarely spend much time on models for it; last fall, for instance, I used only two and meant the contrast between them to point up the casual tone I hoped for and the amount of detail. The first was a little stiff and pretty uninformative. Students could quickly see that the writer's eyes were on the assignment sheet and an imagined form. Here is its beginning (it was only eleven lines long altogether):

> Included herein, are preliminary suggestions to improve the budgeting process presently used by The Student Activities Board. Upon meeting with John McGiver, Director of Financial Administration, Auxiliary Enterprises, Towson State University, he suggested that I develop a budgeting model that would include detailed instructions and examples that would aid the students in formulating their committee budgets for the coming fiscal year.

This writer was standing at attention, very straight, and it is surprising that he could hold his breath long enough to finish this short exercise.

The next one let me sit back and begin to imagine the writer's work situation, to picture what goes on there and get a feel for the atmosphere between people. The first paragraph explained the kind of business, the shifts, the pressures, the work load, and managerial setup. Then followed three short paragraphs explaining the writer's ideas about the project and the ensuing interaction:

> My line supervisor, then, was the logical choice when I needed a person to talk to about my project, if I were to research some aspect of my work. It is sometimes difficult even to make an appointment to see the next person up the hierarchy.
>
> I approached her prepared with two ideas for her to choose from. But as soon as she realized the opportunity I was offering her, she quickly shot down my ideas and suggested one of her own.
>
> Her rejections were reasonable. One idea, she said, would cause political problems because it would involve evaluating the New York Office; the other idea involved an issue which she (as well as others) feel isn't a problem.

The memo was about a page and a half long, full of interesting data about this organization and a description of the problem settled on: "What my supervisor would like me to do is to come up with suggestions of ways to cut down on the confusion by better structuring the turnover of supervision and by better organizing the work and information during the work shift." And although I told students they need not worry about length, I asked them to keep in mind that I needed as much information as they could give me about the situation they were going to use, so that I would be able to help them think about it during the semester.

Reading style through gesture

Voice and interactional style in the first assignment is rarely enough of a problem to warrant spending a class comparing old models and using them to give a context to matters of syntax and structure. But the second memo, even though I ask that the tone and style stay casual, begins to reveal wider differences, giving sensitive readers questions about whether some of the attitudes revealed toward readers and subject matter might find echoes in other writings of the same students. The assignment asks again that the memo be addressed to me and that it detail the problem to be investigated, the plan for research, sources that might be used, and readers for the final report. I asked students to be sure to describe the relationship between writer and reader(s).

Last fall I used the following five memos that gave a wide range of responses to the assignment. In all cases, I left out headings and (in four) gave only the first several lines, assuring readers, though, that nothing in the rest of the individual memos had seemed, at least to me, to change the impression and direction set in the beginnings.

We worked on the first two as a class so that I could model the kind of reading I hoped students would do. I asked them first simply to read the two fairly quickly with the assignment and intended reader in mind, registering a first impression about how these writers sense their relationship to any people that seem to be involved in the project, including the reader of the present memo.

1. The problem in this company is that the owners need someone to inform and explain investment decisions that would be profitable to them. The problem not only lies in investment, but also other business decisions that need to be taken advantage of.

2. In order to suggest procedures and policies that should be implemented in an effort to affect a positive change in productivity within the collections department, I intend to explore the existing variables that ultimately effect the volume of dollars collected by CIT Corporation's Collection Department. [The memo ends here except for a short list of areas in which recommendations will be made.]

The reading took only a few minutes, and I did not ask students to discuss those initial impressions yet. Rather I gave them a new task: Go through each memo once again, this time registering the rhythm of it somehow during the reading, almost as if it is a melody with pitch and stresses, pauses and silences, ups and downs, and punctuations of ideas. Tone and interaction, too. Then I asked the class if they could find a single gesture or posture that seemed to give the gist of the memo's attitudes about the project and the people involved.

I first learned about such physical ways of reading through a friend at the University of Maryland, Patricia French, who had worked with Wendy Atwell (also of the University at that time) in her literature class on the idea of "scoring." Atwell had herself learned the technique from Madeleine Grumet (Grumet, "Curriculum" 57–61; Atwell) in work with theater arts. French describes the scoring or enacting of poses on the first day they worked together with the class:

> [Atwell] explained to the class that we almost always use our bodies to get across meaning. We gesture as we talk on the phone, drum our fingers when we are impatient, roll our eyes when we are disgusted, etc. After demonstrating some of these gestures and their effects, she asked for a volunteer to make a gesture which symbolized that student's written response to [the story]. (31)

Though reticent at first, most of the students in the class became enthusiastic participants in the process as the semester went on, learning how these movements through space and time—the reading through body and facial expressions—get at understanding "quicker than words."

My students needed demonstrations, too, but were willing to suggest gestures for me to enact as we worked backward from words at first: in the first memo they found needy owners with hands outstretched; in the second a writer not looking at reader or people in the collections department, a writer with a wall in front of him. "Businesslike," they said. "Obscure and retreating into abstractions," I added. I closed my eyes and put my head back and up, as the writer seemed to do. They were beginning to get the idea.

For the other three memos I divided students into small reading groups of three or four people and asked them to go through the same process again, reading twice, once for impression, once for gesture, then to present an agreed-on gesture or perhaps two to the class.

3. In searching for ideas for research on my problimatic topic it seemed from my Management/Economic majors standpoint, that Behavior/Industrial Psychology and Management principles could be applied to my topic. The problem at hand is the current tension and ill feeling assocaited and caused by the relationship of the cooks (management) and floor help (employees). Status' [sic] are added to show inner restaurant relationships. Reporting to my

brother, the kitchen manager, I will research alternatives to current relations or suppliment existing ones. Methods used will be reading into Behavior and Industrial Psychology and management methods of first line supervisors. I will also be interviewing people at other restaurants to see what they do about the problem if and when it occurs.

4. I am investigating the problem of easing the transition of Johnson Electric's move to a larger location and increasing employee productivity at the new store.

    To research this problem, I am considering several methods of research. First, I would like to read some management or marketing journals on the subject of expanding a store location. These journals might also suggest methods of increasing employee productivity. I would also like to distribute a questionnaire to employees in an effort to get their suggestions and ideas. Since the employees are the ones who will be affected by the changes, it makes sense to get their input. The third source of my information will be an interview with my boss and primary reader, Mr. Tom Moore. He and I have briefly discussed my project, but I would like to discuss it at length to get a better feel for his needs and how to implement my suggestions.

5. Westminster High School has just built a new Fine Arts building. In this building, a new weight room is being installed. Former Alumni to the school wish to have some access to the new room. My job is to come up with a feasible way of allowing the weight room to be used by the former alumni. There are many little problems that go into this big problem. Some of the problem areas include: liability insurance, proper adult supervision, feasible dates for all, whether to make this free or not, how long this will run during the year and finally if this proposal will work at all.

One group pictured the writer of memo 3 as scrunched down in his chair, reading from his paper, mumbling and not looking at his brother. Another group pictured him as timid, not talking to anyone at the restaurant, *reporting* to his brother rather than talking to him. People in all groups called the writer of memo 4 "he" (the writer was actually a "she"), and pictured "him" sitting in his chair in a relaxed way (they were not yet willing to do stand-up gestures); "normal," they said, "confident," "putting value on his people, giving them credit." Craig Hardesty, a graduate student sitting in on the class, thought that memo 4 brought up questions of power and authority: The writer, he said, was taking charge, not being intimidated by anyone, "there" throughout the two paragraphs. Finally memo 5's writer was imagined standing off at a distance from other people, moving his arms and head busily over his work, but a loner at it, not working with anyone else.

Hindsight gave me an unfair advantage, but I could tell these students that their gestures were astute readings of the semester's work of these three writers. I do not claim that such readings can always find their way to a writer's working habits within his or her rhetorical context, but these three did. The writer of memo 3 never did, throughout the semester of his project, take a really good look at the people in the restaurant; his final report had been mostly undigested material from his library and textbook readings given to his brother-reader, who, he seemed to hope, would himself digest it and find a way to apply it. Memo 4's writer became the manager of the newly relocated Johnson Electric the month after she graduated from Towson; the owner was impressed with her report and believed, she told me, that anyone who could come up with such a good organizational plan should be put in charge of day-to-day operations. The writer of memo 5 *was* a businesslike writer and *did* have some trouble with his contacts: most of the data was found without much interaction with the principal or with any other decisionmaker. I had the feeling that either the principal was not taking this student's idea seriously or that the student was afraid he would not. The final report was adequately researched but not quite alive in its tone or recommendations.

From style to structure

We did not have time that day to move into matters of structure or syntax, but on another day after students have gone through a similar process and perhaps worked on evaluating criteria, I ask them to try to figure out *why* they may have read certain papers in the way they have. What did they find that had led them, somehow, into the senses they had come up with? Whatever other reasons students might give for their reactions at this point, I aim to include among those the possibility that structural matters may have played a part in the rationales, on at least some subliminal level.

During classroom talk on a day such as this, I will use the term "grammar," because I want them to become fearless in the face of what they so often perceive as their old enemy. It is not always an enemy of course, and the edges between structure and usage in students' minds, it is true, are nearly always fuzzy in a way that should keep me from using that catchall term "grammar" for both, when what I want early in a semester is to urge just a sense of structure on them. Nevertheless I use it, because what I want them to imitate (or participate in) is an allegorical doubling that will let a familiar (usually disliked) term resonate with a more pleasurable experience, a second current, or a track, that they themselves participate in creating (and can then participate in finding variations for). Grammar is not a neutral "thing" to them, rather a completely socialized representative of those authorities who *seem* to students to be outside themselves. Embedding it in images, the old rhetorical art of memory, helps them feel its force and animation as their own.

To help them develop a nonthreatening sense of structure, I suggest that we make a class allegory or mental map for whatever piece of writing we are considering. We begin the allegory with the idea that every structure is frozen force, and that in order for grammar to capture attention it needs to move back to the animating force beneath it, one that can be cocreated or multiply created as a stirring movement. I use two motivating ideas. One is from Eugene Hammond's *Informative Writing*, the idea that the basic noun/verb relation of a sentence is "a relation between matter and energy" (94), with both subjects and objects supplying "'matter' we can get hold of," and verbs carrying either kinetic energy (verbs of action) or potential energy (verbs of being) (96). The other motivating idea comes from Ernest Fenollosa and is also related to "transferences of force from agent to object" (Fenollosa 139), a movement he claims constitutes natural phenomena and can be duplicated in imagination for linguistic phenomena as well. The "rapid continuity of this action" is never broken up in nature, claims Fenollosa, and should not be broken up in imagining grammatical movement either. A sentence should be simply a redistribution of force:

> A true noun, an isolated thing, does not exist in nature. Things are only terminal points, or rather the meeting points of actions, cross-sections cut through actions, snapshots. Neither can a pure verb, an

> abstract motion, be possible in nature. The eye sees noun and verb as one: things in motion, motion in things, and so the Chinese conception tends to represent them. (141)

In bringing a sense of visual motion into English sentences from Chinese ideograms, Fenollosa touches Derrida's interest in his work and also in the idea that designs can have mnemonic value (*Of Grammatology* 334).

By bringing sound and sight (and even other senses) together in a classroom grammatical allegory, I hope to help my students begin thinking with the phonetic and nonphonetic elements that Derrida relates to "a fundamental synesthesia" (*Of Grammatology* 89). I want them to sense the simplest kind of force and for this purpose I tap into Mona Brookes' use of five simple shapes presented in the most kinesthetic and visual terms possible. For grammar, the shapes become those places in the reading of a sentence that draw the mind and even the senses into engagement, subliminally, but draw nonetheless. As Thomas Wheeler says, "grammar books ignore the tactile and sensory aspect of writing. . . . But grammar is not separate from the senses, but a form through which the senses find clarity" (92). And it is by analogy, as he claims, that they understand grammar, "not by rote" (94). We will find analogies, then, for those basic shapes to which the mind is drawn: the subject, verb, and two objects. (Later we might add modifier clusters traveling along with those basic shapes.)

Visualizing syntactic patterns

I ask students to choose any narrow traversable body of water, probably a river, imagine the land on each side, and then any kind of boat capable of being rowed fast as their vehicle. The river, I tell them, is the sense of flow they need to get from a sentence; the boat is the verbs that move us along, and the shores are places where the subject gets a start, on the one side, and the objects are affected, on the other (the indirect object getting some kind of force through the direct one). And it is into the bones of the subject rowers—each student imagining herself as a rower—that we now hope to put the sense of a sentence's movements. The class chooses one scene for everyone, with as many sensory details as possible—trees, plants, colors, winds, season, smells in the air. Then I ask students to imagine themselves as boarding the boat and paddling or rowing down the river. I ask them to tell each other (in pairs) for a minute or two about the experience of getting in the boat and rowing (they are usually willing to close their eyes for better images), and then we pause to reread whatever piece we are working on.

Here is a recent one, an introduction to a proposal that had bothered them. (The writer was of course an unknown student from times past.)

> Rules and regulations have become a universal problem for resident living. The resident department doesn't give a student enough time to prove themselves. A student is issued a written warning which is immediately placed on file. This means the area coordinator is notified and knows of the problem. The rules that are enforced are unfair and not beneficial for the resident student. Students feel that they are confined and not given the proper living environment in which to live. The rules are too strict and need to be adjusted. Students are not given a chance to correct their mistakes. If more verbal warnings were given, students will notice their mistakes and correct them. A slight adjustment of the rules can make resident living a learning experience.

Students had already found errors of fact and logic. I asked them to assume four kinds of sentence patterns. In the first one (S/intransitive V), they leave their subject shore and row the boat down the middle of the river, where they simply keep verb-ing (the verbal boat never transfers force to the object shore). In the second, (S/V/ DO), the boat goes on to land downriver on the object shore, with impact appropriate to the verb. The third does the same, with the verb connecting two actions on the object shore (S/V/IO/DO). In the fourth (S/linking V/SC [subject complement]), the boat barely makes it offshore when the rower turns around to come back, having forgotten something, probably.

I tell students that flowing down the middle of the river may feel carefree and good, but—for all those who remember reading *Huckleberry Finn*—though Huck and Jim may have liked the river life, the reader knows that without the adventures on shore, with all the rough and tough dealings with the resistances of life on solid

ground, there would be no *challenging* movement, no plot to follow. And so it is with all of us who move through life or even move
as readers through a sentence. Once people or discourses leave the
womb, no one—not even writers or readers—can simply float or
"verb" through life without material, noun-like challenges, but then
neither can they do without the moves and changes implicit in
verbs.

People need resistance in their lives in order to sense flow at all, I
say to students, and it works two ways: Every verb needs nouns to
anchor it and every noun needs verbs to move it through syntactic
journeys. People do things to other people, and (so Finlay and Faith
would hold) people's language reveals their experience of living on
the giving or receiving end, in a mixing of verb/actions with noun/
people and things, a creating of life stories in which we ourselves
identify with the subjects or objects we use in our language. We can
imagine those two shores in the vision as belonging one to self and
one to resistant others, and hope that writers can identify with (or
carry) active subjects moving swiftly down the river, gathering
objects/people from the other shore, once in awhile staying close to
home shore with the verb "to be," enriching one's self shore with
subject complements. Good writers, I say, feel a sense of aliveness in
their language, and that sense is inevitably translated into syntactic
journeys that have a good balance between entanglements on opposite shores (S/V/O), slowing down of action now and then to stay
near home (S/linking V/SC), and plenty of active verbs to
strengthen the boat's ability to maneuver the currents.

Armed with the four basic patterns and my analogies, then, students climbed into their rowboats to move through the introduction
at hand. It is important during this activity that a teacher balance
precariously between his utmost businesslike seriousness about the
benefits of mnemonic visualization and his utmost readiness to poke
fun at the activity along with students, whose faces are apt to become
red from laughter. But they do create the scenes, and even argue at
its start about whether the water should be blue or muddy, the
season summer or fall, the leaves fallen and musty or still hanging
on. And the time it has taken to set the stage is less than five minutes.

I read the first sentence aloud and asked students to picture
themselves moving in the appropriate manner; not everyone knew
that "become" would put them back on the subject shore, but only a

couple of people who did were needed to direct passage back there for everyone. I suggested that students make outlandish images as much as possible to accord with the content, explaining that the more incongruous the images or the more improbable the combination, the higher the amount of information absorbed. The moving images help people feel syntactic force, and if students are partnered, they can take turns describing them to each other. (I am indebted here to ideas of Win Wenger about learning through describing mental images.) For the first sentence, some students carried books of rules back to the subject shore and deposited them in a bin of "universal problems."

For the second, there was a rowing to the object shore downriver, but the adventure was a pretty mild one, the resident department that visualizers became (or held in their arms) not giving a time/ clock to the poor deprived student on that shore. From this point on the allegory barely moved: students were at first confused about which shore the student was on in some of the sentences, realizing with help that he was actually on the object shore in two sentences using passive voice, and even when he was the subject, that he was a pretty inactive one. There are so many trips back to the subject shore (and verbs and subjects hiding on the object shore) that the adventure never really gets off the ground. The psychological grammar of this student, it could easily be seen, held the seeds for the logical disasters.

As students begin to sense the bare clausal bones, we can begin to add the modifiers that ride with them, gathering around either the subject, the verb, or the completers. In the long run, it is clusters of words in context that I want students to sense, and as they become more and more comfortable with partnered visualizing of outlandish images, they can often come up with additions or changes to the class allegory: Compound sentences, for instance, need two boats and (perhaps) an anchor of some kind, to be manipulated differently for the three kinds of pauses between clauses. Different tenses might call for different placements in the river. Some students would rather find their own images; one of my students who would rather be diagramming sentences than making these images, he tells me, does, after all, decide to use his own pictures, liking the idea of a knight with a sword/verb. Thomas Wheeler has *his* favorite metaphor; he makes writing "anthropomorphic":

> Verbs are the heart because they supply a sentence with energy and allow it to move. A good sentence is balanced, as the body is balanced, with equal weight on either side. The whole weight does not go into a main clause, but into its limbs, allowing the sentence to stretch. Style is like the grace of an athlete or dancer. As the dancer rises, so a sentence ascends toward its importance. It does not come down at the end with a thud, but climbs—as feeling climbs—to a peak. The end of one sentence is a springboard to another. Paragraphs fit together into closely related parts. (92–93).

Students—at least mine—inevitably raise questions about sentence structure that I cannot answer, and I wonder whether or not many teachers avoid the whole subject just because getting caught in ignorance is so embarrassing and just because students usually take grammar as a given that any decent teacher of English should "know." A teacher may thereby avoid the face-threatening, brash bids for power some students engage in when they see fallen authority as an opening for their moves. But a writing course predicated on the idea of negotiated meaning need not raise such a specter; rather, aporias or dilemmas discovered in matters of structure might be likened to whirlpools for the mind, swallowers of meaning but invitations to come back up with a group effort to figure things out. Once we finish these first sentence patterns, I usually turn teaching of either structure or usage over to groups of three or four students at a time, asking—any time a few of them seem to need help with a problem in those areas—that they teach themselves and then the class, in any memorable way they can think of. We have had poems, chants, people acting as words in sentences and others as commas, images, role-playing sessions.

   Do they remember? Are they able to use what they have learned in these sessions? Some do; some do not. Others begin at least to relax a little around the idea of reflecting on their language. I agree with Finlay and Faith that carrying that reflection into larger personal, cultural, and social contexts is finally the most important way to address these issues. But bringing them into writing classes through multiple channels does point up to students that in order to move alertly and in a friendly sense through a piece of writing, readers expect to be drawn *through* the surface conventions we all share *to* rhythms that entrain our minds and let us get at the meaning with ease. When those basic conventions are violated, readers' attention suddenly halts its rhythmic moves and notices the structural defect. What a waste of good meaning.

Structural matters and usage matters are not neutral ones, to be sure, but no writing teacher need ever impose those conventions of Standard English on students as if they were. Learning them is hard work, as is learning a foreign language: one feels, as Alton Becker puts it, a certain "temporary madness," a disorientation (241). But our treating issues of grammar as if they were somehow separate in kind from, and not as important to discuss as, those of the larger units we talk about with our students makes little sense. By creating a climate of anticipation in our classes rather than perpetuating the idea that grammar must always be surrounded by a climate of fear, we set a model for a kind of attitude that trusts success.

Two summers ago, I studied Norwegian with a hard-driving teacher in Oslo whose style of poking fun at our mispronunciations might raise eyebrows among those of us who "know" such a method is an unkind one. But Ivar was not at all unkind, and his students were fond of him. He simply assumed that we *could* learn this language by studying very hard, that we were *absolutely* wonderful people, worthy of respect, ready to share a good Norwegian joke, ready to share with *him* the hard work (and he worked very hard) of communicating with a foreign other, and ready to learn the music and rhythms of this—in his eyes—absolutely wonderful language. His expectant yet relaxed attitude helped us all *want* to work hard. Every difficult step of the way I learned more about my own language as well as about this new one. I do not claim we should begin to poke fun at our students; not many people can make that work as Ivar could, with his good will and kindness. But I do believe our attitudes toward structure to be as important as the methods we choose to teach it, and if we expect our students can learn something about it, they just may.

All my students do indeed have a right to their own language, but I know that whatever that language is, they will be able to see it with new eyes and hear it with new ears from the perspective of those other, written structures that they ought to know too. How much stronger a base for negotiation with a complex, often alienating world they will have, the more multilingual they can become.

9

Conclusion

The scene: an interdepartmental social gathering, nametags being scrutinized, conversations beginning. "Tell me," says a chemist in a group of two, "how is it that you people are calling yourself a discipline when you have no subject matter?" Composition teachers are not unfamiliar with such questions.

So how do we indeed justify our existence in a university setting, when we are often faced with "remediating" what so many of our colleagues believe fifth-grade teachers should have taken care of? How *do* we imagine our teaching lives when so many "authorities" in academia, government, and industry believe our job is to instill form-giving skills into writers' heads, so that those writers can apply the skills to the "real" content or substance—the subject matter—of these authorities' "own" fields?

The status of part-time writing teachers—and often writers—across the many organizations of the professional world bespeaks the status of writing itself in the minds of many of those outside the field. Writing clothes thought. It has no substance in and of itself.

Such anachronistic thinking undermines our working with students and our establishing professional identities. Moreover, gender-related issues surface if we scratch the skin of this age-old belief in the solid, substantive, and publicly important ways in which men think and women add surface touches of form and class to the most-valued other. We writing teachers have talked more than once of this problem, among ourselves, in our journals, with administrators. Many of us are beginning to find politically active ways to deal with it.

Underlying our actions, I think, needs to be a coherent mindset that can leave room at its edges for turbulence and changing of itself, one that can counteract dichotomous and debilitating images of the professional world. A purposeful vision and strong belief system can give us the energy to act as Trojan horses in the midst of those we need to convince, as well as the desire to transform the whole notion of how we might interact with the Trojans, once we stand among them, face-to-face. Here are a few possibilities to consider on the way into and out of the horse.

First, we can make a habit of reflecting on our classroom practices, questioning our reasons for doing whatever we do, noticing what goes on at the borders between what we always thought separate from each other: students and teachers, content and form, cognition and emotion, mind and body, I and the other that seems foreign to me, men and women, birth and death. The list is almost endless. At these borders many scholar's minds are dwelling, interested in what they are calling postmodern culture, a culture penetrating all our lives with questions about boundaries we have thought inviolable: international, institutional, conceptual, and disciplinary ones. When we put our minds into a doubling mode of being, margins explode, new life takes over our thinking. Teachers of composition live on these margins when they are most alive in their practice; in a sense we have a metadiscipline, a home in rhetorical situations themselves, systems of communicational life on which all "substance" depends.

Second, we can define literacy, with Daniel and Lauren Resnick, as "a social transaction mediated by a text" (5), in which the relationship between reader, writer, and text becomes our main concern. We can add to this definition Miles Myers' conviction that the more we are able to work with our writing students in "functional or 'real' situations" (156), the more linguistic power they will gain. Within these situations we can attend stance toward material and readers, and acknowledge too, that in new standards of literacy, our students must be able, in Myers' words, "to shift from one sign system to another to solve problems" (158). Translation itself becomes one of our primary concerns, then, finding ways to encourage moves from one perceptual channel to another, one dialect or language to another, even one art or discipline to another. And because translation will always bring together both differences and samenesses, it will carry seeds of transformation too.

Our field is not without its exciting innovators in this process of translation, people who work with doublings, people who are in the fullest sense rhetoricians of an age-old kind: poised between possible and actual worlds, translating one into the other and even back again.

Wendy Atwell, for instance, came to my informational writing class one day recently to do theater work with students, suggesting to them that they score the rhetorical situations for their projects by directing other students in role plays. They focused on the problems embedded in these situations. (One student worked on the disorder in his restaurant, created when managerial roles were ill defined.) By reading the signs of their own intentions embodied in other people's actions, some students could then begin to improvise changes, understand better their goals, build *possible* worlds.

Valerie Faith does what she calls "kinetic" grammar with her writing classes at the University of Maryland, Eastern Shore. When writing fails to move smoothly for a reader, she tells her students, they might imagine the problem to be one of stage fright with an audience, an uncertainty and discomfort with a performance. Learning the structural elements and practicing variations of them increase the likelihood of a confident on-stage performance later, of an easeful movement between syntax and semantics. Rosemary Gates, at Catholic University in Washington, D.C., works in a slightly different way with syntactic and semantic rhythms, believing that students can develop sensitivity to the way voice in written discourse grows out of emphases and pitch changes in subliminally sensed dialogic exchanges. Single voice is motivated by imagining self answering questions of an other.

Lucille Schultz, Chester Laine, and Mary Savage have worked with interactions between school and college writing teachers, studying ways the frequent cultural hierarchy in such interactions might be transformed into real collaboration. Elyse Eidman-Aadahl, working through the Maryland Writing Project, is forming a multiracial action research group composed of both high school and college teachers. Together they will examine not only ways of teaching composition in multiracial settings, but their own ways of talking with each other in the group itself.

These practices are simply those I either know most about or am thinking about most intently lately. We all hear more and more about innovation in the field, outreaches to communities, experiments nationwide with kinds of writing that carry the potential, as do those above, for double-loop learning in their crossing the borders between text and context, learner and what is learned.

Finally, we need to remember that crossing borders is not easy for us or our students. My informational writing students did not all give themselves over willingly to Wendy Atwell's help with their projects, to the possibilities of changing the way they acted among others. Fear is the most subversive and often the most undetectable element we will deal with on our transformational journeys. Moving into possible worlds or bilingual—even multilingual—conditions is never, once again, without that sense of regression into kindergarten before the move can bear fruit.

How *do* we, then, move into new practices and new visions when there is so much holding us back?

We just begin. And when we find a path that feels right, we inevitably notice that others are already there to make us feel at home.

Designation of Self." *Studies in Symbolism and Cultural Communication* 14. Ed. F. Allan Hanson. Lawrence, Kansas: U of Kansas Publications in Anthropology, 1982. 3–8.

———. *Steps to an Ecology of Mind*. New York: Ballantine Books, 1972.

Battiata, Mary. "Judy Chicago's Tapestry of Birth." *Washington Post*, 13 May 1985: Bl.

Baum, Paull Franklin. *The Other Harmony of Prose: An Essay in English Prose Rhythm*. Durham: Duke UP, 1952.

Becker, Alton. "Text-Building, Epistemology, and Aesthetics in Javanese Shadow Theatre." *The Imagination of Reality: Essays in Southeast Asian Coherence Systems*. Ed. A. L. Becker and Aram A. Yengoyan. Norwood, NJ: Ablex, 1979. 211–243.

Benjamin, Walter. "Allegory and Trauerspiel." *The Origin of German Tragic Drama*. Trans. John Osborne. London: New Left Books, 1977, 159–251.

Bereiter, C., and M. Scardamalia. "From Conversation to Composition: The Role of Instruction in a Developmental Process." *Advances in Instructional Psychology*. Vol. 2. Ed. R. Glaser. Hillsdale, NJ: Lawrence Erlbaum, 1982. 1–64.

Berger, John. *Ways of Seeing*. London: BBC and Penguin, 1972.

Berlin, James A. "Contemporary Composition: The Major Pedagogical Theories." *College English* 44 (1982): 765–777.

———. *Rhetoric and Reality: Writing Instruction in American Colleges, 1900–1985*. Carbondale: Southern Illinois UP, 1987.

Berthoff, Ann E. "Reading the World . . . Reading the Word"; Paulo Freire's Pedagogy of Knowing." *Only Connect: Uniting Reading and Writing*. Ed. Thomas Newkirk. Upper Montclair, NJ: Boynton/Cook, 1986. 119–130.

———. *The Making of Meaning: Metaphors, Models, and Maxims for Writing Teachers*. Upper Montclair, NJ: Boynton/Cook, 1981.

Billig, Michael. *Arguing and Thinking: A Rhetorical Approach to Social Psychology*. Cambridge: Cambridge UP, 1987.

———, Susan Condor, Derek Edwards, Mike Gane, David Middleton, and Alan Radley. *Ideological Dilemmas: A Social Psychology of Everyday Thinking*. London: Sage, 1988.

Bizzell, Patricia. "Cognition, Convention, and Certainty: What We Need to Know about Writing." Rev. of *Cognitive Processes in Writing*. Ed. Lee W. Gregg and Erwin R. Steinberg. *PRE/TEXT* 3 (1982): 213–243.

———. "Composing Processes: An Overview." *The Teaching of Writing*. Eighty-fifth Yearbook of the National Society for the Study of Education, Part 2. Ed. Anthony R. Petrosky and David Bartholo-

References

Argyris, Chris. *Reasoning, Learning, and Action: Individual and Organizational.* San Francisco: Jossey-Bass, 1982.

———, and Donald Schön. *Theory and Practice: Increasing Professional Effectiveness.* San Francisco: Jossey-Bass, 1981.

Aristotle. *The "Art" of Rhetoric.* Trans. John Henry Freese. Loeb Classical Library. Cambridge: Harvard UP, 1926.

———. *Generation of Animals.* Trans. A. L. Peck. Loeb Classical Library. Cambridge: Harvard UP, 1953.

———. *The Nicomachean Ethics.* Trans. H. Rackham. Loeb Classical Library. Cambridge: Harvard UP, 1934.

———. *The Physics.* Trans. Francis Cornford. Loeb Classical Library. Cambridge: Harvard UP. 2 vols. 1929–1934.

———. *The Poetics.* Trans. W. Hamilton Fyfe. Loeb Classical Library. Cambridge: Harvard UP, 1932.

———. *Politics.* Trans. H. Rackham. Loeb Classical Library. Cambridge: Harvard UP, 1932.

Aronowitz, Stanley. "When the New Left Was New." *The 60s Without Apology.* Ed. Sohnya Sayres, Anders Stephanson, Stanley Aronowitz, and Fredric Jameson. Minneapolis: U of Minnesota P, 1984. 11–43.

Atwell, Wendy. "Keeping Body and Soul Together." Paper prepared for American Educational Research Association Conference, Spring 1989.

Auerbach, Erich. "'Figura.'" *Scenes from the Drama of European Literature: Six Essays.* New York: Meridian, 1959. 11–76.

Bakhtin, Mikhail (V. N. Vološinov). *Marxism and the Philosophy of Language.* Trans. Ladislav Matejka and I. R. Titunik. New York: Seminar, 1973.

Bartholomae, David. "Inventing the University." *When a Writer Can't Write: Studies in Writer's Block and Other Composing-Process Problems.* Ed. Mike Rose. New York: Guilford P, 1985. 134–165.

Bateson, Gregory. "Difference, Double Description and the Interactive mae. Chicago: National Society for the Study of Education, 1986. 49–70.

Blair, J. Anthony, and Ralph H. Johnson. "Argumentation as Dialectical." *Argumentation* 1 (1987): 41–56.

Bleich, David. "Cognitive Stereoscopy and the Study of Language and Literature." *Convergences: Transactions in Reading and Writing.* Ed. Bruce T. Petersen. Urbana: National Council of Teachers of English, 1986. 99–114.

———. "Reconceiving Literacy." *Writing and Response: Theory, Practice, and Research.* Ed. Chris M. Anson. Urbana: National Council of Teachers of English, 1989. 15–36.

Booth, Wayne C. *Modern Dogma and the Rhetoric of Assent.* Chicago: U of Chicago P, 1974.

———. "The Rhetorical Stance." *Contemporary Rhetoric: A Conceptual Background with Readings.* Ed. W. Ross Winterowd. New York: Harcourt, 1975. 70–79.

Bracewell, Robert J. "Writing as a Cognitive Activity." *Visible Language* 14 (1980): 400–422.

Braddock, Richard, Richard Lloyd-Jones, and Lowell Schoer. *Research in Written Composition.* Urbana: National Council of Teachers of English, 1963.

Brain/Mind Bulletin 4.13 (1979): 4.

Britton, James. "The Composing Processes and the Functions of Writing." *Research on Composing: Points of Departure.* Ed. Charles R. Cooper and Lee Odell. Urbana: National Council of Teachers of English, 1978. 13–28.

Brookes, Mona. *Drawing with Children.* Los Angeles: Tarcher, 1986.

Brookfield, Stephen D. *Developing Critical Thinkers: Challenging Adults to Explore Alternative Ways of Thinking and Acting.* San Francisco: Jossey-Bass, 1987.

Brown, William R. "The Holographic View of Argument." *Argumentation* 1 (1987): 89–102.

Bruffee, Kenneth A. *A Short Course in Writing.* 3rd ed. Boston: Little, Brown, 1985.

Buck-Morss, Susan. "Piaget, Adorno, and the Possibilities of Dialectical Operations." *Piaget, Philosophy and the Human Sciences.* Ed. Hugh J. Silverman. Atlantic Highlands, NJ: Humanities, 1980. 103–136.

Burhans, Clinton S., Jr. "The Teaching of Writing and the Knowledge Gap." *College English* 45 (1983): 639–656.

Burke, Kenneth. *A Grammar of Motives.* Berkeley: U of California P, 1969.

———. *A Rhetoric of Motives.* Berkeley: U of California P, 1969.

Cameron, Deborah. *Feminism and Linguistic Theory*. New York: St. Martin's, 1985.

Carter, Michael. "Problem Solving Reconsidered: A Pluralistic Theory of Problems." *College English* 50 (1988): 551–565.

Chafe, Wallace L. "Integration and Involvement in Speaking, Writing, and Oral Literature." *Spoken and Written Language: Exploring Orality and Literacy*. Ed. Deborah Tannen. Norwood, NJ: Ablex, 1982. 35–54.

Chicago, Judy. *The Birth Project*. Garden City, NY: Doubleday, 1985.

———. *The Dinner Party: A Symbol of Our Heritage*. Garden City, NY: Doubleday, 1979.

Chodorow, Nancy. *The Reproduction of Mothering: Psychoanalysis and the Sociology of Gender*. Berkeley: U of California P, 1978.

Churchill, Angiola R. *Art for Preadolescents*. New York: McGraw-Hill, 1970.

Cixous, Hélène. "Castration or Decapitation?" Trans. Annette Kuhn. *Signs* 7 (1981): 41–55.

Clifford, John. Review of *Cognitive Processes in Writing*. Ed. Lee W. Gregg and Erwin R. Steinberg. *College Composition and Communication* 39 (1983): 99–101.

Cohn, Carol. "Sex and Death in the Rational World of Defense Intellectuals." *Signs* 12 (1987): 687–718.

Coleman, Linda. "Audience Participation." *Proceedings of the Third Maryland Composition Conference*. Ed. Susan Kleimann, Eric Rice, and Mary Scheltema. College Park: University of Maryland, 1985. 30–45.

Coles, Nicholas, and Susan V. Wall. "Conflict and Power in the Reader-Responses of Adult Basic Writers." *College English* 49 (1987): 298–314.

Coles, William E., Jr. *Composing: Writing as a Self-Creating Process*. Upper Montclair, NJ: Boynton/Cook, 1974.

———. *Composing II: Writing as a Self-Creating Process*. Upper Montclair, NJ: Boynton/Cook, 1980.

———. "Freshman Composition: The Circle of Unbelief." *College English* 31 (1969): 134–142.

———. *The Plural I: The Teaching of Writing*. New York: Holt, 1978.

———. *Teaching Composing: A Guide to Teaching Writing as a Self-Creating Process*. Rochelle Park, NJ: Hayden, 1974.

———. "An Unpetty Pace." *College Composition and Communication* 23 (1972): 378–382.

———, and James Vopat. *What Makes Writing Good: A Multiperspective*. Lexington, MA: Heath, 1985.

Connors, Robert J. "Composition Studies and Science." *College English* 45 (1983): 1–20.

Csikszentmihalyi, Mihaly. *Beyond Boredom and Anxiety*. San Francisco: Jossey-Bass, 1975.

Cureton, Richard D. "Comment and Response." *College English* 47 (1985): 643–645.

Curtius, Ernst Robert. *European Literature and the Latin Middle Ages*. Trans. Willard Trask. Bollingen Series 36. Princeton: Princeton UP, 1953.

de Beaugrande, Robert. *Critical Discourse: A Survey of Literary Theorists*. Norwood, NJ: Ablex, 1988.

———. "Psychology and Composition: Past, Present, and Future." *What Writers Know: The Language, Process, and Structure of Written Discourse*. Ed. Martin Nystrand. New York: Academic, 1982. 211–267.

de Romilly, Jacqueline. *Magic and Rhetoric in Ancient Greece*. Cambridge: Harvard UP, 1975.

Derrida, Jacques. *Dissemination*. Trans. Barbara Johnson. Chicago: U of Chicago P, 1981.

———. "Fors: The Anglish Words of Nicolas Abraham and Maria Torok." *Georgia Review* 31 (1977): 64–116.

———. *Margins of Philosophy*. Trans. Alan Bass. Chicago: U of Chicago P, 1982.

———. *Of Grammatology*. Trans. Gayatri Chakravorty Spivak. Baltimore: Johns Hopkins UP, 1976.

———. *Speech and Phenomena and Other Essays on Husserl's Theory of Signs*. Trans. David B. Addison. Evanston: Northwestern UP, 1973.

———. *Writing and Difference*. Trans. Alan Bass. Chicago: U of Chicago P, 1978.

Descartes, René. *Discourse on Method and Meditations*. Trans. Laurence J. Lafleur. Indianapolis: Bobbs-Merrill, 1960.

Dewey, John. *Art as Experience*. 1934. New York: Capricorn-Putnam's, 1958.

Dillon, George. *Constructing Texts: Elements of a Theory of Composition and Style*. Bloomington: Indiana UP, 1981.

———. "My Words of an Other." *College English* 50 (1988): 63–73.

———. *Rhetoric as Social Imagination: Explorations in the Inter-personal Function of Language*. Bloomington: Indiana UP, 1986.

Dobrin, David N. "What's Technical about Technical Writing?" *New Essays in Technical and Scientific Communication: Research, Theory, Practice*. Ed. Paul Anderson, R. John Brockmann, and Carolyn Miller. Farmingdale, NY: Baywood, 1983. 227–250.

Dodds, E. R. *The Greeks and the Irrational.* Berkeley: U of California P, 1968.

Dreyfus, Hubert L. "What Expert Systems Can't Do." *Raritan* 3 (1984): 22–36.

———. *What Computers Can't Do.* New York: Harper, 1979.

———, and Stuart E. Dreyfus. "Making a Mind Versus Modeling the Brain: Artificial Intelligence Back at a Branchpoint." *Daedalus* 117 (1988): 15–43.

Eisler, Riane. *The Chalice and the Blade: Our History, Our Future.* San Francisco: Harper & Row, 1987.

Elbow, Peter. *Embracing Contraries: Explorations in Learning and Teaching.* New York: Oxford UP, 1986.

———. "Embracing Contraries in the Teaching Process." *College English* 45 (1983): 327–339.

———. "Preface 4: The Doubting Game and the Believing Game." *PRE/TEXT* 3 (1982): 339–351.

———. *Writing With Power.* Oxford: Oxford UP, 1981.

———. *Writing Without Teachers.* Oxford: Oxford UP, 1973.

Elshtain, Jean Bethke. *Women and War.* New York: Basic Books, 1987.

Faigley, Lester. "Competing Theories of Process: A Critique and a Proposal." *College English* 48 (1986): 527–542.

Fenollosa, Ernest. "The Chinese Written Character as a Medium for Poetry." *Prose Keys to Modern Poetry.* Ed. Karl Shapiro. New York: Harper & Row, 1962. 136–155.

Fillmore, C. J. "An Alternative to Checklist Theories of Meaning." *Proceedings of the First Annual Meeting of the Berkeley Linguistics Society.* Institute of Human Learning. Berkeley: U of California P, 1975. 123–131.

Finlay, Linda Shaw, and Valerie Faith. "Illiteracy and Alienation in American Colleges: Is Paulo Freire's Pedagogy Relevant?" *Freire for the Classroom: A Sourcebook for Liberatory Teaching.* Ed. Ira Shor. Portsmouth, NH: Heinemann, 1987. 63–86.

Fisher, Roger, and William Ury. *Getting to Yes: Negotiating Agreement Without Giving In.* 1981. Harmondsworth: Penguin, 1983.

Flood, James, and Diane Lapp. "Reading and Writing Relations: Assumptions and Directions." *The Dynamics of Language Learning: Research in Reading and English.* Ed. James R. Squire. Urbana: Educational Resources Information Center and National Conference on Research in English, 1987. 9–26.

Flower, Linda. *Problem-Solving Strategies for Writing.* New York: Harcourt, 1981.

————, and John R. Hayes. "A Cognitive Process Theory of Writing." *College Composition and Communication* 32 (1981): 365–387.

Foucault, Michel. *The History of Sexuality, Volume I.* Trans. Robert Hurley. 1978. New York: Vintage-Random, 1980.

————. *The Order of Things: An Archaeology of the Human Sciences.* Trans. Alan Sheridan-Smith. 1971. New York: Vintage-Random, 1973.

————. *Power/Knowledge: Selected Interviews and Other Writings, 1972–1977.* Trans. Colin Gordon, Leo Marshall, John Mepham, and Kate Soper. Ed. Colin Gordon. New York: Pantheon-Random, 1980.

French, Patricia. "Reader-Response Theory: A Practical Application." *Journal of the Midwest MLA* 20 (1987): 28–40.

Fulkerson, Richard. "Four Philosophies of Composition." *College Composition and Communication* 30 (1979): 343–348.

Garber, Judy, Suzanne Miller, and Lyn Y. Abramson. "Anxiety and Depression." *Human Helplessness.* Ed. Judy Garber and Martin Seligman. New York: Academic, 1980. 131–169.

Gates, Rosemary. "Defining and Teaching Voice in Writing: The Phonological Dimension." *Freshman English News* 17 (1989): 11–17.

Geertz, Clifford. *The Interpretation of Cultures.* New York: Basic Books, 1973.

Gere, Anne Ruggles. "Teaching Writing: The Major Theories." *The Teaching of Writing.* Eighty-fifth Yearbook of the National Society for the Study of Education, Part 2. Ed. Anthony Petrosky and David Bartholomae. Chicago: National Society for the Study of Education, 1986. 30–58.

Giroux, Henry. "Liberal Arts, Teaching, and Critical Literacy: Toward a Definition of Schooling as a Form of Cultural Politics." *Perspectives* 17 (1987): 21–39.

————. *Theory and Resistance in Education: A Pedagogy for the Opposition.* South Hadley, MA: Bergin & Garvey, 1983.

Glaser, Barney G., and Anselm L. Strauss. "Awareness Contexts and Social Interaction." *American Sociological Review* 29 (1964): 669–679.

Gleick, James. *Chaos: Making a New Science.* New York: Viking, 1987.

Graham, Daniel. *Aristotle's Two Systems.* Oxford: Oxford UP, 1987.

Grassi, Ernesto. *Rhetoric as Philosophy: The Humanist Tradition.* University Park: Pennsylvania State UP, 1980.

Gregg, Lee W. and Erwin R. Steinberg, eds. *Cognitive Processes in Writing.* Hillsdale, NJ: Lawrence Erlbaum, 1980.

Grice, H. P. "Logic and Conversation." *Syntax and Semantics, Vol. 3: Speech Acts.* Ed. P. Cole and J. L. Morgan. New York: Academic P, 1975. 41–58.

Grumet, Madeleine R. "Bodyreading." *Curriculum Inquiry* 87 (1985): 175–190.

———. "Curriculum as Theater: Merely Players." *Curriculum Inquiry* 8.1 (1978): 37–64.

Hairston, Maxine. "The Winds of Change: Thomas Kuhn and the Revolution in the Teaching of Writing." *College Composition and Communication* 33 (1982): 76–88.

Hall, Edward T. *The Dance of Life: The Other Dimension of Time.* Garden City, NY: Anchor Press/Doubleday, 1983.

Halloran, S. Michael. "Technical Writing and the Rhetoric of Science." *Journal of Technical Writing and Communication* 8 (1978): 77–88.

Hammond, Eugene. *Informative Writing.* New York: McGraw-Hill, 1985.

Hampden-Turner, Charles. *Maps of the Mind: Charts and Concepts of the Mind and Its Labyrinths.* New York: Macmillan, 1981.

Harding, Sandra, and Merrill B. Hintikka. Introduction. *Discovering Reality: Feminist Perspectives on Epistemology, Metaphysics, Methodology, and Philosophy of Science.* Ed. Harding and Hintikka. Dordrecht, Holland: Reidel, 1983. ix–xix.

Hart, Leslie A. *Human Brain and Human Learning.* New York: Longman, 1983.

Hartsock, Nancy C. M. "The Feminist Standpoint: Developing the Ground for a Specifically Feminist Historical Materialism." *Discovering Reality.* Dordrecht: Reidel, 1983. 283–310.

Hartwell, Patrick. "Grammar, Grammars, and the Teaching of Grammar." *College English* 47 (1985): 105–127.

———. "Comment and Response." *College English* 47 (1985): 874–877.

Havelock, Eric A. *Preface to Plato.* Cambridge: Belknap-Harvard UP, 1963.

Hebdige, Dick. *Subculture: The Meaning of Style.* London: Methuen, 1979.

Hein, Hilde. "Liberating Philosophy: An End to the Dichotomy of Matter and Spirit." *Beyond Domination: New Perspectives on Women and Philosophy.* Ed. Carol C. Gould. Totowa, NJ: Rowman and Allanheld, 1983. 123–144.

Hirsch, E. D., Jr. *Cultural Literacy: What Every American Needs to Know.* Boston: Houghton Mifflin, 1987.

Holquist, Michael. "Answering as Authoring: Mikhail Bakhtin's Trans-Linguistics." *Critical Inquiry* 10 (1983): 307–319.

Jakobson, Roman. "Concluding Statement: Linguistics and Poetics." *Style in Language.* Ed. Thomas A. Sebeok. Cambridge: MIT P, 1960. 350–377.

Janeway, Elizabeth. *Powers of the Weak.* New York: Morrow Quill, 1980.

Jantsch, Erich. *The Self-Organizing Universe*. Oxford: Pergamon, 1980.

Jaques, Elliott. *The Form of Time*. New York: Crane, Russak, 1982.

Jarratt, Susan C. "Toward a Sophistic Historiography." *PRE/TEXT* 8 (1987): 9–26.

Jones, H. John F. *On Aristotle and Greek Tragedy*. London: Chatto and Windus, 1962.

Kaplan, R. B. "Cultural Thought Patterns in Inter-Cultural Education." *Language and Learning* 16 (1966): 1–20.

Kaufer, David, and Gary Waller. "To Write Is to Read Is to Write, Right?" *Writing and Reading Differently: Deconstruction and the Teaching of Composition and Literature*. Ed. G. Douglas Atkins and Michael L. Johnson. Lawrence: U of Kansas P, 1985. 66–92.

Keith, Philip M. Rev. of *Rhetoric and Reality*, by James Berlin. *Rhetoric Society Quarterly* 18 (1988): 89–94.

Kintgen, Eugene R., Barry M. Kroll, and Mike Rose. Introduction. *Perspectives on Literacy*. Ed. Kintgen, Kroll, and Rose. Carbondale: Southern Illinois UP, 1988. xi–xix.

Kirk, G. S., and J. E. Raven. *The Presocratic Philosophers*. Cambridge: Cambridge UP, 1957.

Knoblauch, C. H. and Lil Brannon. *Rhetorical Traditions and the Teaching of Writing*. Upper Montclair, NJ: Boynton/Cook, 1984.

Kochman, Thomas. *Black and White Styles in Conflict*. Chicago: U of Chicago P, 1981.

Kolln, Martha. "Closing the Books on Alchemy." *College Composition and Communication* 32 (1981): 139–150.

———. "Comment and Response." *College English* 47 (1985): 874–877.

Kristeva, Julia. *Revolution in Poetic Language*. Trans. Margaret Waller. New York, Columbia UP, 1984.

———. "Women's Time." *Signs* 7 (1981): 13–35.

Kroll, Barry M. "Developmental Perspectives and the Teaching of Composition." *College English* 41 (1980): 741–752.

Laín Entralgo, Pedro. *Therapy of the Word*. New Haven: Yale UP, 1970.

Lakoff, George, and Mark Johnson. *Metaphors We Live By*. Chicago: U of Chicago P, 1980.

Lang, Berel. "Style as Instrument, Style as Person." *Critical Inquiry* 4 (1978): 715–739.

Lange, Lynda. "Woman Is Not a Rational Animal: On Aristotle's Biology of Reproduction." *Discovering Reality*. Ed. Sandra Harding and Merrill B. Hintikka. Dordrecht, Holland: Reidel, 1983. 1–15.

Langer, Susanne. *Mind: An Essay on Human Feeling* 1. Baltimore: Johns Hopkins UP, 1967. 3 vols. 1967–1982.

Larson, Reed. "Emotional Scenarios in the Writing Process: An Examination of Young Writers' Affective Experiences." *When a Writer Can't Write*. Ed. Mike Rose. New York: Guilford, 1985. 19–42.

Leonard, George. *The Silent Pulse*. New York: Dutton, 1978.

Lerner, Gerda. *The Creation of Patriarchy*. Oxford: Oxford UP, 1986.

Lévi-Strauss, Claude. *The Savage Mind*. Chicago: U of Chicago P, 1966.

Lewin, Ann White. "Foreword." *Drawing with Children*, by Mona Brookes. Los Angeles: Tarcher, 1986. xi–xiv.

Liddell, Henry George, and Robert Scott, comps. *A Greek-English Lexicon*. Revised by Henry Stuart Jones. 9th ed. Oxford: Clarendon P, 1940.

Lifton, Robert Jay. *The Broken Connection: On Death and the Continuity of Life*. New York: Basic Books, 1979.

Lindemann, Erika. "Ken Macrorie: A Review Essay." *College English* 44 (1982): 358–367.

MacCannell, Dean, and Juliet Flower MacCannell. *The Time of the Sign*. Bloomington: Indiana UP, 1982.

Macrorie, Ken. *Searching Writing: A Contextbook*. Rochelle Park, NJ: Hayden, 1980.

———. *Telling Writing*. Rochelle Park, NJ: Hayden, 1976.

———. *Twenty Teachers*. Upper Montclair, NJ: Boynton/Cook, 1984.

———. *Uptaught*. Rochelle Park, NJ: Hayden, 1974.

———. *A Vulnerable Teacher*. Rochelle Park, NJ: Hayden, 1974.

Martí-Ibáñez, Félix. *Tales of Philosophy*. New York: Dell, 1964.

Maruyama, Magoroh. "Toward Cultural Symbiosis." *Evolution and Consciousness*. Ed. Erich Jantsch and Conrad Waddington. Reading, MA: Addison-Wesley, 1976.

McCrimmon, James M. *Writing with a Purpose*. 7th ed. Boston: Houghton Mifflin, 1980.

Mead, George H. *Mind, Self, and Society from the Standpoint of a Social Behaviorist*. 1934. Ed. Charles W. Morrow. Chicago: U of Chicago P, 1962.

Meerloo, Joost A. M. *Along the Fourth Dimension: Man's Sense of Time and History*. New York: John Day, 1970.

Meyers, Chet. *Teaching Students to Think Critically: A Guide for Faculty in All Disciplines*. San Francisco: Jossey-Bass, 1986.

Miller, Carolyn. "Public Knowledge in Science and Society." *PRE/TEXT* 3 (1982): 31–49.

Millett, Kate. *Sexual Politics*. New York: Avon, 1971.

Moses, Carole. "Comment and Response." *College English* 47 (1985): 645–647.

Myers, Miles. "The Teaching of Writing in Secondary Schools." *The Teaching of Writing*. Eighty-fifth Yearbook of the National Society for the Study of Education, Part 2. Ed. Anthony Petrosky and David Bartholomae. Chicago: National Society for the Study of Education, 1986. 148–169.

Nietzsche, Friedrich Wilhelm. *The Portable Nietzsche*. Ed. and Trans. Walter Kaufmann. Hammondsworth: Penguin, 1954.

Norman, Donald A. "Twelve Issues for Cognitive Science." *Perspectives in Cognitive Science*. Ed. Donald A. Norman. Norwood, NJ: Ablex, 1981. 265–295.

North, Stephen. *The Making of Knowledge in Composition: Portrait of an Emerging Field*. Upper Montclair, NJ: Boynton/Cook, 1987.

Nystrand, Martin. *The Structure of Written Communication: Studies in Reciprocity between Writers and Readers*. Orlando: Academic, 1986.

Ohmann, Richard. "Reading and Writing, Work and Leisure." *Only Connect*. Ed. Thomas Newkirk. Upper Montclair, NJ: Boynton/Cook, 1986. 11–26.

O'Keefe, Daniel Lawrence. *Stolen Lightning: the Social Theory of Magic*. New York: Continuum, 1982.

Owens, Craig. "The Allegorical Impulse: Toward a Theory of Postmodernism." Part 1. *October* 12 (1980): 67–86.

Pattison, Robert. *On Literacy: the Politics of the Word from Homer to the Age of Rock*. Oxford UP, 1982.

Peirce, Charles Sanders. *Collected Papers of Charles Sanders Peirce*. Ed. Charles Hartshorne and Paul Weiss. Vol. 5. Cambridge: Belknap-Harvard UP, 1965.

Perelman, Chaim. *The Realm of Rhetoric*. Trans. William Kluback. Notre Dame: U of Notre Dame P, 1969.

Perl, Sondra, and Arthur Egendorf. "The Process of Creative Discovery: Theory, Research, and Implications for Teaching." *Language and Style* 13 (1980): 118–134.

Petrosky, Anthony R. Review of *Problem-Solving Strategies for Writing*, by Linda Flower. *College Composition and Communication* 34 (1983): 233–235.

Phelps, Louise Wetherbee. "Dialectics of Coherence: Toward an Integrative Theory." *College English* 47 (1985): 12–29.

Piaget, Jean. "Genetic Epistemology." *Jean Piaget: The Man and his Ideas*. Ed. Richard I. Evans. Trans. Eleanor Duckworth. New York: Dutton, 1973. xlii–lxi.

Pirsig, Robert M. *Zen and the Art of Motorcycle Maintenance*. New York: Bantam, 1975.

Plato. *Republic*. Trans. Paul Shorey. *The Collected Dialogues of Plato*. Ed. Edith Hamilton and Huntington Cairns. Bollingen Series 71. Princeton: Princeton UP, 1961. 575–844.

——. *Theaetetus.* Trans. F. M. Cornford. *The Collected Dialogues of Plato.* Ed. Edith Hamilton and Huntington Cairns. Bollingen Series 71. Princeton: Princeton UP, 1961. 845–919.

Polanyi, Michael and Harry Prosch. *Meaning.* Chicago: U of Chicago P, 1975.

Poole, Roger. *Towards Deep Subjectivity.* New York: Harper & Row, 1972.

Potter, Jonathan, and Margaret Wetherell. *Discourse and Social Psychology: Beyond Attitudes and Behaviour.* London: Sage, 1987.

Poulakos, John. "Toward a Sophistic Definition of Rhetoric." *Philosophy and Rhetoric* 16 (1983); 35–48.

Poyatos, Fernando. "Punctuation as Nonverbal Communication." *Semiotica* 34 (1981), 91–112.

Prigogine, Ilya, and Isabelle Stengers. *Order Out of Chaos: Man's New Dialogue with Nature.* New York: Bantam, 1984.

Quilligan, Maureen. *The Language of Allegory: Defining the Genre.* Ithaca: Cornell UP, 1979.

Randall, John Herman, Jr. *Aristotle.* New York: Columbia UP, 1960.

Reiss, Timothy J. *The Discourse of Modernism.* Ithaca: Cornell UP, 1982.

Resnick, Daniel P. and Lauren B. Resnick. "Varieties of Literacy." *Social History and Issues in Human Consciousness.* Ed. A. E. Barnes and P. N. Stearns. New York: New York UP, in press.

Richard, Paul. "'Birth Project': Fetal Visions." *Washington Post,* 28 May 1985: D7.

Rilke, Rainer Maria. "The Panther." *Selected Poems.* Trans. C. F. MacIntyre. Berkeley: U of California P, 1940. 65.

Romanyshyn, Robert D. *Psychological Life: From Science to Metaphor.* Austin: U of Texas P, 1982.

Rommetveit, Ragnar. "Meaning, Context, and Control: Convergent Trends and Controversial Issues in Current Social-Scientific Research on Human Cognition and Communication." *Inquiry* 30 (1986): 77–99.

Rorty, Amelie Oksenberg. "A Literary Postscript: Characters, Persons, Selves, Individuals." *The Identities of Persons.* Ed. Amelie Oksenberg Rorty. Berkeley: U of California P, 1976. 301–323.

Rorty, Richard. *Philosophy and the Mirror of Nature.* Princeton: Princeton UP, 1979.

Rothenberg, Albert. *The Emerging Goddess: The Creative Process in Art, Science, and Other Fields.* Chicago: U of Chicago P, 1979.

Schultz, John. "Story Workshop from Start to Finish." *Research on Composing.* Ed. Charles R. Cooper and Lee Odell. Urbana: National Council of Teachers of English, 1978. 151–187.

——. "The Teacher's Manual" for *Writing from Start to Finish: The*

"Story Workshop" Basic Forms Rhetoric-Reader. Unpublished manuscript.

———. *Writing from Start to Finish: The "Story Workshop" Basic Forms Rhetoric-Reader.* Upper Montclair, NJ: Boynton/Cook, 1982.

Schultz, Lucille, M., Chester H. Laine, and Mary Savage. "Interaction Among School and College Writing Teachers: Toward Recognizing and Remaking Old Patterns." *College Composition and Communication* 39 (1988): 139–153.

Schwenk, Theodor. *Sensitive Chaos: The Creation of Flowing Forms in Water and Air.* London: Steiner, 1965.

Scollon, Ron. "The Rhythmic Integration of Ordinary Talk." *Analyzing Discourse: Text and Talk.* Ed. Deborah Tannen. Georgetown University Round Table, 1981. Washington, D.C.: Georgetown UP, 1982. 335–349.

Searle, John R. *Speech Acts: An Essay in the Philosophy of Language.* Cambridge, England: Cambridge UP, 1969.

Sennett, Richard. *Authority.* New York: Vintage-Random, 1981.

Siebers, Tobin. *The Ethics of Criticism.* Ithaca: Cornell UP, 1988.

Shank, Gary. "Abductive Strategies in Educational Research." *The American Journal of Semiotics* 5 (1987): 275–290.

Smith, Barbara Herrnstein. "Narrative Versions, Narrative Theories." *Critical Inquiry* 7 (1980): 213–236.

Smith, Frank. *Essays Into Literacy.* Portsmouth, NH: Heinemann, 1983.

Smith-Burke, M. Trika. "Classroom Practices and Classroom Interaction during Reading Instruction: What's Going On?" *The Dynamics of Language Learning.* Ed. James R. Squire. Urbana: Educational Resources Information Center and National Conference on Research in English, 1987. 226–265.

Snell, Bruno. *The Discovery of the Mind: The Greek Origins of European Thought.* New York: Harper & Row, 1960.

Solso, Robert L. *Cognitive Psychology.* New York: Harcourt, 1979.

Steinberg, Erwin R. "A Garden of Opportunities and a Thicket of Dangers." *Cognitive Processes in Writing.* Ed. Lee W. Gregg and Erwin R. Steinberg. Hillsdale, NJ: Lawrence Erlbaum, 1980. 155–167.

Stone, Elizabeth. *Black Sheep and Kissing Cousins: How Our Family Stories Shape Us.* New York: Times Books, 1988.

Tannen, Deborah. "What's in a Frame? Surface Evidence for Underlying Expectations." *New Directions in Discourse Processing.* Ed. Roy Freedle. Norwood, NJ: Ablex, 1979. 137–181.

Taylor, Charles. "Interpretation and the Sciences of Man." *Interpretive Social Science: A Reader.* Ed. Paul Rabinow and William M. Sullivan. Berkeley: U of California P, 1979. 25–71.

Toulmin, Stephen. "The Inwardness of Mental Life." *Critical Inquiry* 6 (1979): 1–16.

Untersteiner, Mario. *The Sophists.* Trans. Kathleen Freeman. New York: Philosophical Library, 1954.

Verene, Donald Phillip. "Categories and the Imagination." *Categories: A Colloquium.* Ed. Henry W. Johnstone, Jr. University Park: Dept. of Philosophy, Pennsylvania State U, 1978. 185–207.

———. *Vico's Science of Imagination.* Ithaca: Cornell UP, 1981.

Vico, Giambattista. *The New Science of Giambattista Vico.* Revised translation of 3rd ed. (1744), Thomas Goddard Bergin and Max Harold Fisch. Ithaca: Cornell UP, 1968.

———. *On the Study Methods of Our Time.* Trans. Elio Gianturco. Indianapolis: Bobbs-Merrill, 1965.

Vopat, James B. "Uptaught Rethought—Coming Back from the 'Knockout.'" *College English* 40 (1978): 41–45.

Waller, Gary F. "Working within the Paradigm Shift: Poststructuralism and the College Curriculum." *ADE Bulletin* 81 (1985): 6–12.

Ward, John. "Magic and Rhetoric from Antiquity to the Renaissance." Unpublished essay, 1981.

Wenger, Win, and Susan Wenger. *Your Limitless Inventing Machine.* 3rd ed. Gaithersburg, MD: Psychogenics P, 1979.

Wheeler, Thomas C. *The Great American Writing Block: Causes and Cures of the New Illiteracy.* New York: Viking, 1979.

Wheelwright, Philip, ed. *The Presocratics.* Indianapolis: Bobbs-Merrill, 1960.

White, Edward M. *Teaching and Assessing Writing: Recent Advances in Understanding, Evaluating, and Improving Student Performance.* San Francisco: Jossey-Bass, 1986.

Wiener, Jack, and John Lidstone. *Creative Movement for Children: A Dance Program for the Classroom.* New York: Van Nostrand Reinhold, 1969.

Wilden, Anthony. *Man and Woman, War and Peace: The Strategist's Companion.* London: Routledge and Kegan Paul, 1987.

———. *System and Structure: Essays in Communication and Exchange.* 2nd ed. London: Tavistock; New York: Methuen, 1980.

Williams, Joe. "Comment and Response." *College English* 47 (1985): 641–643.

Winterowd, W. Ross. "Dear Peter Elbow." *PRE/TEXT* 4 (1983): 95–100.

Woods, William. "Composition Textbooks and Pedagogical Theory, 1960–80." Review essay of current theories and texts in the field of composition. *College English* 43 (1981): 391–409.

Yates, Frances. *The Art of Memory.* Chicago: U of Chicago P, 1966.

Young, Richard. "Paradigms and Problems: Needed Research in Rhetorical Invention." *Research on Composing: Points of Departure*. Ed. Charles R. Cooper and Lee Odell. Urbana: National Council of Teachers of English, 1978. 29–47.

——, Alton L. Becker, and Kenneth Pike. *Rhetoric: Discovery and Change*. New York: Harcourt, Brace & World, 1970.

Index